HAPPINESS, PLEASURE, AND JUDGMENT

The Contextual Theory and Its Applications

HAPPINESS, PLEASURE, AND JUDGMENT

The Contextual Theory and Its Applications

Allen Parducci
University of California, Los Angeles

LEA LAWRENCE ERLBAUM ASSOCIATES, PUBLISHERS
1995   Mahwah, New Jersey   Hove, UK

Lawrence Erlbaum Associates, Inc., Publishers
10 Industrial Avenue
Mahwah, New Jersey 07470

Library of Congress Cataloging-in-Publication Data

Parducci, Allen.
    Happiness, pleasure, and judgment : the contextual theory and its
applications / Allen Parducci.
       p.   cm.
    Includes bibliographical references and index.
    ISBN 0-8058-1891-X (alk. paper)
    1. Happiness. 2. Pleasure. 3. Judgment. I. Title.
BF575.H27P37   1995
150—dc20   95-14486
                                                     CIP

Printed in the United States of America
10 9 8 7 6 5 4 3 2 1

Contents

PART III: APPLYING THE THEORY

Preface

What makes a life happy? The essential idea of this book is that *the happy life is one in which the best of whatever is experienced comes relatively often*, regardless of how good that best might be. It matters little whether one is rich or poor, successful or unsuccessful, beautiful or plain: Happiness is completely relative in the sense that the pleasantness of any particular experience depends on its relationship to a context of other experiences, real or imagined. It is the nature of such relationships that makes the difference between happy and unhappy lives. Pleasure with one's normal level of achievement can be diminished by comparison with an occasional great success, but a goodly portion of ecstasy is a crucial ingredient of happiness. At the other extreme, some misery is inevitable; but if sufficiently infrequent, even the worst experiences improve the overall balance of happiness by increasing the pleasantness of other, more frequent experiences. These assertions have grown out of laboratory research in which the effects of different contexts were studied experimentally to discover basic principles of judgment. However, application of these principles requires particular attention to imaginary experiences, anticipations and memories, hopes and fears, and the goals by which we live; for these are the principal players in the drama of happiness.

No research is needed to teach us that the same objective achievement is less pleasing when it falls short of our goals or past achievements, more pleasing when it exceeds them. By such common-sense observations, we each discover for ourselves that happiness is relative. But it is difficult to apply this simple insight to the decisions crucial for our own lives. This volume presents a more highly articulated psychological relativism, with emphasis on its implications for happiness.

Although belief in psychological relativism is rooted in the folk-wisdom of everyday observation, it is treated here within the framework of predictive science. Controlled experiments test between different principles of judgmental relativity, how the rating of any simple stimulus depends on its place in a context of related stimuli. For example, the pleasantness of winning a particular amount of money depends on other wins and losses, real or imagined. This research demonstrates that judgments of pleasantness are highly predictable from simple psychological principles.

Understanding these principles illuminates basic problems of happiness. The essential practical insight, stressed throughout these pages, is that our natural preferences are often a poor guide for our most important choices. What is immediately more pleasing may reduce our pleasure from lesser experiences which, because they occur more frequently, tend to dominate the overall balance between pleasure and pain. Most people can readily accept this for particular examples, such as the disastrous effects of addictive drugs upon certain people. It is harder to give up one's own unhappy patterns of choice.

The contextual theory of happiness presented in this book incorporates the Utilitarian definition of happiness as the balance of pleasure over pain. This is a strictly psychological definition. The theory makes no moral claim that one ought to be happy or even that one is morally obligated to promote the happiness of others. Indeed, an initial concern is whether happiness is even possible, whether pleasure can actually exceed pain over the long run. Contrary to public surveys of happiness, the theory implies that most people are not as happy as they claim to be; but the theory also suggests that happiness could be much more common than pessimists believe.

The basic assumption that ties happiness to the experimental research from which the theory was developed is that psychological experiences of pleasure and pain are internal judgments following the same contextual principles that people follow in their overt ratings of stimuli presented in laboratory experiments. For example, when we experience a rush of pleasure upon hearing some news, we are implicitly judging the news to be good. Insofar as we comment on this experience, either to ourselves or to others, we use a category rating, perhaps "wonderful" or at least "very pleasant!" Just as this overt rating can be predicted accurately by applying the principles of judgment to the appropriate context of related events, so too can the private experience of pleasure be predicted from the same principles.

Detailed implications of the contextual theory of happiness are explored using a computerized game in which the player establishes contexts of related experiences in domains such as work or recreation, with the resulting pleasures and pains represented by wins and losses of points. Most players cannot establish a happy life in the game. As in everyday life, the immediate rewards and punishments encourage choosing what is preferred in the context of choice, even when these choices will establish different contexts that ensure longer-term unhappiness. Although implying severe limits on the possibilities for happiness, the game shows how imaginary experiences, such as pleasurable anticipations of love or success, can contribute to a highly favorable balance of pleasure over pain.

It does not follow that knowing this theory leads to greater happiness. Careful consideration of the arguments should convince the reader that the possibilities for how the theory might be applied in practice are broad enough to encompass different and sometimes even opposed courses of action. Particular assumptions developed for applying the theory may be contrary to the reader's own intuitions. Some actions and modes of thought suggested by the theory may seem difficult to apply.

The following pages present this contextual theory of happiness, explain its foundations in experimental research on judgment, and explore its practical implications. The book is written primarily for those who are curious about the conditions for happiness. Even if unconvinced by this particular theory, some readers may find stimulation in the laboratory research on the relational character of judgment and of pleasure and pain. Readers may also feel encouraged to examine and further articulate their own ideas about happiness.

ACKNOWLEDGMENTS AND APOLOGIES

Those who have helped develop this theory of happiness are so numerous that to list them all would seem to diminish the contribution of those to whom I am most indebted. Therefore, this list is restricted to just two in each of six categories: Charles L. Stevenson and Leo J. Postman who were, respectively, my teachers of analytic philosophy and experimental simplicity; Norman H. Anderson and Irving Maltzman, colleagues who inspired by their very high standards of intellectual honesty; Michael H. Birnbaum and Douglas H. Wedell, former students who continue to teach me the psychology of judgment; and finally, James B. MacQueen and Charles K. Turner, friends who served patiently as sounding boards for these ideas on happiness.

I would also like to make a couple of apologies. The first is to anyone whose ideas I have appropriated as my own. The second is for drawing so heavily upon my own experiences. Somewhat lamely, perhaps, I can only appeal to Thoreau's explanation at the beginning of *Walden*: "I should not talk so much about myself if there were anyone else whom I knew as well."

Allen Parducci

HAPPINESS, PLEASURE, AND JUDGMENT

The Contextual Theory and Its Applications

Introduction

The term *happiness* refers here to the measure of overall hedonic balance, a theoretical average across all pleasures and pains. This sounds like hedonism; but it is not the psychological hedonism that says we act only for our own pleasure, nor is it the ethical hedonism that says we ought to promote pleasure. Rather, this version of hedonism is simply an attempt to define happiness descriptively and suggest how it can be measured.

What then is *pleasure*? Although we all know when we are experiencing pleasure or pain, others can assess our hedonic experiences only by inference, often from what we tell them. At the heart of the contextual theory of happiness is the assumption that pleasantness is a *judgment* for which the underlying dimension represents degrees of preference.

It appears useful to try to understand pleasure as a dimensional judgment because we already know a great deal about how such judgments are formed. My range-frequency theory of judgment was originally developed to explain the *category ratings* people make of simple perceptual stimuli, with an ultimate concern for the pleasantness of what they are experiencing. Category ratings are the overt expression of internal judgments, as when we say that a particular experience is "very pleasant." The research on the pleasantness of winning different amounts of money or imagining different life situations can be explained using the same principles of judgment that explain ratings of simple perceptual stimuli, like lifted weights or sizes of squares.

The orienting assumption of the contextual theory of happiness is that pleasure, like any other dimensional judgment, is always *relative*. In this respect, the theory partakes of the Gestalt approach which holds that perceptual experiences are determined by relationships between different physical parts of the perceptual

1

field. For example, the perceived lightness of a particular rabbit is darker against a background of white snow than against a background of gray slate.[1] So, too, winning a particular sum of money is more pleasant when it is closer to the most that one could win than when it is closer to the least. The research that is presented here supports and adds specificity to this orienting assumption.

Instead of the Gestalt perception of figure against ground, the relativity described by the contextual theory is with respect to frame of reference or *context*. Dimensional judgments are always made relative to a context of similar experiences. For example, consider a simple psychophysical experiment in which the subjects rate the pleasantness of different solutions of lemonade that vary in the amount of sugar that has been added. Each of the succession of presented solutions becomes part of the context determining the pleasantness of any particular solution. This allows the experimenter to control the context so as to better understand how the judgments are made.

Reflecting the ambiguities of its use in everyday discourse, the term *context* is sometimes used rather loosely in this book. The more specific phrase *context for judgment* can sometimes mean the set of external events with which the judged event is compared, as in the laboratory research. But this may suggest that such comparisons are conscious, which is not often the case. More specifically, the phrase *context for judgment* can refer to just those external events that affect the judgment of some particular event. Because these external events are not ordinarily present at the time of judgment, their influence must be mediated by something that is present, something in our heads, like memories or neurological states.

In contemporary psychology and philosophy of mind, it is fashionable to speak of *cognitive representations* of what may formerly have been present physically—without implying that we are consciously aware of such representations. That is the way the term *representation* is used in this book, as when speculating about which prior events are represented in the context for judging some particular event. As a purely theoretical construct, governed by some conditions that are already at least partially understood, the concept of representation is employed here for the purpose of better explaining how judgments are made. For judgments of stimuli that vary on some correlated dimension, like the widths of different squares or attractiveness of different perfumes, the representations can be treated as numerical values reflecting their positions in the contextual range.

With hedonic judgments, it is often useful to postulate contextual representations of imaginary events, such as a successes that have yet to be achieved. Even

---

[1]Demonstrated by the work of Wallach (1948), the Gestalt psychologist who brought brightness constancy under experimental control and developed a quantitative explanation in terms of stimulus ratios that applies even to rabbits on snow or slate.

in the simplest psychophysical situations, it is sometimes necessary to postulate contextual representations of stimuli that have not been presented—as though the experimental subjects had previously been presented with a perfume preferable to any of those they had actually been asked to sniff. On the other hand, when stimuli that were presented much earlier in the experimental session are no longer affecting the judgments of current presentations, it is presumed that they are no longer represented in the context for judgment—even if they can still be recognized or recalled.

The concept of context becomes more slippery when applied to the dimensional judgments we make in everyday life. For example, the pleasantness of a particular bit of news obviously depends on the range of possibilities we had been anticipating, our hopes, and our fears. In applying the contextual theory of happiness, account can rarely be taken of all the considerations determining the context for any particular judgment. However, adopting the contextual approach suggests the sort of consideration that should be taken into account for a better understanding of any particular experience of pleasure or pain.

Perhaps readers will agree that most judgments are relative to their contexts.[2] The next step, then, is to specify exactly how the context determines the judgments. This would permit precise predictions of the effects of different conditions, particularly when the context can be controlled experimentally. The present effort toward specification started with Helson's theory of adaptation level which relates subjective experience to a pooled *average* of contextual stimuli.[3] In its most pristine form, adaptation-level theory implies an equal balance of positive and negative judgments—seemingly denying the possibility for either happiness or unhappiness. The present approach developed from critical experiments that contradicted this and other implications of the theory of adaptation level. Instead, the experimental evidence supported alternative principles relating each judgment to the range and relative frequencies of contextual stimuli. These range-frequency principles are the scientific heart of the contextual theory of happiness, and it is their implications that support the possibility of establishing a positive overall balance of pleasure over pain. The most important implication of this theory is that happiness is directly proportional to the pileup of events toward the upper endpoints of the hedonic contexts in which they are experienced, regardless of the absolute levels of those endpoints.

The following chapters concentrate successively on particular features of the

---

[2]The concern here is with dimensional judgments rather than with categorical judgments like "I judge the ostrich to be a bird rather than a mammal." Although the latter are perhaps less obviously dimensional, they too may reflect the same kind of relativism: For example, MacQueen (1966) explained such categorizations with his K-Mean model which also explains much of the relativity of dimensional judgments.

[3]This theory has a long history, but its most complete presentation can be found in Helson (1964).

theory, the measure of happiness, pleasure and pain as dimensional judgments, the nature of contexts and how they change, the possibilities for (or limitations upon) happiness. The range-frequency principles of judgment and the contextual theory of happiness are then presented in greater detail. Later chapters focus on the logical implications of the theory and how they might be applied to happiness in everyday life.

Many of these implications are derived by means of a computerized game which reverses the usual relationship between experimenter and experimental subjects. In the typical experiment studying contextual effects in judgment, the experimenter establishes the context by selecting which stimuli to present and the subjects express their judgments of these stimuli by category ratings. In the game, however, it is the players who establish the contexts in which the outcomes of their choices are "judged" and the computer that gives "payoffs" representing how pleasant these chosen outcomes would be according to the contextual theory of happiness. Experience with the game reveals a surprising result: Although players typically begin by winning positive points (happiness), with continued play their cumulative average payoff drops increasingly into the negative (unhappiness). This suggests a natural tendency to choose alternatives that, although immediately pleasing, can establish contexts against which their future outcomes compare poorly. Even after hours of play, players fail to change over to a successful strategy. This reflects what is taken to be an all-too-common difficulty: It is hard when making important choices in life to take into account how the future outcomes of those choices will be experienced in their resulting contexts.

This computerized game also demonstrates the consequences of different rules for what gets into the context. For example, the game can be arranged so that the more pleasant outcomes are less likely to be represented contextually. This arrangement is very good for happiness because most outcomes will be relatively high in their contexts. Some of the other implications of the theory are less sanguine, such as the demonstration that if hedonic contexts represented unbiased samples of previous experiences, overall happiness in any stable life could not be very much greater than an exactly even balance between pleasure and pain.

One assumption made for applications of the contextual theory is that most of our pleasures and pains occur while fantasizing, daydreaming, anticipating, or reliving the past in our memories. Insofar as we have more control of our imaginations than we have of external events, the possibilities for happiness are greatly extended. One counter-intuitive implication is that the occasional re-experiencing of some painfully dreadful concern actually helps the overall hedonic balance by enhancing the delight in the great bulk of experiences.

This book concludes with a pair of chapters applying the theory to extended case studies. The first of these describes the unhappy consequences of social planning that failed to take into account the future changes in context. The second examines the attempts of a remarkable man, Henry David Thoreau, to enhance his own opportunities for happiness. Like the briefer examples presented throughout the book (some personal, some familiar to everyone), these extended case studies serve to clarify the key concepts of the theory.[4]

Certain generalizations for everyday life can be drawn from the contextual theory of happiness. One is that there would have to be a great deal of ecstasy in any life for which the overall happiness approaches the level most Americans claim for themselves.[5] Thus, contrary to prescriptions from philosophers such as Aristotle and the classical Utilitarians, trying to avoid ecstasy would be a poor road to happiness. On the other hand, the theory implies that everyone must experience at least occasional misery. A further implication is that the concept of *utility* employed by economists and decision analysts is often not a measure of pleasantness, so that choices that increase expected utility can actually reduce the overall balance of pleasure over pain.

There is another class of practical implications that although not strictly implied by the theory are nevertheless suggested by it. One example is how attitudes conducive to success may work against happiness by setting standards that are only occasionally achieved; the overall balance cannot be positive unless the pleasurable anticipations of success outweigh the disappointments of falling short. Related to this are various possibilities for controlling the imagination, the royal road to happiness. Implications of this sort are particularly conjectural, as any attempt to understand the complexities of everyday life must always be.

---

[4]Gergen (1984) made an interesting argument that a prime function of psychological research has been to further define and clarify the basic concepts of whatever theory is being tested. The same argument should apply to examples of a theory's implications for everyday life.

[5]In the surveys in which people are asked to rate their own overall levels of happiness, self-avowals that the present approach disavows as valid measures of happiness.

A PSYCHOLOGICAL
APPROACH TO HAPPINESS

1 On Defining Happiness: The Balance of Pleasure Over Pain

It is often said that happiness cannot be defined or that it has different meanings for different people. However, we do seem to be communicating when we use expressions like "those were happy days!" or "that poor child is so unhappy!". This suggests that the different meanings have something in common. The definition of happiness as the balance of pleasure over pain is chosen here to reflect this common meaning. Later chapters will clarify the definition's connection to experimental research on dimensional judgments and to the contextual theory of happiness that grew out of this research.

To arrive at a satisfactory definition of happiness, one must resolve a number of questions about how the definition is to function. Is its purpose to dispose people to behave in certain ways? Such a definition would be prescriptive rather than descriptive. The present intention is to avoid prescriptions and thus to keep them out of the definition. To this end, the goal is a *definition in use*, a definition that best catches how the term is actually used. This is not easy, particularly for a psychologist trained in the behavioristic tradition which emphasizes definitions that reduce to physical measurements, such as the overt responses that people give in surveys of happiness. But the present effort is to escape the behavioristic tradition, emphasizing instead the subjective experiences of pleasure and pain that seem basic to the way in which the term *happiness* is most commonly used.

Another question that must be resolved is whether the definition should include something of the conditions either necessary or sufficient for happiness. An affirmative answer to the question assumes that we already know more about the conditions for happiness than now seems likely. It also tends to sneak specific prescriptions for happiness back into the definition. If we can instead first define how we will use the term, then we can more objectively determine what conditions encourage happiness as so defined.

The approach in this chapter is historical, examining different philosophical and psychological definitions of happiness that have withstood the test of time. Starting with the Greek philosophers, we can see how close they were to certain contemporary views. However, we come closest to the definition adopted for the present theory of happiness when we examine how the term was defined by the 19th-century Utilitarians. Although accepting their definition of happiness as the balance of pleasure over pain, the present approach sharpens these concepts by relating them to internal judgments and the contexts in which these judgments occur. Accepting the Utilitarians' definition of happiness does not require acceptance of their advocacy of happiness as the basis for ethical decisions. Questions about how one *ought* to behave are sidestepped here as outside the objectives of the present theory. So too with the Utilitarians' psychological hedonism which has come to seem empty in the light of more recent developments in philosophy and psychology. The alternative of psychological behaviorism is also avoided.

PRESCRIPTIVE VERSUS DESCRIPTIVE DEFINITIONS

Happiness is a "glow" word. It is better to be happy than unhappy. People seem to be confessing failure when they admit to unhappiness in any important domain of life, such as work. "If he is so unhappy with his job, why doesn't he find a different one?" The good salesperson tries to appear happy in his or her success, "I love selling this product!" And because *happiness* carries such glowing connotations, it is often used prescriptively to express moral judgments, such as "happiness is doing what is right" or "happiness is being kind to others."

The classical Greek philosophers used the term prescriptively. As presented by Plato, Socrates identified happiness with virtue: an evil man could not be happy.[1] Although this seemed self-evident to Socrates, it puzzles contemporary students who, steeped in the mysteries of personality deviations, suspect that even truly evil people may sometimes be happy. But Socrates thought that happiness depended on wisdom, the ability to choose wisely. He also believed that one could never choose to behave badly if one were truly wise. Thus, virtue and happiness were intimately related for Socrates and Plato, with wisdom a necessary and sufficient condition for behaving well and being happy.

Aristotle, Plato's most influential student, adopted much the same position in his *Nicomachean Ethics* (340 BC/1986). However, Aristotle added the notion of

---

[1]For example, in Plato's dialogue "Gorgias," Socrates tells Polus, "The men and women who are gentle and good are also happy, as I maintain, and the unjust and evil are miserable" (Plato, 360BC/1892 trans., p. 529).

fittingness. Our nature is such that it is fitting for us to behave in certain ways. Man is a rational animal, and thus the happiest life is one of rational thinking, philosophical contemplation. Today, this may seem like intellectual elitism; people even say of certain mentally retarded children that they are a joy to be with because their happiness is so contagious.

It is not clear how central pleasure is to the Platonic and Aristotelian conceptions of happiness. Although both philosophers believed that happier people actually experience more pleasure, neither identified happiness solely with pleasure. In fact, many of the Platonic dialogues pit Socrates against sophists, teachers of rhetoric and pragmatic success, who made personal pleasure the ultimate criterion against which one's behavior was to be evaluated. Thus, as with so many other philosophical issues that continue to our own time, we find already articulated in ancient Greece the issue of whether happiness is a moral condition, how one *ought* to be, or a sequence of psychological states constituting what a happy person experiences. This contextual theory of happiness takes the descriptive rather than the prescriptive approach.

Much of the Hebraic-Christian tradition is more prescriptive than descriptive. Happiness is serving God, living in accordance with God's wishes as learned from holy scripture or by personal revelation. However, for certain sects, happiness is a psychological state that is achieved in an afterlife, in a heaven that is either the reward for good behavior or the result simply of God's grace. Thus, there is still, for many of our contemporaries, the old Greek conflict between prescriptive and descriptive conceptions of happiness.

The Utilitarian Definition.   Bentham (1789/1948), the founder of Utilitarianism, combined the prescriptive with the descriptive when he defined the good in terms of pleasing consequences: that action is best that leads to the greatest happiness of the greatest number. Happiness itself was defined by Bentham as a favorable balance of pleasure over pain. He thought of hedonic experiences as measurable quantitatively, permitting the estimation of how much pleasure or pain would result from each of the different possible courses of action.

Although rarely accepted without reservation, Utilitarianism continues to be an important part of contemporary thinking about happiness. Many would not want happiness to be the *sole* criterion of right and wrong, good and bad. For example, American (as compared with British) jurisprudence is said to give greater weight to innate rights than to consequences for general happiness. Others are dissuaded by the difficulty of knowing how much happiness would result from different choices.

Without accepting the Utilitarian approach to ethics, the contextual theory of happiness presented in this book starts by defining happiness as *a theoretical summation over separate momentary pleasures and pains*. This is clearly a descriptive rather than a prescriptive definition. Rather than prescribe specific rules for behavior, the contextual theory provides a psychological foundation for thinking about pleasure and pain and about how happiness, conceived as a measure of their sum total, is affected by the conditions established by different choices.

Measuring happiness as the algebraic sum of pleasures and pains requires some specification of time. We may speak of the happiness of a moment or of a day, but we often reserve the term for much longer periods: a happy period in one's life or, indeed, a happy life. The happiness that Aristotle identified as the ultimate goal, the end for which everything else is but a means, is a long-term happiness. Still earlier, Solon asserted that the happiness of a life cannot be known until it is over.

Whatever the period encompassed, it is theoretically divisible into smaller units of time, at least some of which can be located on the hedonic dimension of pleasure and pain. The happiness of any period is a conceptual summation of these separate hedonic values, positive and negative, divided by the duration of that period. This duration can include temporal intervals in which neither pleasure nor pain is being experienced, or it can be restricted to just the hedonic moments. The choice depends on how the concept of happiness is to be applied, on whether one is more concerned with the richness of the period in hedonic experiences, or just with the pleasantness of those experiences that are hedonic.

A bigger problem, one that was never recognized by the classical Utilitarians, is how numbers can be assigned to represent degrees of pleasure and pain. This is the problem of measurement. The solution adopted for the contextual theory of happiness is presented in the next chapter.

Global Assessments.   The Utilitarian definition of happiness should be distinguished from the one adopted, sometimes explicitly, by social scientists doing survey research on happiness. In these surveys, people are typically asked to attempt global assessments of how their lives have been going over some recent period, such as the last few weeks. The researchers then use these global assessments as the operational measure of happiness.[2] However, this may be quite a different sense of happiness than a purely theoretical summation over momentary experiences of pleasure and pain, as required for the Utilitarian definition adopted here. Self-avowals of global happiness could hardly be based on this kind of summation, for it would require that people recall each of their separate hedonic

---

[2]There is a vast literature on self-avowals of happiness, summarized independently by Diener (1984) and Veenhoven (1984a, 1984b). A number of recent books on happiness leaned heavily on this type of survey (e.g., Argyle, 1987; Eysenck, 1990; Freedman, 1978; and Myers, 1992). Although each presents interesting ideas about the conditions for happiness, I do not think that the validity of these ideas can rest on the survey results. Problems with surveys and their implicit definition of happiness are discussed later in this book.

experiences and somehow come up with an average. We should not be surprised if this overall assessment differed greatly from a true average.[3] For example, an optimistic person might have suffered through a painful period but when now asked to characterize this period might recall only the optimistic moments during which the suffering seemed to be for the best. Although the acceptance of such global assessments would greatly simplify the problem of measuring happiness, the measure it gives may have validity only for how the person feels when asked to make an overall assessment. The contextual principles of judgment that explain momentary experiences of pleasure or pain can also explain these overall assessments. However, the overall assessment has no particular relationship to the theoretical sum or average of momentary experiences—beyond the momentary pleasure or pain experienced while making it.

Psychological Hedonism.   Adoption of the Utilitarian definition of happiness does not imply acceptance of the theory of motivation that historically accompanied it. Bentham asserted that pleasure and pain are the supreme masters, reducing motivation to the quest for pleasure and escape from pain. Current skepticism about this psychological hedonism concentrates on its lack of explanatory or predictive power.[4] Consider heroes who sacrifice their lives to save others, presumably eliminating their own chances for future pleasure. The psychological hedonist can explain these apparent exceptions by saying that such heroes are simply avoiding the pain of being labeled cowards; but then if they had failed to sacrifice themselves, the explanation would be that the prospect of death evoked an even greater fear. Once the behavior in question has occurred, the psychological hedonist can always provide a plausible "explanation." Such post hoc accounts are like those of the financial experts who always have a reason for why the market rose or fell but who seem to perform no better than chance when predicting its rise or fall.

No part of the theory of happiness presented in this book should be confused with psychological hedonism or with any other theory of motivation or choice. There is no pretense here of being able to predict what choices people will make.

---

[3]In what may be the most suggestive research bearing on this point, Diener, Sandvik, and Pavot (1991) reported a .60 correlation between the average of momentary reports (described in chap. 2) and a measure of global happiness. This would be a high correlation between measures of two different psychological characteristics, the validity of one for predicting the other. However, it is a low correlation for alternative measures of the same characteristic, their consistency or reliability. Although some of the same biases in reporting may distort both measures (but with greater distortion of the global reports), both should agree on extreme cases, like the chronically depressed. This could account for much of the correlation.

[4]This conception of scientific explanation is taken from Popper (1959), where the proposed criterion for measuring explanatory power was *falsifiability* (i.e., the possibilities for proving the explanation wrong).

The concern is only with how experiences of pleasure and pain depend upon the contextual relationships established by choices. In this sense, it aspires to be scientific, with the distinct possibility of being proven wrong. The underlying theory of judgmental relativity has survived rigorous experimental tests in the simpler laboratory situations in which it is possible to control the contexts for judgment. Less testable is the theoretical speculation about what gets into the contexts for the everyday pleasures and pains experienced in the private worlds of our own imaginations.

The reader should also be careful not to confuse the term *hedonic*, as used in this book, with the idea of a life devoted to pleasure, as when someone is said to be an unabashed "hedonist" or to be "extremely hedonistic." Rather, hedonic is used here simply to mean "having to do with pleasure." Thus, we can speak of the "hedonic" dimension of experience when referring to its pleasantness and of "hedonic" contexts when referring to the contexts for judgments of pleasantness or painfulness. None of these uses should be construed as support for a sybaritical life that exalts pleasure over any other good. Perhaps defining happiness in terms of pleasure encourages such misconstrual, particularly among those who, like Aristotle, think of happiness as the ultimate goal. I can only plead, as I have regularly done with my students, that I would rather that people be good than that they be happy.

Pleasure as a Common Denominator for Happiness. Different approaches to personality and psychotherapy have emphasized different personal goals, including self-esteem, self-fulfillment, closer correspondence between perceived-self and ideal-self, peace of mind, love, and so on. The list could be very long. Although each of these personal goals may seem crucial to happiness, none provides an adequate substitute for "pleasure" when trying to understand happiness in general. Consider self-esteem. Some of our worst moments occur when self-esteem is temporarily shattered, and even our apparent failures do not seem so bad when we have a strong sense of self-esteem. However, self-esteem seems unrelated to many of our most gratifying or disappointing experiences, such as the satisfaction of basic biological needs. If one is terribly thirsty, as when a desert hike has taken much longer than expected, finding water can be deliriously gratifying—an ecstatic experience that is usually unrelated to self-esteem. The pain of the dentist's drill can be agonizing, even if one does not blame oneself for the bad tooth. What physical agonies and ecstasies have in common with experiences of self-esteem, or lack thereof, is that they all partake of pleasure or pain.

For anyone who is not a Utilitarian with respect to morality, there are difficulties in reducing the moral component of a dimension like self-esteem simply to pleasure and pain. Some acts have basic moral value even though their consequences may be unpleasant. For example, it seems right to divide a limited amount of food equally, even though the division satisfies no one (or even though some might be satisfied with less than their "fair share"). Similarly, it would seem wrong to punish an innocent person—even if doing so would add to the total amount of pleasure in the world. Certain behaviors may lower a person's self-esteem and yet give that person real pleasure, as when Dostoevsky's Fyodor Karamazov revels in his own buffoonery, all the while recognizing how he is degrading himself.[5] Similarly, we sometimes take delight in the reprehensible behavior of rascals (providing we are not their victims), all the while knowing that what they are doing is morally wrong.

Pleasure and Value.   An overly narrow concentration upon physical pleasures may be at the root of a common objection to treating pleasure and pain as the essential ingredients of happiness. People speak of a love being "merely physical," meaning that although sensually pleasurable it lacks the nonphysical attributes of a more complete love. Some of these other attributes, such as commitment and responsibility, may seem right or fitting or reassuring, though not always pleasant. Thus, a couple that shares the same psychological problems may confess, "we both suffer so much and that is why we belong together." The pleasantness or painfulness of nonphysical attributes, like character, imagination, and abstract ideas, may seem too different to be lumped with physical sensations.

The contextual theory of happiness presented here is itself based on a theory of judgment that applies to all kinds of evaluative dimensions, not just to pleasure and pain. An emphasis on a broader, less hedonic conception of value would be just as consistent with the underlying experimental research on dimensional judgments. Thus, the dimension of experience basic to happiness could have been labeled *value* or *subjective value*. However, use of the term value would risk taking us back to the normative considerations that have drawn attention away from the psychological character of happiness. The term *value judgment* has an ethical ring. If we say that a musical composition is "very good," there is an implication that others *ought* to like it: Such value judgments thus have a hortatory component.[6] Even avowals of happiness have something of this normative flavor: other things being equal, we think better of a person who seems happy than of one who seems unhappy, as though we still sub scribed to Plato's association of happiness with virtue. This association may produce a strong positive bias in surveys of happiness. People want to appear *socially desirable*, that is, they try to make themselves seem better (and hence happier) than they are. But there need be no implication that I approve of what pleases me, or that others ought to approve of it. My own particular recreational activities can give me pleasure without my thinking that others have any duty to pursue the same recreations.

---

[5]For example, in the famous scene at Father Zossima's cell in *The Brothers Karamazov* (Dostoevsky, 1880/1966) where Fyodor Karamazov disgraces his sons.

[6]This is the emotive theory of ethical language developed by Stevenson (1944).

To summarize, this has been an attempt to carve out from the plethora of notions about happiness a particular definition that catches what seems common to most of them. The definition is in terms of the hedonic dimension of experience, pleasure and pain. Happiness is thus conceived as a psychological state, or rather as a theoretical summation or average across many momentary psychological states, each with a certain degree of pleasure or pain. It is not identified here with the global assessments that people make when asked to rate their overall happiness. Nor is there is any mention of objective criteria for happiness. Indeed, as argued in the next chapter, pleasure and pain are subjective judgments determined by the place of the particular event that is being experienced in its context of related events. This is why useful specification of the conditions for happiness must be at a level of abstraction that takes into account these contextual relations.

CONDITIONS FOR HAPPINESS

People frequently include the conditions they believe conducive to happiness when attempting to define it: "happiness is making progress toward one's goals," "happiness is being in love." The fact that different people specify different conditions explains much of the skepticism about reaching a common definition of happiness, and even the same person may find different conditions essential at different times: When sick, health seems essential to happiness; when really hungry, it is food; the existentially hopeless emphasize the sense of meaning or purpose; and the ambitious believe that it is success that one needs in order to be happy.

One source of confusion about the conditions for happiness issues from the enormous differences in time-span subsumed under the simple term, *happiness*. Buying a new car can make one "happy," in the sense that it is immediately gratifying. Any improvement in one's material circumstances is likely to be pleasant in this sense; but although there is an immediate increase in happiness, the long-term effect may actually be toward unhappiness. For example, addictive drugs can produce immediate psychic highs, but their longer-term effects are often extremely unhappy. One implication of the contextual theory of happiness is that we regularly learn the wrong thing from our gratifications: Because certain conditions give us immediate pleasure, we mistakenly infer that they elevate our total, long-term happiness.

We rarely give sufficient attention to the *relational* character of experience. For example, where a child might be delighted to find a dime on the sidewalk, an adult might question whether a dime was worth retrieving. It is the same dime, but what it can buy is likely to be more pleasing for the child. So too with adults whose financial circumstances change. The little apartment that was once so satisfying becomes incommensurate with one's improved status. We all know about such relativism, but it is hard to incorporate relational considerations into our thinking about what counts most in life. *The primary aim of this book is to explore the implications for happiness of a thorough-going psychological relativism.*

The pleasantness of any particular event depends on how it compares with those related events that form its immediate context for hedonic judgment. The overriding dependence of pleasure on context means that the correlation between happiness and the usual sociometric indicators, like wealth or health, must always be low. This dependence on context may be an important reason why empirical surveys do not find substantial correlations between objective material measures and self-avowals of happiness.[7] It also argues against defining happiness in terms of any absolute conditions.

It would seem an endless task to enumerate the specific concrete conditions in which different people appear to be happy. Such a goal encourages *the psychologist's fallacy*, mistakenly assuming that others are like oneself. For example, the attractions of philosophical contemplation, so strong for Plato and Aristotle, may be felt by only a few people. Philosophers may experience their greatest enthusiasms while contemplating universal truths or wrestling with deep philosophical problems, but most people would be quickly frustrated by the effort. We know that people are different, that "one man's meat is another's poison," and that what is satisfying at one period of one's life may be dissatisfying at a later period. This book does not attempt to detail specific conditions for happiness. People must do that for themselves. Rather, the goal here is to specify, at a more general level, those relationships that must hold between one's experiences and their respective hedonic contexts to produce happiness—regardless of the absolute level or nature of whatever elicits one's hedonic experiences. An additional goal is to encourage speculation about how changes in hedonic contexts might improve one's overall balance of happiness.

ATTITUDES AND HABITS

The Greek philosopher Epicurus developed a psychological approach for avoiding unhappiness.[8] Where Aristotle had allowed that a certain amount of health and wealth is essential to happiness, Epicurus prescribed an attitude toward life that would provide psychological insurance against a loss of health or wealth, a loss that would otherwise leave one unhappy. His prescription was to establish an ascetic detachment from material conditions so as to minimize the pain of their

---

[7]This is my empirical generalization after reviewing the extensive survey research on self-avowals of happiness, including the summary reviews cited in Footnote 2. See, for example, the classic study by Campbell, Converse, and Rodgers (1976). Similar assessments can be found in Cantril (1965) and Easterlin (1973).

[8]For an introduction to the philosophy of Epicurus, see Russell (1945) and Smith (1934).

loss. Although Epicurus claimed that a man could be happy even on the rack,[9] it is not clear that he believed genuine happiness to be possible.

Epicurus' emphasis on internal attitude rather than on external conditions has had wide appeal, often in other, more materialistic forms. Belief in "the power of positive thinking" (Peale, 1952) is popular psychology. Be optimistic rather than pessimistic! Describe your glass as half full rather than half empty! Act as though you were happy, and you will, in fact, be happier! This is like Shakespeare's Hamlet admonishing his mother to assume the cloak of virtue so she might actually become more virtuous or James' (1910) admonishing the depressed to act out a more cheerful part so as to actually become more cheerful.

This kind of self-therapy seems a characteristic part of contemporary American culture. The socially acceptable response to the question "How are you?" is "Fine, and how are you?" (to which you must in turn respond that you too are fine). When practiced assiduously, this positive approach to life can give a superficial impression of happiness. It is less clear that one actually becomes happier. An extreme case is provided by the young cultists who accost people in airports with their "happy" smiles. Former cultists have reported that while smiling on the outside, they had been crying on the inside.[10]

The behavioristic approach to happiness seems subject to the same limitation. Reinforcement theorists in psychology, such as the once enormously influential Clark Hull, posited that it is the reduction of tissue needs that is the basis for all rewards or reinforcements for behavior. Others have applied related behavioristic approaches to happiness.[11] However, reinforcement principles seem more obviously applicable to certain examples of overt behavior than to the private experiences of pleasure identified here with happiness.

THE CONTEXTUAL APPROACH

This approach to understanding happiness begins with the relational nature of hedonic experience. It tries to separate happiness, conceived as a theoretical summation over momentary pleasures and pains, from the multitude of different conditions that can be conducive to happiness. One person's happiness may depend largely on friendships, another's on success at work.

What these happy conditions have in common is their setting up of favorable

---

[9]Russell (1945) asserted that Epicurus preceded the Stoics with this oft-quoted claim.

[10]This skepticism about the value of trying to appear happy should be distinguished from the real possibility that those who are genuinely optimistic are indeed happier. Myers (1992) made a persuasive case for the latter proposition (cf. Taylor, 1980, on their also being healthier).

[11]Hull's (1943) behavioristic theory dominated scientific psychology, particularly in the 1950s, until it came to seem untestable—even by the simple animal experiments for which it had been developed. It was Skinner (1948, 1971) and Houston (1981) who applied the behavioristic approach most directly to happiness.

contexts. It does not matter for long-term happiness how much money we make. What counts is how each of our earnings, including anticipations of income, stacks up against our own past earnings, the earnings of our friends or competitors, and against our hopes and fears in this domain. It is the representation of these in the context for judging our own earnings that determines how pleased we will be with what we actually make. Pleasures will outweigh pains in this domain only to the degree that our monetary gains are high relative to the levels with which we compare them.

SUMMARY

A review of prominent philosophical and psychological conceptions of happiness suggests a defining role for hedonic experience, pleasure and pain. In the spirit of how the term is most often used, *happiness* is defined here as a theoretical summation or average of all the separate pleasures and pains experienced over whatever period is being considered. Although this psychological definition is taken directly from the Utilitarians, the contextual theory of happiness incorporates neither the ethical nor the psychological hedonism of classical Utilitarianism: Happiness is defined descriptively with no implications for how one ought to behave, nor does the contextual theory assume that people try to maximize pleasure. Rather, the theory focuses on those contexts in which pleasures and pains are experienced and on how different contextual relationships contribute to happiness.

2 Pleasure as an Internal Judgment

Defining happiness as the balance of pleasure over pain has a frustrating looseness that allows for many possible interpretations. What is meant by *pleasure* and *pain*? How can they be measured? What can it mean to assess the balance of pleasure over pain? These questions are the concern of this chapter.

A BRIEF HISTORICAL INTRODUCTION

It was not until a little more than a century ago, when psychology was first breaking away from philosophy, that subjective experiences of pleasure and pain began to be studied experimentally. Pursuing a program that had been proposed by the 17th- and 18th-century philosophers of empiricism, Locke and Hume, Wundt founded the world's first laboratory of experimental psychology at Leipzig in 1879. Wundt used controlled introspection as the scientific basis for his dimensional theory of feeling. The hedonic component of each experience of feeling is represented in Wundt's theory by the dimension of pleasure and pain: each experience, real or imagined, has a specific location or value on this dimension.[1] Wundt was close to common sense in believing that he not only experienced pleasure and pain directly but that he could discriminate degrees of

---

[1]Osgood, Suci, and Tannenbaum (1955), using the *semantic differential* to collect and factor analyze ratings, found virtually the same underlying dimensions of connotative meaning that Wundt found, with the hedonic dimension usually predominant; Miller (1962) pointed out the interesting congruence between results obtained by Wundt's classical introspection and by Osgood's more behavioristic analysis.

intensity along the hedonic dimension. Before him at Leipzig, Weber and Fechner had worked out psychophysical methods for measuring subjective sensations. Wundt and his students used these methods in their attempts to build a quantitative, experimental science of the mind.

As Fechner predicted, we are still arguing about how subjective experiences should be measured. The history of scientific psychology presents a strange but revealing story on this question. Psychologists working in the tradition of Wundt could not agree on the fundamental nature of pleasure—for example, whether it is a quality of sensory experience or a unique type of conscious element; and the introspective reports seem unduly influenced by training and theoretical preconceptions. Exasperated by such controversies and by the slow development of theory, experimental psychology came to reject introspection. Indeed, for half a century (roughly 1915–1965), the dominant American theoreticians in experimental psychology derided any concern with subjective experience, rejecting it as outside the domain of science. This was our behavioristic period. If conceptions of pleasure and pain were to have any scientific respectability, these measures would have to be defined in terms of publicly observable behavior. Watson (1913) had urged psychologists to stop "deluding themselves in thinking that private mental experiences could be the object of scientific study" (p. 160). Under the influence of the logical positivism of philosophers like Carnap and the early Wittgenstein, the radical behaviorists, for whom Skinner became the most outspoken representative, attempted to define pleasure as a disposition to behave in certain ways. For example, where the influential educational psychologist Thorndike (1910) had first hypothesized that pleasure stamps in the connection between the response and whatever stimulus precedes it, he later made this formulation more acceptable to behaviorists by defining pleasure as a characteristic of anything the organism would approach.

The promissory notes presented by Skinner and the positivistic philosophers, their bold offers to catch the meaning of subjective terms like *pleasure* and *pain* with behavioristic definitions, were never satisfactorily delivered—although not for lack of effort, as in the philosophical analyses by Ryle (1949) and Cowan (1968), and the efforts by Tolman (e.g., 1950) to define *expectation* experimentally.[2] Meanwhile, psychologists continued to perform psychophysical experiments designed to measure subjective experiences, like pleasure, using variations upon the methods devised in the 19th century. It is this research, it seems to me, that provides the best foundation for a theory of happiness defined as the

---

[2]Ryle (1949), like a behavioristic psychologist, argued that most of what is meant by pleasure and pain is simply overt behavior, including verbal expression. This may satisfy the concern with how we recognize the pleasures and pains experienced by other people; but for oneself, it would be almost a joke to question whether or not the toothache was painful and then to conclude that "because I told the dentist that it is painful, it must be." What is epiphenomenal is not our private hedonic experience but rather the overt behaviors with which we may or may not report it.

average level of pleasure. Now, the postbehavioristic climate of cognitive psychology encourages the development of theories about the judgmental processes underlying subjective experiences of pleasure and pain.

PSYCHOPHYSICAL EXPERIMENTS

Although often outside the mainstream of experimental psychology, which has tended to concentrate on learning and memory, psychophysics continues to be one of psychology's most successful fields of scientific research—as measured both by substantive findings and predictive theory. In a typical psychophysical experiment, simple physical stimuli (such as auditory tones) are presented in random order; observers, usually human, are instructed to report subjectively on each presentation. This report may simply be whether or not the observer detects the presence of a stimulus, but often the instructions ask the observer to report how loud, large, or pleasant the stimulus seems. For example, the observer may rate a particular odor 6—*slightly pleasant* on a scale from 1—*very, very unpleasant* to 9—*very, very pleasant.*

Such experiments can provide extraordinarily systematic data, as systematic as any in experimental psychology. The theories devised to explain these data, such as Thurstone's (1929) theory of discriminal dispersions, the closely related theory of signal detection (Swets, Tanner, & Birdsall, 1961), and Anderson's (1981) theory of information integration, are among the most sophisticated of psychology's explanatory systems, with the greatest predictive success. Each of these theories must deal with the determining influence of the stimulus context. For example, the same solution of sugar in a soft drink may be rated *sweet* when tasted along with drinks having less sugar, *flat* when the other drinks have higher concentrations of sugar. It is from these shifting reports that the theories have succeeded in abstracting constant scale values to represent the stimuli.[3] However, it seems self-evident that it is the verbal reports themselves, untransformed by theory, that best reflect the actual subjective experiences; for they are the way in which we ordinarily report these experiences, whether with respect to loudness, sweetness, or pleasantness.

---

[3]The special appeal of these inferred scale values is that they often remain constant under variations in experimental conditions that radically affect observers' reports of particular stimuli, permitting a parsimony of explanation (Anderson, 1981; Birnbaum, 1982; Mellers & Birnbaum, 1982). They thus represent psychologically constant features of the stimuli, analogous to physical measures like length and weight. This stability became the goal sought by many psychophysicists (e.g., Poulton, 1989; Stevens, 1971), but it is not basic to the measurement of pleasure. A related concern was expressed by Campbell and his collaborators who have attempted to separate perceptual from semantic shifts in judgment experimentally (e.g., Krantz & Campbell, 1961; Harvey & Campbell, 1963).

PLEASURE EXPERIENCES AS DIMENSIONAL JUDGMENTS

The Utilitarian theory of pleasure (Bentham, 1794/1948) conceptualized the stream of consciousness as a succession of experiences, each of which has a certain degree of pleasantness or unpleasantness. There was no attempt to describe the special nature of the hedonic experience: This was taken as a given, undefined, perhaps undefinable, but something of which readers could be as certain as they were of sensory qualities, like the color red. It seems to me that Bentham was right. Although people would find it difficult to define hedonic experience, they have no difficulty describing its intensity, particularly when the pleasure or pain is extreme.

Bentham did not take account of the relational character of pleasure, how the pleasantness of anything depends on the context in which it is experienced. The relational orientation driving this book encourages the assumption that pleasures and pains are always dimensional judgments,[4] reflecting relationships to contextual events on the dimension of preferability. The fact that verbal reports of the degree of pleasantness are so highly predictable from the immediate context argues for identifying the experience itself as a judgment. However, we are not ordinarily aware of making such judgments; the pleasure or pain is itself the immediate conscious experience. It is when we try to understand the experience, to predict the verbal report of pleasure or pain, that it becomes clear we are dealing with an internal judgment.

Music can be painful when it is too loud, lemonade unpleasant when either too sweet or not sweet enough. The physical correlates of the pleasure dimension can be enormously complex. Even for something as simple as a sip of lemonade, pleasantness is affected by the amount of sugar and lemon, the temperature of the drink, the drinker's state of thirst, the level of each of these for the more recent prior experiences with lemonade, and a host of other, somewhat correlated conditions. If this seems forbiddingly complicated, imagine the complexity of what is being judged when we take pleasure in feeling loved or in our success at making progress toward some intellectual goal! Rather than attempt such an endless analysis, the present effort takes a radically different direction.

We begin with the assumption, for which there is actually considerable evidence,[5] that whenever pleasure is experienced, the event that is pleasant compares favorably with other events in the context in which it is experienced. These

---

[4]This should not be confused with the *judgmental theory of feeling* developed by Peters (1935) and Carr (1925), whose more behavioristic approach attributes the judgment to observation of one's own tendency to approach or avoid.

[5]The ratings of pleasantness obtained in carefully controlled experiments can be predicted with considerable accuracy from the stimulus context: change the context and the same stimulus, whether it is a particular sum of money, an odor, or a life event (like cutting yourself while shaving), receives a predictably different hedonic rating.

contextual events differ on a scale of preference, from least to most preferred. This underlying dimension of preference is what differentiates hedonic judgments from other dimensional judgments, such as the experienced loudness of a piece of music or sweetness of a sip of lemonade. Preference is the measure of utility, the measure of subjective value or worth, that is basic to the theory of subjective expected utility. This theory is the contemporary version of classical Utilitarianism that is so popular with economists and students of decision making.[6] The utility of some particular event can sometimes remain constant under changes in context that shift the hedonic experience from pleasant to unpleasant; but within any particular context, the more preferred event is always more pleasant.

To get from preference to pleasure, appeal must be made to a process of hedonic judgment. The judged event is compared with the context of related events on the dimension of preference or utility. This process of judgment reflects the place of the judged event with respect to the range and relative frequencies of the other events in the context. The judgment follows well-established principles that are described in later chapters. Although the experience of pleasure is itself conscious, we are rarely aware of applying these principles of judgment or even of the context to which they are applied.

When we try to describe the pleasantness of something, we ordinarily make a verbal categorization, such as *somewhat pleasant* or *very unpleasant*. This category rating is predictable from the context, using the principles of judgment developed to explain the results of laboratory experiments. These are the experiments that led to the contextual theory of happiness. With the happiness for any period defined as the hypothetical mean across all the hedonic judgments (that is, across all the ratings of pleasantness that could have been made during that period), the theory can predict the effects on this happiness of different hedonic contexts. The later chapters of this book are primarily concerned with the practical possibilities for establishing happier contexts.

THE PSYCHOPHYSICS OF PLEASURE

Consider a laboratory experiment in which human subjects are presented a series of odors (sniffing chemicals stored in bottles) under instructions to rate the pleasantness or unpleasantness of each presentation. Subjects have little diffi-

---

[6]See Raifa (1968), Savage (1950), Von Neumann and Morgenstern (1947). This modern version of utility theory, so basic to much of contemporary thinking (especially in economics), places emphasis on the maximization of utility, as inferred from consistent choices. Its conception of utility is radically different from the conception of pleasure presented here or indeed as used by the man on the street (see Kahneman & Varey, 1992). The preferences revealed by actual choices are also different from moral preferability: We say it is morally preferable to turn the other cheek even when our actual choice is to hit back.

culty making such ratings, and their behavior seems consistent with these verbal categorizations. For example, if the series of odors includes a true stench, some subjects supplement their low ratings with less formal exclamations, such as "phew," or with gestures, even holding their noses. An occasional subject has refused to continue with the experiment, complaining that the stench is too revolting. At the other end of the scale, a subject may describe a particular odor as "absolutely divine!" One graduate student liked to "start each day euphorically" with a whiff from the bottle containing extract from vanilla bean. Perfume companies strive to capitalize on such attractions.

Within the constraints of the behavioristic framework, these reports are not indicative of private experience, at least not any experience accessible to science. However, the experimental subjects know they are trying to report what they feel, and they certainly know when they experience an extremely pleasant or unpleasant odor. What they may not know is that the experimenter has considerable control over the pleasantness of any particular presentation. For example, the experimenter can make a neutral test odor (like plain water) unpleasant by presenting it on alternate trials with odors that the subject rates "pleasant." This was first demonstrated by Beebe-Center (1932).[7]

Beebe-Center's findings have since been extended to dozens of other types of psychophysical stimuli. My range-frequency theory of judgment allows the experimenter to predict with some precision the changes in the category rating of any stimulus, depending on the changes in the set of stimuli with which the stimulus is presented. The evidence for this is reviewed in chapter 5. Here, the reader is asked to take on faith the empirical generalization that category ratings are *highly* predictable from the stimulus context which, in psychophysics, is often the particular series of stimuli presented for judgment.

Consider a variation on Beebe-Center's experiment, a variation in which the subject is not asked to report the pleasantness of each of the successive presentations, only to sniff them. Finally, after a lot of sniffing, the subject is given the usual instructions for judgment. Even the very first rating will be predictable from the preceding context. Indeed, it will be the same rating the subject would have given after making overt ratings from the beginning. This encourages the assumption that each presentation naturally elicits an internal judgment, whether or not it is overtly reported in the form of a category rating, and that this internal judgment follows the same contextual principles as do the overt ratings.

In everyday conversation, we may say that we find a particular perfume "enchanting." This verbal categorization communicates that its odor is very pleasant. The pleasure would ordinarily have been experienced whether or not we tried to describe it, either to ourselves or to others. This conception of

---

[7]Described by Beebe-Center (1932) in his landmark book, *The Psychology of Pleasantness and Unpleasantness*. Beebe-Center's (1929) *law of affective equilibrium* is an early formulation of the theory of adaptation level, a prominent contextual theory of judgment, examined in chapter 4.

pleasure as an internal judgment does not require any particular overt behavior, only that we could report our pleasure if so motivated. Sometimes, the report is a silent verbal category, such as *very pleasant*, made only to ourselves. More often, there is no report at all, either public or private: We simply experience some degree of pleasure or pain, usually as an attribute of some real or imaginary stimulus event.

MEASURING PLEASURE

Although the Utilitarians assumed the quantifiability of pleasure and pain, they did not explain how hedonic intensity might be measured. Supposedly, the numeric representations of different degrees of pleasure or pain could be added and multiplied, just like fundamental physical measures. However, no method was presented for actually arriving at numbers.

A solution to this problem of measurement is suggested by psychophysical research. Just as psychophysicists use their subjects' category ratings to measure in the laboratory the effects of different manipulations of the immediate context upon the pleasantness of a particular stimulus, the same type of rating provides a measure of the effects of different contexts upon the pleasantness of everyday experiences. People ordinarily employ verbal category ratings to describe their everyday pleasures and pains to themselves and to others. Although ratings are rarely given in numerical form outside the laboratory, even when trying to be as precise or accurate as possible, experimental research demonstrates that verbal categories can be transformed to numbers whose theoretical addition or averaging produces predictable values—and hence, a meaningful measure of happiness as we are defining it.

Consider how such measures might be used to assess the overall balance of happiness for some extended period of a life. We can imagine recording a category rating of the pleasantness or painfulness of each successive experience, immediately after it occurred. But to record the countless number of successive ratings required for such a complete assessment would soon become tedious, even if it were practically possible. Instead, one could take a representative sample of one's experiences: Every time a randomly programmed alarm sounded, a rating could be recorded of the degree of pleasantness of what one had just experienced.[8]

---

[8]This procedure was developed in the 1970s by Csikszentmihalyi who used it in conjunction with an extensive questionnaire. This Experience Sampling Method (ESM) was employed successfully in numerous studies (e.g., Csikszentmihalyi, 1990; Csikszentmihalyi & LeFevre, 1989; Csikszentmihalyi & Massimini, 1985; Diener, Larson, & Emmons, 1984). It is not clear from the published reports how many ratings were exactly at neutral, indicating neither pleasure nor pain. Another problem, one that I have experienced myself, is that the sounding of the alarm may be an unpleasant interruption that reduces the validity of the ratings.

This would be an interesting exercise, but it would also be frustrating because on most occasions one would not be able to report any genuine pleasure or pain. Perhaps only a very small minority of our experiences are genuinely hedonic. Neutral experiences could all be assigned a 0, with the occasional pleasure or pain reported on a scale from -10 to $+10$. Later, all these randomly sampled ratings could be numerically averaged. According to the Utilitarian conception of happiness, this average would approximate the degree of happiness for the period of time sampled—provided, of course, that these ratings were accurate representations of the pleasures and pains actually experienced.[9]

This averaging across ratings of randomly sampled moments would come much closer to an assessment of happiness in the Utilitarian sense than do the more global assessments obtained in surveys of the quality of life. In these surveys,[10] people are asked to select from a restricted set the particular category or numerical rating that best represents their degree of happiness for some recent period. Americans typically claim to be almost two thirds of the way up from the bottom of the scale, well over on the happy side. Few confess to being unhappy.[11] This would all be wonderful, if true; but the overall picture strikes me, as it does most other psychologists with whom I have discussed these reports, as unrealistically rosy.

If these self-avowals were supposed to represent happiness in the Utilitarian sense, the task would seem impossibly difficult. How could anyone be expected to remember the various pleasant and unpleasant events occurring over a long period (or even a representative sample of them), to assign each a numerical rating on a scale of pleasantness, and to compute the average for all of these ratings, accomplishing this mnemonic and arithmetic feat while the interviewer is impatiently waiting for an answer? Although the interviewer rarely fails to elicit a rating, these ratings may be simply what the interviewees think is expected, what they think might make a good impression, or what the immediate interview situation seems to demand. Therefore, this type of global report may not provide a very valid measure of happiness in the Utilitarian sense.

---

[9]A simpler, rough-and-ready assessment of whether a particular period has been happy or unhappy for you could be made using the following method. Begin the period with 10 pennies in your left pocket and 10 in your right. Every time something seems really pleasant (7 or above on a 9-point scale), transfer a penny from the left pocket to the right. Every time something seems really unpleasant (3 or less on the same scale), transfer a penny in the other direction, right to left. When all 20 are in the same pocket, you know at least the direction of imbalance for that period.

[10]Reviewed by Diener (1984) and by Veenhoven, (1984a, 1984b). For earlier massive studies, see Andrews and Withey (1976), Campbell (1981), and Cantril (1965).

[11]I once prevailed upon Gerald Shure, an indulgent colleague, to conduct a random telephone survey in which interviewees rated the pleasantness of what they had been experiencing just before the phone had rung and also rated their overall happiness. As predicted, ratings averaged significantly higher for overall happiness. Like a number of investigators, I found (in classroom demonstrations) that, on average, students rate their own happiness higher than they rate the average happiness of their fellow students.

Therein lies a basic problem for practical research on happiness. If people's global self-avowals are not to be credited, how can we determine which conditions are conducive to happiness? Empirically, global ratings correlate poorly with general conditions, like health and wealth. These low correlations are consistent with the contextual theory which relates happiness to context rather than to absolute levels. Also consistent is the finding that avowals of happiness tend to increase slightly with wealth within a particular country but that wealthier countries are not necessarily happier than poorer countries by this measure. The contextual interpretation would be that people are more likely to judge their own material status in a context of others within their own country and closer to themselves.

A radically different approach was taken in developing the contextual theory of happiness. It began with the study of contextual conditions determining immediate experiences, concentrating on category ratings of well-specified stimuli. These momentary ratings are more believable because they are focused on immediate experience. They are also more systematically related to definable contextual conditions, providing principles useful for predictive theorizing. The goal of the contextual theory is to articulate conditions governing immediate hedonic experience which can then suggest, at the most general level, contextual conditions conducive to happiness.

Commensurability of Pleasures.   A common objection to the Utilitarian emphasis on the summation of separate hedonic experiences is that qualitatively different pleasures are not commensurate. An example of this objection is illustrated by John Stuart Mill's (1863/1939) introduction of qualitative distinctions, a major retreat from Bentham's simple quantitative approach. Thus, Mill maintained that it "is better to be Socrates dissatisfied than a fool satisfied" (p. 902), evidently considering a given amount of intellectual pleasure to be worth more than the same amount of sensual pleasure. Mill justified this by the following *thought experiment*: Imagine a person of broad experience who has lived two lives, one as Socrates, the other as a fool; even if both lives included the same amount of pleasure, would not such a person choose the life of Socrates?

This appeal to informed choice is basic to the modern utility theory and neoclassical economics. Utilities are inferred from choices. Utility theory assumes that people are rational, in the sense of being consistent in their preferences; it then follows that people's subjective values are revealed by their choices.

A problem with this modern version of Utilitarianism is that people often choose unwisely. Not only can people be systematically inconsistent in their choices,[12] but they often ignore the effects of future contexts upon how the outcomes of their choices will be experienced. Comparing both lives, a philoso-

---

[12]Schoemaker (1982) reviewed experimental demonstrations of this inconsistency.

pher would no doubt choose the life of Socrates. But the fool does not know how Socrates lives, Socrates' delight in dialectic, the ecstasy of Socrates' mystical contemplations. And what the fool does not know cannot enter into his context for pleasure. Once the fool's limited context is extended to include the life experiences of Socrates (as in Mill's case of the person who has lived both lives), the choice between the two no longer reflects the pleasures or pains peculiar to each one.

Mill's retreat from Bentham's Utilitarianism reflects a common observation: The intense pleasure from gulping down a cold drink when very thirsty is qualitatively different from the intense pleasure of first learning that the one you love also loves you. Bentham could have argued that the difference is simply one of duration: The cold drink gives pleasure for only a moment, the excitement of reciprocated love endures much longer. But there are other differences. One seems to be primarily a physical sensation, the other a cognitive appraisal (albeit with physical concomitants). These differences are undoubtedly of far-reaching importance, affecting how we talk about the experience and even our subsequent choices. But are qualitative differences crucial to the measurement of pleasure? Can these apples and oranges really be counted together as so many delights to be tasted?

The simple answer is that they can. The relationship of the best among one's physical sensations to its context of other sensory experiences is the same as the relationship of the best among one's cognitive-social experiences to its context of other cognitive-social experiences. The relationship of each experience to its own context is what determines how each is judged. If the hedonic component of experience is this judgment of pleasantness, then the degree of pleasantness is the same for all experiences that bear the same relationship to their respective hedonic contexts on the dimension of preference. However, when a single new context includes qualitatively different experiences, as when a person who has lived both lives compares Socrates' pleasures with those of the fool, then qualitative preferences become crucial. It is the differences in preference or utility, differences that become relevant only when the qualitatively different experiences are compared with each other (i.e., within the same, larger context) that led Mill to deny that the two lives could be equated with respect to pleasantness.

Qualitative differences between types of pleasure become crucial when their eliciting events are judged in a single context. Then, the preference of one over the other is reflected in a difference in pleasantness. Consider an example drawn from my own experience. I love to windsurf on a small sailboard, and I ordinarily prefer this type of sailing to sitting on the beach. However, small-board windsurfing is only enjoyable when the wind is strong—above 15 knots. With less wind, trying to windsurf becomes a frustrating experience. On the other hand, just lounging on the beach can be enjoyable, especially when there is little wind and no temptation to sail. This suggests a simple rule: Sail when the wind is strong, lounge on the beach when the wind is light.

Oh, that it were so easy! Like so many other windsurfers, I sometimes attempt to sail when the wind is too light. At the moment of this foolish choice, the prospect of even mediocre sailing seems preferable to lounging on the beach. And it is preferable, given that the two activities are being compared and are thus in the same context. But once out on the water and suffering the frustrations of insufficient wind, the context for sailing no longer includes lounging on the beach. Instead, it consists mostly of other sailing experiences when the wind has been much stronger. The beach would have yielded much more pleasure than sailing if I could have excluded the prospect of sailing from my context of beach experiences. The essence of this argument about ignoring qualitative differences is that these differences become important only when events with the different qualities are compared, for then the difference in pleasure is affected by the difference between their positions on a scale of preference.

Consider an example that is experienced by almost all of us who work. We do not ordinarily compare our work with our recreational pastimes. There are pleasant and unpleasant experiences at work, just as there are pleasant and unpleasant experiences when we are playing. A good experience at work may have little effect, either positive or negative, on our recreational pleasures: The respective contexts for these two domains are ordinarily independent. But this independence does not preclude their being incorporated into a single context. Suppose that one day we have the choice between working and playing. Then, the different activities of working may be compared with those of playing. Perhaps most people would have little difficulty with such a choice, providing there would be no punishment for skipping work that particular day; most take all the paid vacation time they are allowed. And yet, many of these same people may actually have a greater balance of satisfaction at work than at play.[13]

If we must work, we should avoid conditions that encourage comparison with a preferred activity such as play. Better not to have our friends call us at work, particularly not with invitations to join them in our favorite recreations! The pleasure of working is maximized when the activities of work stack up well against the other events in the same context. These other events will typically be related to work, including what happened on other recent days at work. It may seem odd to suggest that these events could, on the average, stack up well against themselves; but that is a basic implication of this theory of happiness, and it is what has been repeatedly demonstrated in experimental studies of judgment: To the degree that the most preferred of the events in the context come relatively often, the overall balance tips toward pleasure over pain.

---

[13]A psychological hedonist might ask why, if this were the case, they do not choose to work rather than to play. Possible reasons for people choosing an alternative that yields less pleasure are considered in later chapters, particularly in chapter 8 where such "irrationality" is characteristic of most players of the Happiness Game.

The Problem Of Neutral Pleasures.   As described by Miller (1962), Wundt's best known research on the measurement of pleasure was performed with the ticks and tocks of a metronome. Varying their rate, he experienced different degrees of pleasantness or unpleasantness. That Wundt could find pleasure in these ticks and tocks suggests his complete immersion in the experiment, with the different rates of the metronome becoming his entire context for judgment.

In the broader contexts of everyday life, the metronome would seem hedonically neutral, devoid of real pleasure or pain. Perhaps an overwhelming proportion of our experiences are just as neutral. Although Bentham (1789) may have been right that pleasure and pain are the "supreme masters," their occurrence may be much less frequent than he assumed.

This paucity of hedonic experience need not be disturbing for Utilitarians: Any experience could be rated on a scale of pleasantness, even though most experiences would be rated at the neutral point (i.e, as neither pleasant nor unpleasant). However, if these neutral experiences were to be averaged in when computing the overall level of happiness, they could overwhelm the relatively infrequent pleasures and pains. Suppose that 90% of our experiences were neutral and that we assigned each of them a 5 on a scale from 1 to 9. Suppose also that the remaining 10% averaged to a happy 7 for one life, an unhappy 3 for another. The overall average would then be 5.2 for the happier life, 4.8 for the unhappier life. The difference would be only 5% of the difference between agony and ecstasy (i.e., between 1 and 9). Could such a small difference be all that differentiates happiness from unhappiness?[14] If we could somehow restrict such comparisons to averages, ignoring the component experiences (which could go from 1 to 9), even such a small difference might indeed seem important.

Experiences that are not hedonic should be distinguished from those that, although neither pleasant or unpleasant, are nevertheless hedonic (i.e., those having an hedonic value that is "neutral"). An example of an hedonically neutral experience might be a sip of a particular wine that it is neither pleasant nor unpleasant; this is a judgment made in a context of other wines, some of which would be preferred to it, whereas it would be preferred to others. Another example might be an hedonically neutral reaction when receiving a perfunctory "thank you," perhaps having hoped for more, but also having feared that one would get less. Such hedonically neutral experiences cannot be overwhelmingly

---

[14]How could we discriminate happy from unhappy periods of our own lives if the difference were really so small? The answer comes from psychophysical research demonstrating that discriminability is inversely proportional to contextual range (Braida & Durlach, 1972; Parducci & Perrett, 1971). This relational characteristic of judgment ensures remarkable powers of discrimination when the range of experienced differences is very small. For example, on tropical islands where the temperature is almost always in the 80s, the natives are sensitive to differences that seem hardly noticeable to us; thus, they complain of the extremes, of the heat when the temperature is in the high 80s, of the cold when it is in the low 80s.

frequent, at least not according to the judgment principles of the contextual theory of happiness.[15]

Much more frequent are experiences that do not seem to be in any sense hedonic, those whose lack of both pleasantness and unpleasantness is due to their not being experienced in a context of events that vary in preferability. As illustrated by the numerical example, these might be frequent enough to overwhelm the genuinely hedonic experiences. Averaging them into the hypothetical computation of happiness would tend to trivialize differences on this measure. But they must be included when we are considering the hedonic richness or fullness of life. Consider two lives, both of which have twice as much pleasure as pain but one of which has a much higher proportion of experiences that are nonhedonic in the sense of lacking the potential for pleasure or pain. If the total duration of conscious experience were the same for the two lives, would not the one with a smaller proportion of these neutrals be happier?

This seems to catch what people mean when they say that they "want to experience life more fully," even if there must be some additional pain along with the expected increase in pleasure. A happy life would become still happier in spite of there being no change in the overall balance of all genuinely hedonic experiences. Living more fully, in this sense of living more hedonically, is perhaps the most obvious road to a happier life.

SUMMARY

The scientific study of pleasure and pain began scarcely a century ago, following the program of research envisioned by the philosophers of British Empiricism. Psychophysical experiments permitted experimental control of the context for hedonic experiences. This research led to the present conception of pleasure as an internal judgment elicited by an experience, real or imaginary, in a context of other experiences that vary on a scale of preference or utility. The contextual nature of pleasure is demonstrated by experiments studying judgments of simple perceptual stimuli, like odors, and also judgments of symbolic or imaginary events. The pleasantness is typically experienced as an attribute of what is being judged, just as blueness is an experienced attribute of a clear sky. Like any dimensional judgment, the hedonic experience can be verbalized as a category rating. These verbal ratings transmit quantitative information: for example, *slightly pleasant* can be equivalent to a rating of 6 on a 9-point scale. Category ratings thus provide a quantitative measure of different degrees of pleasantness that can be averaged, hypothetically, across qualitatively different experiences to calculate the degree of happiness. This average need not correspond to a self-avowal of happiness of the type collected in surveys of subjective well-being.

---

[15]Not even if virtually all experiences were concentrated at the midpoint of an hedonic context.

Reports of immediate hedonic experience are much more direct and thus more believable than the more global self-avowals of happiness that could hardly be the product of an overall averaging process. In spite of their central importance for happiness, hedonic judgments comprise only a small proportion of all experiences. Increasing this proportion would make a happy life still happier, unless the ratio of pleasure to pain was thereby reduced.

3 The Context for Judgment

As with all dimensional judgments, pleasures and pains are experienced contextually. This assumption underlies the contextual theory of happiness: Pleasures and pains are determined by relationships between events, real or imaginary, in the same way that psychophysical ratings are determined by relationships between the stimuli presented by the experimenter. These events are represented as a context or frame of reference for judgment, with the degree of pleasure or pain depending on the place of the experienced event in this context.

Some contexts are happier than others, and contexts change, so that what seems like the same eliciting event can yield either more or less pleasure, depending on the context at the time it is experienced. This psychological relativism may seem obvious, but people balk when relational explanations are applied to concrete examples from their own lives. Such explanations are the functional purpose of the contextual theory of happiness.

Consider, as a perhaps distant and therefore more easily accepted example, a young woman from a poor village in Mexico who is offered temporary employment in the home of a prosperous family in the United States. This will mean a higher standard of living and the seemingly limitless possibilities of the affluent society. She will learn how easy it is to wash dishes by machine, to prepare prepackaged foods, and that expense need scarcely be considered when planning a menu. These material advantages may impress her less than differences in social relationships, especially the greater independence of women; but the material considerations are sufficient to illustrate how changes in context affect her life.

Before leaving Mexico, the overall distribution of her experiences in the domain of eating could be represented as evenly balanced with respect to pleasure and pain. Hunger was among the worst of her experiences, but such days were balanced by days of plenty, fiestas when there was more than enough to eat. Most days fell between these extremes, the daily occupations of her village life, grinding corn, preparing tortillas, and trying to make do with very little.

If we restrict our attention to her first weeks in the United States, we can see how satisfying the new abundance might be in the context of what she had been experiencing. Now she can eat all she wants, what she wants, and when she wants it. She may scarcely think of the hunger she has escaped, but it continues to operate as a contextual determinant of her present pleasures. As long as it does, each new day is almost like another fiesta, with pleasures comparable to the best she had experienced back in her village.

As the weeks and months go by, her context changes. It is no longer so delightful to open the refrigerator packed with delicacies: She has done it so many times, and she knows that it need never be empty. The piling up of experiences near the upper end of her contextual range reduces the pleasure of any particular experience. This adaptation intensifies as events from the village drop from her context. Now the lower endpoint of the context determining her pleasures in this domain is no longer the hunger occasioned by lack of food in her village but the self-imposed hunger she experiences when emulating her dieting employers. She becomes fussier about what she eats, disappointed when the family orders food that she does not really like. There must be a worst in any context; and insofar as this worst occurs as often as the best of the same context, the overall balance is unlikely to be very happy. For this young woman from Mexico, the new pains may come to be as frequent as the new pleasures so that the balance between pleasure and pain becomes roughly equal, just as it had been back in her village. It is not that she would be indifferent in choosing between abundance and want. However, her happiness may be at roughly the same level in these two, very different contexts.

Suppose that she must now return to her village. Along with the memories of her affluent life in the United States, she will bring a context in which most of her village experiences will rate very low. The first time there is nothing to eat will be distressing indeed; but it will have the beneficial effect of extending her context back downward, reducing her aversion to the monotonous diet of tortillas and frijoles. After the initial culture shock, when everything is low in the context she brings from the United States, she may slowly return to her former even balance. However, as long as the abundance of her experience in the United States remains in her context, the poverty of the village will continue to be more painful than the same poverty had been before she went north.

This tragic scenario illustrates how changes in context, even when based on improved circumstances, can lead to further changes detrimental to happiness. Everyone experiences such changes in one or another of life's important domains: People find new jobs and new friends. The contexts for work and for social relationships change accordingly. The immediate improvement in circumstances often produces contextual changes inimical to happiness.

However, the temporary move to the United States could have entrained a different scenario. Instead of the poverty of her native village dropping so quickly from the context, it could have remained indefinitely, perhaps rejuvenated in the context by occasional trips back home to her village. This would have improved her overall balance of happiness during this period of her life. Once she had returned permanently to the village, marriage or some other irrevocable decision to remain there, would hasten her readjustment to the routine of village life. Much of this book is concerned with the analysis of such changes, exploring the implications of different hypotheses about what is represented in our everyday contexts for pleasure and pain.

Defining Context

The term *context* refers to a conceptual representation of the set of events, real or imaginary, determining the dimensional judgment of any particular event. This representation is the context in which the judgment is made. It provides the standards against which a particular event is evaluated.

We are not ordinarily conscious of the context while making a judgment—although we have experienced each of the events represented in the context at some earlier time. Even subjects in a short psychophysical experiment are frequently unable to report contextual comparisons: When asked why they rated a particular concentration of sugar in lemonade as "pleasant," they typically say only that "it tasted good" or that "it was just the right level of sweetness." When I tested myself in this experiment, even though I have a specific theory for how the context determines the pleasantness of each experience, the pleasantness seemed an intrinsic property of the lemonade, with no conscious comparisons having been made.[1]

Subjects in a psychophysical experiment are also unaware that their judgments are so predictable from the context of presented stimuli. An occasional subject may plead, "Please don't use my ratings; my mind was wandering, and my random responses would just mess up your experiment." But when the ratings by such a subject are tabulated, they turn out to be no less predictable from the context than ratings by other subjects. The basic process of judgment is not open to direct introspection. Like the context on which this process operates, it must be inferred from the overt category ratings.

Constituents of Context

Applying *Occam's razor*—that is, postulating no more theoretical entities than necessary—we must assume that the context for any judgment is restricted to just those events necessary and sufficient for predicting that judgment. In experi-

---

[1] Ironically, this poverty of introspective experience may be the phenomenal basis for the behavioristic analysis of pleasure, as developed by Ryle (1949) and Cowan (1968).

ments on category ratings of the type I have made a specialty, the physical values of the presented stimuli are all we need to predict the category rating of each separate stimulus. By properly selecting the stimuli the experimenter can elicit any desired rating for a particular stimulus. For example, consider a weight-lifting experiment in which each weight in a long series of presentations is rated on a scale from *very light* to *very heavy*: If the presented weights vary between 100 and 300 grams, the 300-gram weight will be rated *very heavy*; but if they vary from 300 to 900 grams, the same 300-gram weight will be rated *very light*. It is this ease of manipulating and controlling the context that makes the psychophysical experiment a particularly attractive source of contextual principles of judgment—and hence for the contextual theory of happiness. Although the contexts of everyday life are usually more extensive and complex than the simple set of recent psychophysical presentations, the same contextual principles should govern the pleasures and pains of everyday life.[2]

In psychophysical research, each of the successive stimuli presented for judgment is consciously experienced by the experimental subjects, right at the time it is presented. Each new stimulus immediately becomes a member of the context for subsequent judgments. In some experiments, however, certain stimuli are always present, such as the background for visual presentations. Such stimuli assume a greater importance in determining the judgments. It is as though these more important stimuli were represented with higher frequency than were any of the regular stimuli the subject is rating. Importance is thus represented contextually by frequency, the more important stimuli being experienced more frequently.

Restrictions.   An exception to the rule that each stimulus is represented in the context was demonstrated by Sarris in a convincing series of experiments studying the effects of an extreme *anchoring stimulus* presented on alternate trials. He found that when the anchor was too extreme, too different from the other stimuli on the dimension of judgment, it was less likely to be incorporated into the context for subsequent judgments—in the sense of affecting these judgments (e.g., Sarris, 1967; Sarris & Parducci, 1978). Thus, even in such a simple psychophysical situation, the members of the context must share a certain similarity. With the more complex events of everyday life, the similarity may not be with respect to a single sensory dimension.

Another restriction is the limitation on the number of different presentations that can be represented in the context. When the same stimuli are presented repeatedly in a long, randomly ordered series, the relative frequencies of contextual values may be representative of only the last dozen or so presentations. The

---

[2]An argument for this consideration, one to be developed more fully in chapters 4, 5, and 6, is that rigorous tests of theories can be conducted only in situations simple enough to permit a high degree of experimental control. This would seem to preclude rigorous tests of a theory of happiness in the bewildering complexity of everyday life.

hypothesis that the context can be restricted to such a small sample of previously presented values is based on experiments in which the relative frequencies of the different stimuli are suddenly shifted.[3] This small sample is sufficient for accurate predictions of the ratings, provided that earlier endpoints (the two extreme values of the stimulus set) are assumed to remain much longer in the context. Functionally, the size of this sample may be limited by people's capacity for processing information so that no more is included than would be required for efficient characterization of the position of any particular stimulus in the whole frequency distribution of presented stimuli (Fabre, 1987; Parducci & Wedell, 1986). As new stimuli are experienced, they replace prior ones in the context. Thus each contextual representation (with the exception of the two, crucial endpoints) has a limited life—perhaps only a dozen trials. And even with this restriction to such a small set, there also may be a limit to how many different examples of a particular stimulus can be members of the same context.

We need not assume that contexts for judgment of the more complex events of everyday life must also be limited to the most recent experiences. Things that have happened in the distant past can be represented in an everyday context, even though there have been thousands of intervening events coming in and out of that context. For example, I was once paid for private consulting at a rate 20 times my regular salary. It was many years before I was tempted to do any consulting again, the proposed fees seeming grossly inadequate even though still much higher than my regular salary. In this case, there was probably a special context restricted to the different rates earned consulting—so that the hundreds of intervening paychecks from the University were not coming in and out of that particular context. In memoirs by Russian emigres who had lost their wealth when fleeing the 1917 revolution, it seems that some of them continued to feel impoverished for the rest of their lives; this suggests that their lost wealth continued to be part of the context for evaluating their reduced material circumstances in exile.

Related examples can be illustrated for the sense of *romantic tragedy* in which nothing seems satisfying in comparison with some great ideal. This ideal or dream, perhaps the hope for a magical world without evil, ensures the romantic's dissatisfaction with the world as it is. In some cases, the romantic ideal has had an earlier basis in reality, such as a lost loved one who remains permanently fixed in the context against which others are evaluated. Perhaps to hold its place in the context, the lost love must occasionally be experienced again, if only in the imagination. For some romantics, this enjoyable reliving may occupy a large enough portion of their conscious experience to tip the overall balance of plea-

---

[3]Wedell (1984) found that the rate of adjustment to the new frequencies was independent of the number of preshift presentations beyond 12 to 20; This hypothesis of a small context also provides a basis for explaining the effects of number of categories and number of stimuli (Parducci & Wedell, 1986).

sure and pain toward happiness. This could have been the case for the young Mexican woman in the example at the beginning of this chapter: After returning to her native village, she might have continued to experience in her imagination the pleasures of her life of abundance back in the United States, the pleasantness of these daydreams perhaps outweighing the pain of her reduced level of objective circumstances.

Imaginary Contexts.   The psychophysical paradigm is one in which the experimenter selects the stimuli that are presented to the subject for judgment. In many experiments, these appear to be the only stimuli represented as context, there being no need to hypothesize additional contextual representations to explain the ratings. However, nothing prevents subjects from generating their own imaginary stimuli that could become important parts of their contexts for judgment. Indeed, certain experimenters have encouraged subjects to create additional contextual representations, usually with more complex materials: "Imagine an action much more evil than any of those you are rating!" Such an injunction makes those actions actually described for judgment seem less evil, as though the imagined action were actually a member of the set presented for judgment (e.g., Dermer, Cohen, Jacobsen, & Anderson, 1979; Hunt, 1941; McGarvey, 1943).

In other experiments, the stimuli actually presented for judgment evoked imaginary possibilities that also become part of the context. In one of ours, subjects evaluated the pleasantness or unpleasantness of different outcomes in a pseudogambling game (Marsh & Parducci, 1978). When the actual outcomes included wins of up to $200 but no losses bigger than $100, the ratings ranged from *Very, Very Satisfying* for the biggest win to only *Moderately Dissatisfying* for the biggest loss. Although $100 was the biggest possible loss, it was as though subjects said to themselves, "If one can sometimes win as much as $200 in this game, it could just as well have been arranged to include a $200 loss; against that possibility, my $100 loss isn't so bad." In the part of the research studying judgments of morality, we found the same symmetrical extensions of the contextual range for different acts of behavior.

In everyday life, our imaginary worlds can evoke powerful experiences of pleasure and pain. Thurber's (1945) story, "The Secret Life of Walter Mitty," describes the imaginary triumphs of a man for whom being brought back to his modest reality was experienced as a disappointing letdown. In this appealing psychological portrayal, imaginary events became part of the context for judging real events.

More typically, our daydreams form their own separate contexts, safely distanced from reality, with little influence on our reactions to the external world. This does not imply that they are irrelevant for happiness. When a daydream is pleasant in its own context, this pleasantness must be included in any accounting of the overall balance of pleasure and pain. But daydreams vary in their pleasantness, and some may be very unpleasant. If daydreams were always pleasant, their contexts would have to include representations of lesser events from real life.

Even when pleasant daydreams do not enter into the contexts for judging publicly observable events, they can distract us from worldly affairs. Some would call this wasting time, time that could be better spent accomplishing things in the workaday world. But if the independent world of our imagination is sufficiently satisfying in itself, it may still be good for our overall balance of happiness. This is another example of a possible conflict between success and happiness.

Representations Never Experienced Hedonically.   Although events that were once consciously experienced are represented in various contexts that are themselves unconscious, there may also be contextual representations of events that were never consciously experienced. Bevan and Pritchard (1963) demonstrated that a subliminal tone—one too soft for even its presence to be reported—entered the context so that the supraliminal tones of the regular series were rated louder after it had been presented. For the symmetrical extensions of the context around the neutral point in the pseudo-gambling experiment, subjects may not have felt the pain of a loss they knew could not occur: The symmetrical contextual endpoint may have been evoked without ever having been experienced hedonically.[4]

Representations of events that enter the context without ever having been experienced would greatly enhance the possibilities for happiness.[5] Suppose that, in what must be the best of all possible worlds, we could regularly incorporate into our contexts terrible possibilities that we never had to experience, even in our imaginations. Because the worst of any context would be experienced as very painful, not having to experience it would permit a much greater balance of satisfaction. Against this perhaps overly optimistic possibility is the more likely assumption that no representation, whether of something real or only hypothetical, can become part of an hedonic context without first having been experienced as either pleasant or unpleasant. This would place a much tighter limit on the possibilities for extreme happiness, especially if the pain had to be experienced again and again. However, if representations of our most painful experiences could remain semipermanently in their contexts, having to be reexperienced only very rarely, the overall balance could be almost as favorable.

---

[4]This interpretation may also be applied to the stimulus-evoked counterfactuals hypothesized by Kahneman and Miller (1986).

[5]In certain versions of the Happiness Game that allow for evoked contextual items that are almost never themselves experienced, overall happiness can be much greater than what is possible when all contextual items must themselves be periodically reexperienced. These and some of the other possibilities suggested in this chapter are treated more specifically in chapter 9 which explores their quantitative implications.

Information-Based Contexts: Social Comparisons.   Conceptual verbal information may partially substitute for the perceptual experiences that are more ordinarily represented in the context for psychophysical judgments.[6] So too with more complex hedonic judgments. You hear that a colleague received a prize or promotion. Perhaps you feel glad for your colleague, putting yourself in his or her shoes, empathically experiencing joy at the good news; then, your subsequent evaluation of your own success could, as a result, be much less pleasant. However, your initial reaction could have been much less empathic, so that instead of joy for your colleague you experienced disappointment with yourself. You did not actually lose anything, nothing bad happened to you; nevertheless, the news of your colleague's promotion signified a certain failure on your part. This would have been especially likely if you had hoped, with some justification, to win that prize yourself. Although immediately painful, and repeatedly so insofar as you dwell upon it, this would make more pleasant those other events that are experienced in the same context.

Instead of a prize or promotion, the news might have been that your colleague had been fired. Having yourself experienced the fear of being fired, the news might bring the representation of this painful experience back into the context without your having to reexperience it. If you now take pleasure in the fact that you are not the one who was fired, you are getting a free ride—gain without pain!

The moral uneasiness of these examples of social comparisons calls for reiteration of the distinction between *psychological* and *ethical* relativism. This book deals only with how people feel, not with how they ought to feel. One ought to take pleasure in another's good fortune, and we are morally uneasy about getting pleasure from another's misfortune. The distinction between psychology and ethics, although philosophically straightforward, may not be so clearcut psychologically. Russell (1930) asserted in *The Conquest of Happiness* that people who get genuine pleasure from the pleasures of others tend to be happier as a consequence: When completely genuine, their empathic behavior ensures that other people will enjoy their company, in turn providing pleasant social support. Although appealing, Russell's claim is no more convincing to the modern skeptic than is Socrates' identification of virtue with happiness. The world would be more just if these claims were true.

Expectations, Goals, Hopes, Fears, and Standards.   The research literature on contextual effects gives a large place to the role of expectation. For example, Crespi's (1944) rats ran faster or slower to a given amount of food, depending on whether it was more or less than what they had received for previous runs. He

---

[6]This is exemplified by certain kinds of experimental instructions: for example, telling participants that the larger sizes would not reappear facilitated adjustment to the restricted series—although participants never completely adjusted to the restriction of range (Parducci & Hohle, 1957).

ascribed this elation or depression to a contrast with the rat's *level of expectation*, identified by the amount of food the rat received in the recent past. There are two ways in which Crespi's concept of *expectation* could be incorporated into the present treatment of context: a) recent experiences of food would normally be represented in the context, and b) there may also be additional representation of other amounts of food, either expected or desired. With the rat, the context might be restricted to recent experiences; but with humans, cognitive inferences and goals might deviate markedly from the levels obtained in the recent past. For example, if the meteorologist had incorrectly predicted a drop in temperature, we may experience the actual weather as warm—even though it is just a continuation of recent, normal temperatures. In this case, the context includes representations of expectations based upon the meteorologist's prediction.

The present treatment also differs from Crespi's in that the context is always a range of values, a frequency distribution, rather than just a single value, like a level of expectation. It would be conceptually simpler to characterize the context by a single value. However, as I show in the next three chapters, the conception of context as a set of representations of different events provides a more powerful basis for understanding dimensional judgments and happiness.

The pleasure derived from any event or outcome is also dependent upon anticipations—what we had been hoping for or what we had been fearing. How might these motivational states be represented contextually? Suppose, for example, that you have a tennis match scheduled against a player whom you fear is much too expert for your own level of play. You anticipate his or her shots whizzing past while you are left in helpless disgrace. Such unpleasant anticipations are likely to be represented in your context for self-evaluations of your actual play. As a consequence, even if your opponent turns out to be the expert you feared, these contextual additions reduce the level of your own embarrassment. As with other kinds of events, anticipations probably have to have been experienced hedonically before they can be represented in a context for hedonic judgments. The mere knowledge that a prospective opponent has a reputation for being very good may not be enough. You may have to feel the humiliation of being completely outclassed, if only in your imagination.

Goals and plans can also be represented in your context. You enjoy going over and over again in your imagination the wonderful things you plan to do on your vacation. In spite of increasing the likelihood of your being disappointed with the actual vacation, each pleasurable reexperiencing of the goal adds something to your sum total of pleasure. Whether or not these pleasures of anticipation outweigh the resulting disappointment depends on the relative strengths and durations of the respective pleasures and pains.

How might personal *standards* serve as context? In the present theory, a standard is just a single value, perhaps an average, that summarizes a whole distribution of contextual values. In the 1980s, for the first time in my experience, students were heard making materialistic remarks like "I know I couldn't be happy making less than $50,000 a year." But the figure of $50,000 was just a rough approximation. The context of future incomes presumably covered a range of values, with the estimated breaking point between satisfying and dissatisfying close to $50,000. Such projections of future contexts are conjectural, and the students would probably not have wanted their professed standards to be taken so seriously.

Changes in Contextual Representations.   Anyone who has participated in a rugged outdoor adventure, such as hauling a heavily loaded backpack over a steep mountain pass, may resonate to what seems a common observation: The adventure grows better in the telling so that the painful climbing, the heat, the aching muscles, the resolutions never to make such a strenuous climb again, all seem to lose their negative qualities. We enjoy describing our trials to others, and with time we even find ourselves looking forward to repeating the adventure.[7]

This seems to exemplify the systematic shifts that are so characteristic of memory. But if this is what happens to conscious memory, might it not also be happening to the various representations in a context for judgment? Psychophysical experiments demonstrate how the effective value of a standard drifts toward the values of other stimuli presented in the same experimental session.[8] In addition, there are more general, systematic shifts, upward or downward. Such shifts may have important consequences for the effects of different contexts upon happiness. Life would be better if the contextual representations of past experiences shifted downward, thereby enhancing the pleasantness of present experiences. However, the shifts may often be upward. Just as we remember the past as better than it was, as in the example from backpacking, past experiences may be represented at similarly enhanced levels in our current context for judgment; and upward drifts in contextual values would make for unhappiness.

Contexts Evoked by Particular Events.   In many of these commonplace examples, the context was evoked by the particular event being experienced. The warm day in winter can evoke a context of summer days rather than, or in addition to, the more recent colder days of winter. In this sense, the analogy to the simplest psychophysical experiments can be misleading. In such research, it is the experimenter's selection of prior stimulus presentations that establishes the context, so that there is already a context when a particular stimulus is presented for judgment. Although representations of recent experiences are important com-

---

[7]One reason the retelling or remembering may be enjoyable is that one's present comfort is compared with the trials of the adventure—also, a certain amount of self-gratification is likely to accompany the retelling: how strong and courageous one must have been to have survived such a test!

[8]Parducci, Marshall, and Degner (1966) and Parducci and Haugen, (1967) illustrated such historically well-known "drifts," explained in these cases by the range-frequency theory presented in Chapter 6.

ponents of the context for events outside of the laboratory, Kahneman and Miller (1986) speculated that a particular event can evoke a context quite different from the simple representations of the recent past.[9]

Some of this evoked context may consist of events pulled out of the more distant past. This is the case when the warm day in winter is compared with summer days. The warm day in winter may also elicit associations that become part of the context: For example, we may remember the last time that we were in this particular location, how warm it was then, and now it seems cool by comparison. However, we are usually unaware of the elements composing the context. Tulving and Schacter (1990) characterized as *implicit memory* the effect of past experience upon how we perceive the present, a type of unconscious memory that is not revealed by the usual tests for recall or recognition.

Other features of the evoked context may have been experienced only fleetingly and then only in the imagination. Suppose that you occasionally indulge in an evening of poker with several friends. Sometimes you win, sometimes you lose, but never more that $15 or $20 either way. Then, one of your friends really lucks out and goes home with $50 in winnings. Everyone is impressed. Perhaps a month later, you wind up the evening $30 in the hole. This is twice as much as you have ever lost before, more even than anyone in the group has ever lost. As the worst in your experience with poker, it should feel just awful. But this is not the way it goes when the previously described phenomenon of symmetrical extension of the range applies. Your friend's winning $50 may have evoked the possibility that one could also lose $50, against which your $30 loss does not seem so bad.[10]

More generally, certain experiences evoke possibilities that, though perhaps experienced only in the imagination, can become important elements in our present context for judging a real-world event. This evocation may be strictly intellectual: if you can win $50, you can also lose $50. As asserted previously (see footnote 5), this kind of counterfactual offers dramatic possibilities for getting the range-extending advantages of a new low event without having to experience the pain again and again. Even if a brief, one-time pain must be experienced, some bad experiences give greater contextual mileage than others. A possible loss might be experienced as awful but never be evoked as context for subsequent events. Another, no worse, might be repeatedly evoked as an endpoint of an hedonic context, enhancing the pleasantness of whatever was actually being experienced. With respect to improving happiness, only the latter pain was useful.

---

[9]A host of intriguing possibilities were presented by Kahneman and Miller (1986), illustrating their seminal notion of stimulus-evoked contexts. Although they used the term *norm* in place of *context*, it represented for them, also, a distribution of values.

[10]From the standpoint of overall happiness, each of the pleasures and pains experienced during the course of a game would have to be weighted by their durations: For example, if the reaction to each gain or loss was brief, but if the net loss of $30 was relived again and again in memory, this net loss would have to be weighted more heavily. Moreover, there might be additional negative consequences, such as deciding that you now should forgo a planned evening at the baseball stadium.

Some constituents of an evoked context may be independent of the past experience represented by the usual psychophysical context. Parts of the evoked context may not even have existed before the immediate event that evokes its own context. For example, an immediate loss of $30 might itself suggest the possibility of a still greater loss, perhaps $100.

However, evoked contexts can be representations of selected collections of actual past events. In Brown's (1953) experiment, ratings of the heaviness of small, weighted cylinders were not affected by lifting the much heavier tray on which they were arranged. However, if the experimental subjects had been asked to rate the heaviness of the tray, it would presumably have evoked a context of other trays in which this particularly tray might even have been rated as light. This is like the example of my evaluating a fee for consulting in a context of other fees rather than in a context of my more recent university paychecks.

Inferring the Context

The assumption that the constituents of a current context may not be immediately accessible to consciousness and may not even be recalled or recognized raises the practical question, how can a context be identified and controlled in the interests of happiness? Even those experiences that can be remembered may long since have been dropped from the context. This would seem to leave the concept of context as a deus ex machina that can be brought in to explain any experience of pleasure or pain but that lacks the predictive power characteristic of useful scientific theories. Perhaps there must always be this lack of power in explanations of the complex psychological phenomena of everyday life. However, the basic idea of context does have enormous explanatory power in the psychophysical laboratory: One can accurately predict what the category rating of any particular stimulus will be, knowing only the other stimuli with which it is presented.

Often, we can at least partially identify the context for an everyday judgment, even though the separation in time between the successive events represented by the context may have been months or years rather than just the seconds or minutes separating stimuli in a psychophysical experiment. When someone says of a 6'2" basketball player that "it is a shame he is so short," we can be pretty certain that the speaker's immediate context is the heights of other basketball players. If the speaker then adds, "but he's really a tall man," we know that the context has shifted to represent the heights of all men. People have little difficulty shifting back and forth between contexts.[11] In such cases, we can infer the different contexts in a general way—at least the type of events that the contexts represent. When we share particular contexts, such as the heights of basketball stars or of all adult males, there is no problem inferring the context. However, if a foreigner were to tell us that our summers seem warm, we would infer that

---

[11]Stevens (1957) used the striking example of the large mouse that ran up the trunk of the small elephant.

most of the other summers in his or her own context for judging summers were cooler, or perhaps that at least one of these past summers (the lower endpoint of the visitor's contextual range) had been much colder. When our judgments of particular days are extreme, as when we say that "today is really a scorcher," the inference is that we are at an endpoint of the range of the context for that particular experience.

In such inferences of context, the contextual representations need not have been experienced personally. We may have read that the summer weather in San Francisco is cooler than in other parts of the country; consequently, if we learn that the temperature there is 80 degrees, we might say that "this is a scorcher for San Francisco." It would probably not have felt hot if we had just driven in from the desert: We might then have said that "although it feels deliciously cool, it is actually quite hot for San Francisco." Not all such ratings express our own hedonic experiences. In the realm of happiness, it is the experiences of pleasure and pain that count, not our cognitive grasp of what we would have felt if we had someone else's context, such as a San Franciscan's. The heat will be unpleasant only insofar as it is judged so in our own immediate context. The same temperature might be unpleasantly cold for people living near the equator. On the Micronesian island of Ponope which is almost on the equator, I was told of a bitter night back in 1915 when the temperature dropped to a record-breaking 69 degrees! We can predict with reasonable certainty that Ponopeans would suffer from the cold if they were to visit San Francisco.

If we feel depressed when looking in the mirror, our context probably includes an image of a much younger self. By estimating a crude running average of our pleasures and pains for a particular type of experience, we can also infer some things about the frequency distribution of events in the contexts for this type of experience. When the pains greatly outbalance the pleasures, events close to the upper-endpoints of their respective contexts must be infrequent. We may not be reexperiencing that image of a younger self, but it is still there in our context— promoting our dissatisfaction with what the mirror so callously reveals.

Occasionally, it may be hard to specify what event one is experiencing, much less its context. Walking alone, thinking about nothing in particular, I occasionally feel overcome with gladness, the euphoric feeling of Browning's (1939, p. 531) "God's in His heaven—All's right with the world." But the euphoria does not seem to be elicited by any particular external event or even by some private thought, so that I have no idea why I am euphoric. Perhaps it is the warm sun on my face.[12] At such moments, it is difficult to identify the context for judgment.

---

[12]I first heard this idea proposed years ago by Sylvan Thomkins in a lecture at UCLA, and later, a possible explanation by Robert Zajonc who theorized that relaxing the facial muscles changes the blood supply to parts of the brain, thereby affecting the sense of pleasure. Or perhaps some chemical change at the synapses between neurons in the pleasure centers of the brain is responsible for this kind of unexplained euphoria.

A more elegant example is Proust's (1922) famous description of an unexplained pleasure occasioned by a piece of a petite Madeleine:

> I raised to my lips a spoonful of the tea in which I had soaked a morsel of the cake. No sooner had the warm liquid, and the crumbs with it, touched my palate than a shudder ran through my whole body, and I stopped, intent upon the extraordinary changes that were taking place. An exquisite pleasure had invaded my senses, but individual, detached, with no suggestion of its origin. And at once the vicissitudes of life had become indifferent to me, its disasters innocuous, its brevity illusory—this new sensation having had on me the effect which love has of filling me with a precious essence; or rather this essence was not in me, it was myself. I had ceased now to feel mediocre, accidental, mortal. Whence could it have come to me, this all-powerful joy? I was conscious that it was connected with the taste of tea and cake, but that it infinitely transcended those savors, could not, indeed, be of the same nature as theirs. Whence did it come? What did it signify? How could I seize upon and define it? (p. 58)

What seems most unusual about this type of euphoria is the inability to identify its source. Proust could not credit the taste itself as anything more than the occasion for such an all-consuming pleasure. In the more usual case, one is aware of what it is that pleases or displeases but cannot identify the context in which it is experienced. For example, you may have guests for an evening party at home and find the people to be unpleasantly reserved. You suggest a parlor game of charades to help everyone loosen up. As your guests throw themselves into ridiculous contortions and become demonstratively excited when partners seem to be coming closer to the secret words they are portraying, you are pleased that it had been such a good suggestion to play the game. And yet, you remain slightly dissatisfied. You still sense a certain stiffness. In what context is the present situation being evaluated? When the game began, your appreciation of its relaxing effects occurred in the context of the earlier reserve. That was obvious. But how can that context have evolved to leave you dissatisfied with the same relative degree of relaxation? The context has perhaps lost some of its earlier representations of stiffness, but it may also have extended upward. Perhaps something in the present game evoked unconscious contextual representations of other occasions when you had played the same game with people much better at letting themselves go. In a context that includes representations of these other occasions, the present one is less than satisfying.

Multiple Contexts

This example illustrates a drift from one context to another, with behavior that was actually becoming more relaxed evoking a context that made it seem to be growing stiffer. This suggests a gradual, unidirectional shift in context. There can instead be sudden shifts back and forth between contexts: The hilarity of the game is sometimes in a context of the earlier reserve; but at other moments, the context includes livelier games from the past, with switches back and forth between the two, perhaps triggered by some element (such as a fleeting memory) from one or the other class of events. Similarly, the impoverished Russian emigres who made invidious comparisons with their prerevolutionary wealth must sometimes have felt elated by finding any job, however menial. There might have been the initial pulse of satisfaction on landing a job, followed shortly by the sobering reflection: "Here I am, a countess, thrilled by the chance to wash other people's laundry!" From the context of being unemployed and in desperate need, there has been a shift back to the larger context that included her wealthy position in the distant past, in Czarist Russia.

When more than one dimension underlies the hedonic judgment, the same event may be experienced in more than one context at almost the same time. Your guests who seem stiff or relaxed may also seem clever or stupid. The guests' stiffness is painful, but their cleverness is pleasing. The net effect depends on the relative intensities of pleasure and pain and also upon their durations. Your concern to liven up the party suggests that the pain had been prevailing.

The initiation of a judgment is an entry into an evaluative mode, an entry that evokes a context for whatever judgment will be elicited by the particular event that is being judged. The nature of this context depends upon various factors, including your interests at the moment, such as whether you want to liven up the party, and where your attention happens to be directed—perhaps to a clever remark made by one of the guests. You may even rate the same event with respect to more than one context: "In spite of its cleverness, that remark was pretty tense." This does not mean that the contexts for cleverness and stiffness are experienced simultaneously. It is not clear that we can ever simultaneously experience both pleasure and pain, but sometimes the separate hedonic experiences seem to come in close succession.[13] Instead, the combination of cleverness and stiffness may elicit a single hedonic experience in a context of such single, integrated experiences.[14]

Controlling the Context

We say that "everyone talks about the weather, but no one does anything about it!" Let us return to the example of how the way in which we talk about the weather can reveal our selection of contexts, this time with a concern for the possibility of controlling how the weather affects us. When applied to happiness, the crucial practical question becomes one of how much control we have over our

---

[13]Chuck Turner, who contributed many useful suggestions for this book, raised with me the complicating possibility that even within very short durations, perhaps only a second or so, we can experience a succession of different levels of pleasure or pain.

[14]Using psychophysical stimuli, Mellers and Birnbaum (1982) demonstrated both of these possibilities and a method for discriminating between them (see also Wedell, 1990).

hedonic contexts. Can we make a typical summer day more pleasant by consciously choosing to experience it in a context of other summer days that were
much too hot?

Assuming that we can achieve considerable understanding of how contexts
determine our pleasures and pains (the aim of this book), the practical question
is, how can we use this understanding to control hedonic contexts? Even in
laboratory work with simple perceptual stimuli, there is evidence that people can
control their contexts. In an experiment on judgments of size (Parducci, Knobel,
& Thomas, 1976), different sizes were presented in the form of either a circle or a
square, on alternate trials. Participants were remarkably successful in establishing separate contexts for the two forms when instructed to do so: Although the
smallest circle was larger than the largest square, it received a much lower rating;
and ratings of either circles or squares were completely independent of the
relative frequencies with which the different sizes of the other form were presented. However, those instructed to ignore the difference in form included both
in the same context, so that the largest square and smallest circle were both rated
"medium."

The fact that these participants could follow the experimenter's injunctions to
either segregate or combine contexts suggests that we have some control over our
more important hedonic contexts outside of the laboratory. This possibility could
make sense of the conjecture, sometimes attributed to Abraham Lincoln, that
most people are about as happy as they want to be. However, even in the
simplified version of the computerized Happiness Game in Chapter 8, few players succeed in establishing contexts that make for happiness. Indeed, many
players get worse with practice! If life is really governed by the contextual
principles of judgment on which this game was constructed, we could never learn
these principles from observing life in all its complexity. It is only by simple
laboratory experiments in which different features of the context are manipulated
independently that we come to an understanding of how relationships between
contextual stimuli determine our pleasures.

How much conscious control do we have over the immediate context for
judgment? In Porter's (1913) story for children, Pollyanna tried to make the best
of minor misfortune by, among other techniques, encouraging invidious comparisons with much greater misfortunes. We smile indulgently at Pollyanna, not
really believing that her "game" would work for us. Our own parents tried to
make us appreciate the Brussels sprouts by telling us that the starving children of
China would be grateful for such a delicacy. It did not work. Yet we do believe
we have some control over our contexts.

There is one kind of contextual control that is commonly attempted. People
tend to associate with members of their own social class,[15] one reason being that

---

[15]Indeed, a sociological tradition, initiated by Centers (1947), identifies one's social class by the
people with whom one associates.

they fear that comparisons with people of higher status would leave them discontent. In contextual terms, experiencing the higher status of others would extend one's own context upward, lowering one's sense of self-worth. I remember, as a 12-year-old, being offered a scholarship to an elite private art school; my father turned it down, admonishing me that association with richer boys would make me feel deprived. Perhaps he was wrong, but do not most people believe, like my father, that they can control important contexts by choosing their associates?

This kind of contextual control is difficult because small differences in status become large when the context shrinks to include only people of similar status. The neighbors' new car makes yours seem a sign of poverty, even though their income is no greater than yours. To avoid feeling impoverished, we evoke downward-looking contextual considerations: "Now the poor souls have big monthly payments!"

Efforts to restrict the upper contextual endpoint may conflict with efforts to acquire outward symbols of success. People imagine that association with those who are more successful will facilitate their own advancement. Apart from any direct help, the association may lend status: "Look who I hang around with!" Furthermore, having successful people as standards may encourage higher levels of achievement, just as practicing with tennis players who are more advanced than oneself is supposed to improve one's game.

An important implication of the contextual approach to happiness is that there is often a tug of war between efforts to succeed and efforts to be happy. The high achievement that constitutes worldly success seems to be facilitated by upward extensions of the context, anticipations of success that, although themselves pleasurable, reduce the pleasure from actual achievements. Wisdom consists in reaching the right level of compromise, not setting standards so high that disappointment with one's actual achievements outweighs the pleasure of the unrealistically high anticipations.

Another example suggesting some degree of contextual control occurs while waking up but still in a state between sleep and waking. In this hypnogogic state, I occasionally have a powerful sense of wasting my life away, utterly failing in what I am trying to do. However, these negative thoughts quickly disappear if it is already morning and I get up. Once fully awake, I seem to have a control that I did not have while half asleep: The same level of achievement that seemed painfully inadequate now seems much better, suggesting that the contextual comparisons evoked in the waking state are more conducive to positive self-evaluations. Although I am not consciously trying to evoke lower standards or to direct my attention to the more positive aspects of my life, I may be unconsciously doing what Pollyanna tried to do consciously.

This kind of protection against pain is much more highly developed in adults than in children. Children experience greater extremes of feeling. The reduced proportion of extreme "lows" may be a positive by-product of aging, but older people also seem to experience fewer "highs." If so, the greater contextual control is not likely to yield greater happiness. Older people may be more content, more resigned, readier to accept reality. However, they may not have a more favorable balance of pleasure over pain.

SUMMARY

The amount of pleasure or pain elicited by any particular event, real or imaginary, depends on its place in a context of related events. Although rarely experienced themselves, contexts change with new experience so that the same event may be satisfying on one occasion, dissatisfying on another. Recent events are the most likely to be represented contextually, but hedonic contexts may also include events from the distant past, particularly those extreme enough to be contextual endpoints. Goals, fears, expectations, and even hypothetical logical possibilities may also be represented in the contexts determining pleasure or pain, and certain events evoke their own contexts at the time they are experienced. Insofar as the lower endpoints of hedonic contexts are experienced only rarely, they enhance the possibilities for happiness. Practical implications center on our ability to control contexts in the more important hedonic domains.

II CONTEXTUAL THEORY AND RESEARCH

4 Life as an Even Balance Between Pleasure and Pain

My childhood coincided with the Great Depression of the 1930s, but my family experienced more than the usual financial losses. Perhaps to soften any sense of relative deprivation, my father erected a powerful psychological antidote:

> Don't envy the other boys! They have grown accustomed to their bicycles and expensive toys so that they no longer have the fun you think you are missing. The more one has, the more it takes to be satisfied. Pleasure and pain are strictly relative. No matter what you have or what happens to you, your pleasures and pains must balance each other out. In the long run, no one is happier than anyone else.

A similar psychology had been articulated by Mark Twain (1916/1962b) in *The Mysterious Stranger*, written in his later, more pessimistic years:

> Every man is a suffering-machine and a happiness-machine combined. The two functions work together harmoniously, with a fine and delicate precision, on the give-and-take principle. For every happiness turned out in the one department, the other stands ready to modify it with a sorrow or pain. . . . (p. 350)

We cannot know how thoroughly Twain subscribed to this psychology. He also wrote that when the balance is not even, it is always tipped toward unhappiness. My father was not so pessimistic, and he may not really have believed in the necessary character of an even balance. But for an impressionable child, this relativism was powerful stuff.

By the time I had left home for college, I was already convinced that the psychological relativism inherent in the meaning of terms like "pleasure" and "pain" entailed an even balance. This balance seemed an axiomatic truth, impervious to contrary evidence. I remember one of my college roommates remonstrating with me: "But Allen, can't you see that one moves to a higher level of happiness when one succeeds, when one becomes rich?" None of his examples of apparently happy or unhappy people could convince me. He went on to become a wealthy captain of industry. I went on to study psychology.

In psychology, it was easy to find grist for my mill. I read of Crespi's (1944) experiment with laboratory white rats for whom the incentive value of any given amount of food appeared to be determined by the ratio between that amount and how much they had previously been getting—so much so that, although deprived of food for 24 hours, some rats actually refused to eat when their reward for running was reduced. In my first research as a graduate student, I was able to observe this astonishing phenomenon myself, replicating many of Crespi's findings.[1] I also saw the film of Tinklepaugh's monkey, trained to retrieve a piece of lettuce (which it then ate) it had seen placed under one of two boxes. But once, after letting the monkey see him place a banana (much preferred to lettuce) under one of these boxes, Tinklepaugh surreptitiously substituted the usual lettuce for the banana. The film showed the monkey retrieving the lettuce but, instead of eating it, turning immediately to the other box, finding nothing, picking up the lettuce, examining it with disgust, and finally throwing it at Tinklepaugh. A most impressive portrayal of the relativity of pleasure!

These demonstrations with animals seemed consistent with the relational ideas underlying the notion of an equal balance. However, it was Helson's theory of adaptation level that finally opened my eyes to the possibility that the notion was subject to empirical verification (e.g., Helson, 1938, 1947, 1964). Helson's theory was a quantitative development of the averaging notion implicit in my father's philosophy—although earlier, less quantified versions of this theory had been presented by a number of influential psychologists (including Beebe-Center, 1932; Hollingworth, 1910; Johnson, 1949, 1955; and Woodrow, 1933). As Birnbaum summarized so succinctly: the essence of Helson's version is that the stimulus that is experienced as "neutral" or "average" (the adaptation level), is simply the average stimulus; other stimuli are judged higher or lower in proportion to their differences from this average. Put mathematically, the theory in its simplest form asserts that the adaptation level is equal to the arithmetic mean of all stimuli represented in the context for judgment.[2] The judgment, Ji, of any particular stimulus, Si, is then:

---

[1]However, I did find strange genetic interactions in which rats from some litters appeared more prone to this relational determination of incentive value.

[2]Helson's actual equations (e.g., Helson, 1964) equated the adaptation level to the logarithmic mean, reflecting his acceptance of Fechner's Law which transforms the physical values of stimuli logarithmically to represent their psychological values. The present treatment of Helson leaves open the form of this transformation, substituting in Helson's equations the psychological values of the stimuli. For simplicity of exposition, the two constants of the linear equation were dropped.

$$Ji = Si - \bar{S}, \tag{1}$$

where $\bar{S}$ represents the arithmetic mean of all the stimuli. Since the algebraic sum of deviations from the mean must equal 0, adaptation-level theory, in this pristine form, provides a precise articulation of the theory of a perfect balance: The algebraic sum of all the judgments, positive and negative, is equal to zero.[3]

I should have been delighted by Helson's mathematical articulation of what I so firmly believed; however, I was more impressed by the possibility of testing the theory. Helson advocated an empirical approach, and he showed how his theory could be tested experimentally by having subjects rate simple perceptual stimuli, like lifted weights. Although not extensive enough to be completely convincing, his own data and those of Johnson (1955) were consistent with adaptation-level theory.

More important for me was the realization that the data could have been inconsistent with the theory, that the notion of a perfect balance could be wrong! What had seemed an axiomatic truth was revealed, instead, to be a testable empirical generalization. A faint suspicion of doubt invaded my soul. Could the notion of an exactly even overall balance between pleasure and pain be unnecessarily restrictive? Must psychological relativism preclude the possibility of an overall tipping toward happiness?

Besides articulating the notion of an equal balance as a quantitatively scientific theory, Helson demonstrated how the theory could be tested. The trick was to establish experimental control of the context for judgment. To do this, Helson (like Johnson and others before him) adopted the research strategies of psychophysics. These require the selection of simple perceptual stimuli that, like lifted weights, can vary on a single dimension, like heaviness. The different stimuli are then presented to the experimental subject, in random order, eliciting a judgment of how heavy each one seems. It turns out that in such an experiment, the context for judgment is effectively the set of weights selected for presentation. When this is the case, adaptation-level theory implies that the particular weight that seems "neutral" (i.e., neither "heavy" nor "light") is the mean of all those presented and, most important to me, ratings of "heavy" and "light" will exactly balance each other out.

Using Helson's psychophysical methods, I began laboratory research to test his theory. This work will be described in the next chapter. Some of my early data were consistent with adaptation-level theory: adaptation level tended to be

---

[3]Although never actually derived by Helson, I first published this implication of adaptation-level theory in the *Scientific American* (Parducci, 1968); it was also inferred, independently, by Brickman and Campbell (1971). The opponent-process theory, developed by Solomon (1980), might lead to the same implication, although starting from different principles. Solomon posited two physiological processes, one for pleasure, the other for pain, which in combination tend to bring the affective state back to neutral. With Solomon's help, I once tried, unsuccessfully, to find some link between opponent-process theory and my own range-frequency theory of judgment.

close to the mean of the stimuli, just as the theory asserted. However, the ratings for skewed or asymmetrical sets of stimuli were not balanced at "neutral" or "average." Instead, the overall balance tipped toward the higher categories when the stimuli were packed more closely toward the upper end of the contextual set. This was because, contrary to the basic premise of adaptation-level theory, the ratings of the different stimuli were often *not* proportional to their differences from adaptation level. Instead of the predicted linearity, plots of ratings against stimuli steepened or flattened in accordance with how densely packed the stimulus presentations were in different parts of the range. The form of these plots suggested a compromise between two principles of judgment: (a) ratings divide the range of the presented stimuli into equal subranges, each successive category assigned to the next subrange; and (b) the different categories are each assigned to the same frequency of stimulus presentations.

The first principle implies that the stimulus rated "average" or "neutral" is at the midpoint of the range of contextual stimuli, that is, halfway between the two extremes of the presented stimuli. The second principle implies that this "average" stimulus is at the median (50th percentile) of all the stimulus presentations. Neither gives any importance to Helson's mean which, however, often falls between the midpoint and median.

This compromise between the two principles became the central feature of my range-frequency theory of judgment. Since the early 1950s, I have been demonstrating (with my collaborators) the predictive value of range-frequency theory for various types of psychophysical stimuli (size of squares, number of dots, length of lines, heaviness of weights, pleasantness of odors or tastes) and also for more complex cognitive materials (judgments of the morality or psychopathology of different behaviors, the pleasantness of getting different amounts of money or exam grades, and even the pleasantness or painfulness of more general life situations). The earlier predictive success of adaptation-level theory now seems an artifact of the mean being intermediate between the midpoint and median for many natural distributions.

The evolution of my thinking was thus first to recognize that the theory of an equal balance was not true by definition, that it was an implication of the scientific theory of adaptation level which could be tested experimentally. I then found that adaptation-level theory failed crucial experimental tests. I thus came to reject this theory even though it articulated what had long been for me an a priori truth, the necessity of an equal balance between pleasure and pain. However, my basic faith in the relational character of hedonic experience (or of any other dimensional judgment) remained unchanged. What did change was my understanding of how the relativism works.

With respect to the contextual theory of happiness, the most interesting implication of range-frequency theory was derived algebraically: the mean of all the judgments, $\bar{J}$ (on a 0-centered scale), is equal to the difference between the mean and the midpoint of the contextual stimuli, divided by their range:

$$\bar{J} = (\text{Mean} - \text{Midpoint})/\text{Range}. \tag{2}$$

This equation implies that the mean of the judgments will only be zero for distributions for which the mean of the stimuli is right at their midpoint.[4] It also implies that the mean of the judgments will be positive to the degree that stimuli are concentrated toward the top of the range, negative insofar as the pileup of stimuli is toward the bottom of the range. This implication directly contradicts the belief in the inevitability of a perfect balance, the belief with which I grew up. The experimental evidence supports this implication. The way to elicit a positive balance of judgments is to concentrate the stimuli near the top of the range. It is only this relative piling up that counts, not whether the context is high or low relative to other contexts.

With respect to the assumption of an overall balance of hedonic judgments, the amount of pleasure being exactly balanced by the amount of pain, the contextual theory of happiness (incorporating these principles of judgment) implies that the balance can be tipped either way. This is supported by the laboratory experiments in which positive and negative ratings are equally balanced only for symmetrical distributions of stimuli. The fact that much of this evidence was obtained in psychophysical experiments for which adaptation-level theory had been developed encourages rejection of its implication of an equal balance. The same experiments demonstrate that the experimenter can tip the balance one way or the other simply by the direction of skewing of the distribution of stimuli presented for judgment. This is exactly what is entailed by range-frequency theory, with precise predictions of the individual judgments and hence the degree of overall imbalance. The demonstration that this control of judgment can be established in the laboratory with highly predictable effects encourages speculation about how we might increase the happiness of our everyday lives.

How Could There Have Seemed to be an Even Balance?

It remains curious to me now that I could ever have thought that judgmental relativity required an equal balance of pleasure and pain. But when I present the logic of the equal-balance notion to a large class of undergraduates, I find that about one third avow complete agreement. This same third also expresses agreement with the following statement: "It is only an illusion that some people are happier than others." I remember one brilliant student who could not be dissuaded from the notion that pleasure had to be exactly balanced by pain, even after he had been presented the empirical evidence on the effects of contextual

---

[4]Note that this equation assumes that the context for each judgment is representative of the entire set of stimuli presented and judged. See chapter 6 for a more detailed exposition of range-frequency theory and this algebraic implication.

skewing. No evidence could be relevant to his belief which he held to be true *a priori*, a necessary consequence of defining pleasure and pain relationally. Perhaps the earlier psychophysical experiments on adaptation level would have seemed irrelevant to me had they not been supportive of the notion of an even balance.

If everyday experiences of pleasure and pain reflect range-frequency principles, why is not this already obvious to everyone? The answer, proposed in the previous chapter, was suggested by what happens to players of the Happiness Game developed to illustrate the application of the contextual theory of happiness: Many players do not shake their losing patterns of play, even after hours of failure. The immediate rewards they gain from extending the range upward seem to obscure its basic consequence—namely, that unless this new best is experienced relatively frequently, the overall balance of pleasure and pain becomes more negative. This suggests that people could never learn range-frequency principles by simply observing life in its usual, uncontrolled complexity. The power of simplification, the primary appeal of the laboratory experiments, was crucial for discovering the principles of judgment incorporated into the contextual theory of happiness.

SUMMARY

My own attempts to understand happiness began with the discouraging assumption that one's total amount of pleasure is always balanced by an equal amount of pain. This assumption seemed a necessary, a priori consequence of psychological relativism. However, Helson's theory of adaptation level showed me that this assumption could be tested empirically. The results of crucial experiments then proved more consistent with a simple compromise between two simple rules of judgment: (a) categories segment the context into equal subranges, and (b) categories segment the context into subsets of equal frequency. As incorporated in the contextual theory of happiness, this range-frequency compromise ensures that the overall balance of pleasure over pain is greater when events occur more frequently near the upper endpoints of their contextual ranges—regardless of what absolute levels of preference those upper endpoints may represent.

5 Experimental Research on Contextual Effects

As described in the previous chapter, the principles of judgment embodied in the contextual theory of happiness grew out of experiments conducted in the psychophysical laboratory.[1] This research began with a preconceived theory, one which the experiments were designed to test. The theory failed the tests. A new theory was developed to explain this failure. This chapter is primarily concerned with how this new theory has survived experimental tests with a wide variety of dimensional judgments. But like the old theory, the new one will outlive its usefulness and be replaced, in turn, by a better theory. This is the way of science. In the meantime, the experiments that led to the new theory encourage speculation about the relational character of dimensional judgments, experiences of pleasure and pain, happiness.

Category Ratings

How do we ordinarily express our happiness or unhappiness in words? It is by expressions like "life is wonderful," "I feel pretty bad," "that was an awful day," "when I am with that woman, I am deliriously happy," and so on. Each of these statements expresses an hedonic judgment in the form of a category rating. Verbal categories describe the relative positions of events with respect to some

---

[1]This chapter does not attempt to review the voluminous literature on contextual effects in judgment but only those laboratory studies from which the principles of judgment incorporated into the contextual theory of happiness were developed and only a sample of those on which they were tested. Some of the closely related research on scaling, anchoring effects, sequential effects, and social judgments are treated in other chapters.

attribute, such as height, loudness, pleasantness or happiness. If pressed, we can put these ratings in numerical form: the meeting that we describe as "unpleasant" would be rated "2" on a scale from 1 to 5, "-5" on a scale from -10 to $+10$. The use of numbers in experiments on judgment facilitates precise tests of quantitative theories; however, it does not seem to matter whether the numbers are assigned by the experimental subjects themselves or whether the subjects' verbal categories are tabulated by their numerical ranks in the set of available categories. Both procedures lead to the same interpretations of the data.

Number Judging

The philosophy of experimental simplicity suggests that if we want to understand how judgments depend upon context, we must find a situation in which the context for judgment can be manipulated independently of other conditions. Psychophysicists eliciting ratings of simple perceptual stimuli usually find that their subjects adapt quickly to the particular set of stimuli presented for judgment, so that in choosing this set psychophysicists are effectively controlling the context for judgment. The simplest situation that I have found manipulates the immediate context for judgments of numerical magnitude, with experimental subjects rating how large or small each of the numbers is—in comparison with a contextual set of other numbers.

There are several advantages to studying judgments of numbers rather than judgments of the pleasantness of meaningful events, such as a first date or the birth of a child. Besides the ease of creating the stimulus materials (simply typing the numbers on a page), there is the fact that the context for abstract numbers can be more completely controlled by the experimenter than can the contexts for more meaningful stimuli. Consider the number 500. Is it large or small? The answer depends on the context: As the number of pages in a book, 500 might seem large; but as the population of a town, it is likely to seem very small to anyone who has been living in an urban metropolis. In the experiments to be described next, the subjects (usually students in classrooms) are each presented a sheet of paper on which is printed a list of numbers that are purely abstract, not referring to any particular class of objects like books or towns. The task is to record a category rating beside each number, in accordance with how large or small it seems in comparison with the other numbers on the page. In a typical experimental condition, the subject might be restricted to six categories: *Very Small, Small, Slightly Smaller than Average, Slightly Larger than Average, Large,* and *Very Large* (recording just the capitalized letters as abbreviations). When the experiment was performed in a lecture class of some 300 University students, 10 different contexts were employed, with each of the contexts given to approximately 30 student subjects.

What are the contexts? For each subject, the effective context for judging any particular number turns out to be simply the particular list of numbers printed on the page that he or she received. This means that the judgment of each number on the page can be accurately predicted from its position in the list of other numbers on the same page.

In the study to be described first, the lists differed only in the spacing of successive numerical values between 100 and 1,000 (Parducci, Calfee, Marshall, & Davidson, 1960). There were 48 numbers in each list, arranged in order of increasing magnitude. For a positively skewed context, the spacing progressively increased, for example, 100, 103, 107, 119, 128, 143 . . . 787, 833, 902, 1,000. For a negatively skewed context, the spacing progressively decreased, for example, 100, 198, 267, 313 . . . 957, 972, 981, 993, 997, 1,000. Other lists were not skewed but symmetrical, the numbers in a normal context being spaced more closely in the middle (i.e., between 400 and 700), those in a context with a U-distribution being spaced more closely near the two ends. An evenly spaced (rectangular) context served as a baseline against which the effects of the various spacings could be assessed.

Subjects were instructed to record next to each number a category representing their immediate impression of its size, not bothering with arithmetic calculations. Most completed the task within 5 minutes. After the sheets were collected, the experimenter asked the subjects to describe how they had performed the task. Some reported dividing the range of numerical values into six equal subranges, each corresponding to a successive category; because the total range is $(1,000 - 100) = 900$, and $900/6 = 150$, the first category, *Very Small*, would extend from 100 to 250, *Small* from 250 to 400, and so on. I describe this rule as judging in accordance with the *range principle*. It is simple, logical . . . and no one actually did it! Except for the baseline context in which numerical values were evenly spaced, the subranges of numbers to which the respective categories were applied were always unequal.

Another rule that is sometimes reported by student subjects is to divide the contextual set of numbers into successive subsets of equal frequency: Because there are 48 numbers and 6 categories, there must be $48/6 = 8$ numbers in each category. The eight smallest numbers would thus be rated *Very Small*, the next eight *Small*, and so on. I describe this rule as judging in accordance with the *frequency principle*. Like the equal-subrange rule, the equal-frequency rule is simple, logical . . . and no one actually followed it (again, excepting those given the evenly spaced set).

Instead, every subject struck a compromise between these two rules. If, for a particular context, the switch from *Very Small* to *Small* would be at 250 following the equal-subrange rule but at only 150 following the equal-frequency rule, subjects would make this break close to 200, that is, $(250 + 150)/2$. This range-frequency compromise occurs for each of the contexts studied and for each of the limens or breaks between adjoining categories.

Evidence Against Adaptation-Level Theory.   The research on number judging was designed to test the theory of adaptation level described in the previous chapter. Remember that adaptation-level theory is based on the common-sense notion that what seems average, the adaptation level, is simply the average of the contextual stimuli and that each stimulus seems above or below average in proportion to its deviation from this average stimulus. When the stimuli are scaled in proportion to their psychological values, the theory asserts that the adaptation level is equal to the arithmetic mean of the stimulus values. One attraction for using abstract numbers as the stimuli is that the numbers are already properly scaled for adaptation-level theory: When the contextual distribution is equally spaced between 100 and 1000, the equality of the category widths above and below adaptation-level supports this assumption.

The first tests of adaptation-level theory (Parducci et al., 1960) concentrated on what the subjects rated average (the numerical value at which subjects switch from *Slightly Smaller than Average* to *Slightly Larger than Average*).[2] This measure of adaptation level was recorded for each subject and then averaged across all subjects judging a particular contextual set of numbers. The theory of adaptation level implies that this measure should approximate the arithmetic mean of the numerals on the same page. An initial plot showed that although adaptation levels were indeed linear to the means, the slope was less than 1 (i.e., adaptation levels were higher than predicted insofar as the mean of all the numbers was low, lower than predicted when this mean was high). Although the overall linearity seemed to lend partial support to adaptation-level theory, these systematic errors of prediction were puzzling. More damaging was the finding that particular categories were narrower when they were applied to numbers that were spaced more closely, for this is directly contrary to adaptation-level theory's assumption that each rating is proportional to the difference between the rated stimulus and adaptation level. The actual width of each category was about halfway between what it would have been following the frequency principle and what it would have been following the range principle, as summarized in the preceding chapter.

When the overall measure of judgment was not the adaptation level but rather the mean of all the ratings (representing each rating by its rank in the set of six), 28 of the 29 students given the positively-skewed set had lower overall mean ratings than 15 of the 30 subjects given the negatively skewed set. This dramatic difference contradicts the discouraging implication of adaptation-level theory that the mean of all ratings is independent of context, that is, always at the middle of the rating scale. Instead, it supports the compromise between range and frequency principles, a compromise entailing that the mean of all the ratings for any context is proportional to the piling up of stimuli toward the top of the contextual range. This provides a more optimistic basis for the contextual theory of happiness.

If ratings conformed strictly to the equal-frequency rule, the middle break or

---

[2]In this early research (Parducci et al. 1960), five categories were actually used to rate 44 numbers between 108 and 992; adaptation level was taken as the mean of those numbers rated *medium*. The example of six categories for rating 48 numbers between 100 and 1,000 is employed here to simplify the exposition.

adaptation level would be at the median of the stimulus context, that is, at the break between the 24th and 25th of the 48 numbers. But if ratings conformed strictly to the equal-range rule, adaptation level would be at the midpoint of the contextual range—at $(100 + 1,000)/2 = 550$. With an equal compromise between the two rules, adaptation level for any context would be halfway between the midpoint and median of all the numbers in that context. This would explain the partial success of adaptation-level theory with the initial data, because the mean is intermediate between the median and midpoint for these sets (as for most distributions found in nature).

To provide a more powerful test of adaptation-level theory, the next experimental tests studied ratings of abstract numbers in contexts for which the mean, midpoint, and median varied independently. For example, two lists of numbers might have the same midpoint and median but different means; or the means might be the same, but either the midpoints or medians would be different. Lower midpoints were produced by having the numbers vary between 100 and 700, between 100 and 300, or even between 10 and 100; higher midpoints were produced by having the numbers vary between 300 and 1,000, 700 and 1,000, or even 1,000 and 10,000. Utilizing some 40 different sets, the resulting adaptation levels were subjected to powerful statistical analyses.[3]

The results were clear-cut: Contrary to the theory of adaptation level, variation of the mean had no effect on adaptation level when the midpoint and median did not vary; however, with the mean held constant, variation in either the midpoint or median had dramatic effects on adaptation level. The best-fit acombination of predictors was close to an equal weighting of midpoint and median, that is, halfway between them. Thus, the hypothesized compromise between range and frequency principles was confirmed. Subsequent analyses of these same data supported the range-frequency compromise at each of the other breaks between categories, between *Very Small* and *Small*, between *Large* and *Very Large*, and so on.

The Form of the Judgment Function.   Although many subjects made their breaks between categories at the same points, there were, of course, individual differences. A procedure that is most useful with psychophysical judgments is to average the ratings made by different subjects. With six verbal categories, each is transformed to its rank from 1 to 6, and these ranks are averaged across subjects to obtain a mean rating for each of the stimuli presented in a particular context.

The left panel of Fig. 5.1 shows an example of the results of such averaging for two unusually spaced sets of numbers (cubic functions, labeled -C and C) rated with nine categories: the nonlinearity of the respective ratings functions is particularly striking because of their double crossovers. As Birnbaum (1974) demonstrated algebraically, no monotonic rescaling of the stimulus and response

---

[3]This multivariate analysis was described, along with the details of the some 30 different contexts studied, in the research article by Parducci et al. (1960).

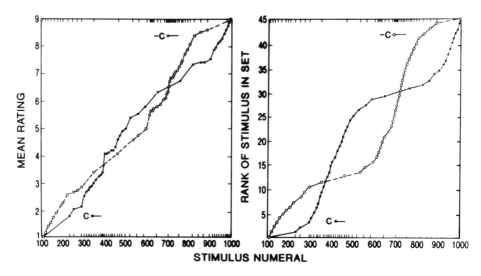

FIG. 5.1. Left panel (adapted from Birnbaum, 1974), shows mean rat-ings of two sets of numerals, C and −C, whose spacings are indicated on upper and lower abscissas, respectively—ratings inconsistent with adaptation-level theory because they shift more rapidly where numer-als are spaced more closely, producing double crossovers. Right panel shows what these ratings would have been following just the frequen-cy principle, with ratings proportional to ranks in respective sets.

scales could produce the parallelism required to make the data consistent with adaptation-level theory. It should be clear that both functions are steeper wherev-er the stimuli within their respective contexts are spaced more closely.

The right panel of Fig. 5.1 magnifies this relationship between the steepness of the rating function and the spacing of the numbers by showing what the rating functions would have been if subjects had simply followed the frequency princi-ple: insofar as each small difference on the average rating scale corresponds to the same number of stimuli, the mean rating of each stimulus would be propor-tional to its percentile rank (i.e., to the proportion of all contextual numbers that are smaller than the number being rated). Comparison between the left and right panels of Fig. 5.1 shows that each actual mean rating is about halfway between its frequency value and its range value (i.e., the proportion of the range below it which would have been shown as its position on the diagonal). This is the range-frequency compromise.

Psychophysical Experiments

When the research on number judging was first published, there was concern that the range-frequency compromise might work only for stimuli presented in numerical form. Skeptics asked whether it would also be found using simple perceptual stimuli like the lifted weights and auditory tones traditionally studied by psychophysicists, for these do not come with numbers already attached to them. Subjects judging psychophysical stimuli would be unlikely to articulate equal-subrange and equal-frequency rules and therefore, according to the skeptics, less likely to apply them.

The logic of the experimental tests using numbers on a page was therefore transferred directly to the psychophysical laboratory for crucial experimental tests between adaptation-level and range-frequency predictions. An early monograph (Parducci, 1963) reported experiments in which subjects rated either the heaviness of lifted weights, the numerousness of dots projected visually, or the sizes of squares. In each case, the mean, median, and midpoint of the contextual stimuli were manipulated independently.[4] The results confirmed the conclusions drawn from the research on numbers: Contrary to adaptation-level theory, variation of the mean had no effect upon the empirical adaptation level (the physical stimulus rated *average*) when the midpoint and median were held constant; however, as implied by the range-frequency compromise, adaptation level varied directly with both the midpoint and the median when the mean was held constant. In addition, the nonlinearity of the functions relating ratings to stimuli took the forms implied by the range-frequency compromise.

The most extensive psychophysical tests (Parducci & Perrett, 1971) concentrated on ratings of the sizes of squares, projected visually, one at a time, in long randomized sequences. Figure 5.2 shows characteristic results for ratings of the different sizes of squares. The left panel of Fig. 5.2 shows the mean ratings for squares presented with equal frequency but whose spacings (differences separating successive sizes) were skewed either negatively or positively; the right panel shows the ratings for two additional sets of squares with the same unequally spaced sizes of squares, but for which the skewing was increased by presenting the more closely spaced stimuli more frequently (numbers on respective abscissas represent stimulus frequencies). In both panels, the ratings (points) are accurately predicted by the simple compromise between equal-subrange and equal-frequency rules: Ratings are lower with negative skewing (and much lower with the greater difference in skewing), and the overall mean of all the ratings is higher (by one quarter of the range of possible categories) for the extreme negative than for the extreme positive skewing. This is contrary to the notion of an even balance implied by the theory of adaptation level. However, as will be explained in the next

---

[4]In calculating these measures of central tendency, the physical values of the stimuli were first transformed logarithmically. For example, the difference between lifted weights of 100 and 110 grams is just about as easy to discriminate as is the difference between 500 and 550 grams. This is in accordance with *Weber's Law*, first established in 1834, as elaborated upon by Fechner (1860). A log transformation turns equal ratios into equal differences. Helson (e.g., 1964) incorporated this transformation into his equations for adaptation-level theory, in which the adaptation level was assumed to be equal to the physical stimulus corresponding to the mean of these log values, taken across all members of the experimental series, namely, the context.

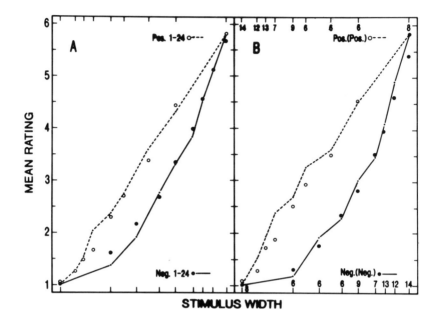

FIG. 5.2. Mean ratings (points) for sets of nine squares varying with respect just to spacing (left panel), to both spacing and relative frequency of presentation (right panel). Rating functions (lines) predicted from ratings of single rectangular set, assuming range-frequency compromise. From Parducci and Perrett (1971).

chapter, it is just what is implied by the range-frequency compromise.

In other research (Riskey, Parducci, & Beauchamp, 1979), subjects rated the sweetness of different solutions of lemonade that varied in the amount of sugar that had been added. Different groups of subjects received the solutions in sets that were either unskewed, positively skewed or negatively skewed. The ratings conformed closely to predictions from a simple range-frequency compromise.

Taken as a whole, the research with psychophysical stimuli shows that these rules are as useful for predicting simple perceptual ratings as for ratings of abstract numbers.[5]

Frequency and spacing. The range-frequency compromise implies a trading relationship between different methods of varying the frequency distribution of contextual stimuli: The effects upon judgment can be produced by experimental

---

[5]The accuracy of these predictions indicates the power of these principles to go beyond common-sense notions, like *assimilation* and *contrast*, that describe the direction of contextual effects but not their magnitude. Adaptation-level theory, which does deal with magnitude, incorrectly predicts that these functions would all be parallel lines.

manipulation of either the frequencies or spacings of the stimuli presented for judgment or, as we just saw, by combining the two. In what is perhaps the most convincing test of this trading relationship, the respective effects of spacing and frequency canceled each other out when sizes from a normal distribution of spacings (i.e., more closely spaced in the middle) were presented with a U-distribution of frequencies (i.e., middle sizes presented less frequently).

Category and Stimulus Effects.   More recent research with size judgments of squares (Parducci & Wedell, 1986) argued for distinguishing the effects of inequalities in frequency and spacing. Although the effects of skewing the spacings of the stimuli were independent of both the number of categories and the number of stimuli, the effects of frequency skewing varied inversely with the number of categories (the *Category Effect*) and directly with the number of stimuli (the *Stimulus Effect*).[6] Both effects are explained by Wedell's *consistency model* (Wedell, 1984; Wedell & Parducci, 1985; Parducci & Wedell, 1986) which postulates a limit on how many representations of the same stimulus can be kept in the effective context for judgment. This limit, which depends on the number of categories and stimuli, reflects a tendency to use categories consistently, that is, to efficiently identify which stimulus is being judged.[7]

Wedell's model differentiates between the entire set of stimuli presented by the experimenter and representations of a much more limited sample that compose the actual context for judgment. It is as though the context could represent in working memory only a limited number of past experiences, perhaps as few as a dozen: For consistency of judgment, past experiences with a particularly frequent stimulus are dropped from the context when to retain them would lead to using more than one category for that stimulus. Because both Category and

---

[6]Surprisingly, these do not change substantially the overall mean of the ratings; consequently, neither Category nor Stimulus Effects are incorporated into the theory of happiness presented in this book. Wedell suggested to me that the expected changes in the overall mean are counteracted by changes in the effective endpoints of the context.

[7]Haubensak (1992) developed in Germany a different consistency model theory to explain both Category and Stimulus Effects. Although incorporating both range and frequency principles (along with the postulated tendency toward consistency), Haubensak's theory emphasizes associations established when the context is first developed. The consistency resulting from this fixation of associations seems a possible explanation of cases in which changes in the spacings or frequencies of stimuli during the course of the experimental session are slow to change the ratings of particular stimuli. It is still not clear how the implications of this alternative might be different from, or perhaps more useful than, Wedell's consistency model which is much closer to range-frequency theory. In a crucial test between the two approaches, the results were more consistent with range-frequency predictions (Parducci, 1992a). Haubensak's associative model does evoke the possibility that ratings might not reflect changes in psychological experiences when this would make them appear inconsistent with earlier ratings of the same stimuli. Another model emphasizing a somewhat different conception of consistency was developed by Fabre in France (Fabre, 1987, 1993; Parducci & Fabre, 1995). Although also simulating both Stimulus and Category Effects, this model has not yet been subjected to crucial tests.

Stimulus Effects occur with more complex stimuli rated for pleasantness, the idea of a highly limited context seems applicable to the joys and sorrows experienced with everyday events occurring outside the narrow confines of the psychophysical laboratory.

Judgments of Pleasantness

Skeptics about the applicability of the range-frequency compromise to questions of happiness call attention to the unrepresentative simplicity of psychophysical stimuli. They also contrast the nonhedonic character of judgments of size (whether of abstract numbers or of squares) with the hedonic judgments underlying happiness. It is only an assumption that the apparent relativism of everyday experiences of pleasure and pain reflects the range-frequency compromise governing these simple, nonhedonic judgments. Therefore, it is important to study whether or not the same compromise holds for judgments of pleasantness, of both simple and more complex stimuli.

Pleasantness of Odors.   One of our early studies (Sandusky & Parducci, 1965) used odors as stimuli, selected because of their ability to evoke strong hedonic experiences. For example, one stench was so bad that an occasional subject refused to continue with the experiment. A graduate student in a neighboring lab found our vanilla extract so pleasant that he started his working days "on a euphoric note" by sniffing the particular bottle in which it was stored. The different odors were chemically complex, so that there was no simple characterization of their positions on physical dimensions; nor did subjects agree in their preferences among the different odors. We found that a separate ranking by preference had to be determined for each subject. Each subject was later run in two conditions: in the narrow-range condition, only the middle 6 of the 12 ranked odors were presented for judgment; in the wide-range condition, the subject rated all 12. The task in both conditions was to rate the pleasantness of the different odors, just as in Beebe-Center's (1932) pioneering work. To the degree that the range-frequency compromise applies to hedonic judgments, the lowest and highest odors among the middle 6 should elicit more extreme ratings (*Very Unpleasant* or *Very Pleasant*) when presented in a series that included just these middle 6 than when presented with the entire set of 12. And that was what we found.

Monetary Outcomes.   In another study, subjects rated their satisfaction with different monetary payoffs in a pseudo-gambling experiment. The subjects, again university undergraduates, were told that on each of a series of trials they could turn over any one of three cards, finding on the reverse side the value of their monetary payoff for that trial. Unknown to them, all three cards yielded the same payoff on any particular trial. This permitted complete experimental control of the frequency distribution of actual payoffs. Two different sets of payoffs were used, with each subject getting payoffs in only one of the two. For the positively skewed set, payoffs varied between 7 and 27 cents per trial, the lower values occurring much more frequently. For the negatively skewed set, payoffs varied between 1 and 21 cents per trial, the higher values occurring much more frequently. The mean payoff was 14 cents for both distributions, so that subjects averaged 14 cents per trial regardless of the experimental condition to which they were assigned.

After each choice of a card, the experimental subject rated the pleasantness of the resulting monetary payoff. In conformity with the range-frequency compromise, the overall mean of these pleasantness ratings was lower for the positively skewed set of payoffs, with 15 of the 20 in this condition having lower overall means than any of the 20 in the negatively skewed condition. Furthermore, the range-frequency predictions for these two overall means (3.5 and 4.5, respectively, on the 1-to-7 rating scale) is close to what was actually obtained from the subjects (3.4 and 4.6). The special interest in the mean of all ratings reflects the conception of happiness as the overall balance of pleasure to pain, the mean of all hedonic judgments. If the range-frequency compromise accurately predicts the ratings or judgments of each individual stimulus in each of the different contexts, then it must also predict the overall means. The individual ratings are lower for the same payoffs in the negatively skewed set; but, because the more pleasing of its payoffs come so much more frequently in this set, their overall mean is predictable higher. It was for this reason that my *Scientific American* article describing this research (Parducci, 1968) was given the tongue-in-cheek subtitle, "Happiness Is A Negatively-Skewed Distribution."

In more extensive research (Marsh & Parducci, 1978), the pleasantness of monetary outcomes was rated in a win-lose situation. In this special case, the hedonic neutral-point appears anchored to the break-even point. Separate applications of the range-frequency rules to outcomes on each side of the neutral-point nevertheless accounted for the ratings—but only by assuming the symmetrical extension of the contextual range described in chapter 3, so that the upper endpoint of the context for wins was as far above the break-even point as the lower contextual endpoint for losses was below it. This extension of the contextual range beyond any of the payoffs actually experienced provides a basis for some of the speculation in later chapters about the role of evoked contextual stimuli in determining everyday experiences of pleasure and pain.

Pleasantness in Aristotelian Domains.   More recent experiments have tested the applicability of the range-frequency compromise to hedonic judgments on dimensions for which subjects prefer some intermediate level.[8] Klusky (1990) found support for the compromise when subjects rated the pleasantness of

---

[8]In the earlier research on the judged sweetness of lemonades (Riskey et al., 1979), other groups of subjects were asked to rate the pleasantness of the solutions in these same sets; systematic shifts were found in their preferences: the most pleasant level of sweetness was higher for the negatively skewed set, lower for the positively skewed set. This shift in the order of preferences is contrary to the assumption, usually made by economists, that preferences or utilities remain constant.

solutions of lemonade varying in sweetness and also for musical motifs varying in loudness. Similar results were obtained when they rated the pleasantness of different facial expressions of an actress simulating different degrees of friendliness (Parducci, 1989). In these cases, an intermediate level on the correlated dimension, sweetness, loudness, or friendliness, was the most pleasant for many subjects, with progressively less pleasantness for both higher and lower levels. These experiments suggest that a single context was established by each subject, with the different stimuli ordered by preference, that is, by degree of difference from the level that was most preferred, without respect to the direction of difference. This supports the assumption that pleasures and pains are experienced with respect to a context whose hedonic representations are distributed along a scale of preference. And because Aristotle's golden mean seems characteristic of many real-life pleasures, finding that the range-frequency compromise operates upon the dimension of preference (rather than upon the underlying physical dimension) encourages its more general application to understanding the pleasures and pains of everyday life.

Pleasantness of Life Events.   Perhaps the closest approach to the cognitively complex hedonic events of everyday life was undertaken in a large-scale study in which college students rated the pleasantness of everyday events described by brief verbal phrases (Wedell & Parducci, 1988). The students were asked to imagine that they were experiencing these events as they might occur in a typical day (e.g., "You wake up and find the shower won't rise above lukewarm," "You are late for your discussion section and get a zero for the quiz that was given," "You eat lunch with a friend," "You and some of your friends then go to the beach and relax in the sun," "Traffic isn't too bad on the way home"). Each student rated the pleasantness of each of 65 such events, segregated to represent 5 successive days, each of which encompassed 13 events. As in the psychophysical research, the context was manipulated experimentally by presenting a preponderance of more-preferred experiences to some students and a preponderance of less-preferred experiences to others. And, in accordance with the range-frequency compromise (and, also, in this case, with common-sense notions about hedonic contrast), the same experiences were rated less pleasant when the more-preferred experiences predominated. But more crucial for the contextual theory of happiness, the mean of all ratings was predictably higher for the negatively skewed context.

This effect upon our measure of happiness would hardly have been predicted without the more precise range-frequency principles. Other features of the data, too technical to be detailed here, also supported the conclusion that the principles developed in psychophysical research apply equally well to ratings of the pleasantness of real-life events. One finding that was not necessarily expected: Students' assessments of the week as a whole were also higher for the negatively skewed context. In this case, the students seemed to know what made them happy. This had not been the case when they were given a choice between negatively skewed and positively skewed distributions of outcomes in the pseudogambling experiment, for there they chose the positively skewed distribution (even though it had elicited lower ratings, overall).[9]

Judgments on Other Value Dimensions.   A variety of experiments have demonstrated the range-frequency compromise with other types of value judgments. The work of Mellers (1982, 1990) on judgments of equity or fairness provides such examples, especially interesting in that she obtained dramatic contextual effects for subjects expressing their judgments of merit by allocating different amounts of salary, a continuous scale. Other experiments (Mellers & Birnbaum, 1982; Smith, Diener, & Wedell, 1989) demonstrated the range-frequency compromise with evaluations of scholastic performance. Wedell, Parducci, and Geiselman (1987) showed similar contextual effects upon ratings of facial attractiveness judged from photographs. Russell and his collaborators found contextual effects on ratings of emotion; for example, Russell and Fehr (1987) demonstrated that the same neutral face is rated "happy" when presented with a sadder face, "sad" when presented with a happier face. Even assessments of psychopathology are subject to these contextual effects: Campbell, Hunt, and Lewis (1957) and Perrett (1972) demonstrated that in spite of admonitions to maintain their standards using an apparently well-anchored scale, professional psychotherapists were just as affected by the skewing of the immediate context of case histories as were untrained undergraduates.

Moral judgments seem to exhibit the same dependency on immediate context. Though instructed to ignore the context and stick to their own personal set of values, my college students systematically assigned a harsher rating to any particular act, such as "poisoning a neighbor's dog whose barking bothers you," when it appeared in a set of more innocuous items, such as "registering in a hotel under a false name," than when it appeared with more outrageous acts, such as "murdering your mother without justification or provocation."[10]

These and other studies provide a compelling answer to one basis for skepticism about the contextual theory of happiness. Although range-frequency princi-

---

[9]Most players of the Happiness Game choose the positively skewed distribution of incomes when these are higher—even though they win points for maximizing pleasure rather than income. However, Mellers and Cooke (in press) demonstrated that students' choices between apartments that varied in rent and distance from the campus (rather than choices between different distributions of rents and distances) can reflect the same range-frequency rules developed to explain dimensional judgments. This is described further in chapter 7.

[10]This was first reported in Parducci (1968). Successful replications have subsequently been reported to me by both high school and college teachers in various parts of the United States. In a later study that presented good as well as bad acts of behavior (Marsh & Parducci, 1978), we also found the neutral-point anchoring described previously for ratings of the pleasantness of monetary outcomes.

ples were developed and first tested with nonhedonic ratings of abstract numbers and simple psychophysical stimuli, they appear quite general in their applicability. I know of no evidence suggesting that the principles of judgment are different for complex hedonic situations than for the simplest laboratory stimuli. As argued in subsequent chapters, the differences are primarily in what goes into the context for judgment—with the role of imagination becoming a much bigger factor in determining the pleasures and pains of everyday life.

SUMMARY

Experiments manipulated crucial features of the context for judgment, measuring the effects of these manipulations on category ratings. Contextual sets of abstract numbers provided the simplest test. The results suggested that each rating reflects a compromise between two principles of judgment: (a) division of the contextual range into equal subranges, and (b) assignment of the same number of contextual values to each category.

Ratings of various types of simple psychophysical stimuli, including size of squares, heaviness of lifted weights, and numerousness of dots, all conform to the range-frequency compromise. Using more complex stimuli, the same contextual effects were demonstrated for moral judgments, judgments of facial attractiveness and of scholastic performance, and even judgments of psychopathology made by trained experts.

In the realm of hedonics, the range-frequency compromise governs the pleasantness of monetary outcomes, odors, tastes, musical motifs, and simulations of friendliness. In each case, the context for hedonic judgment represents the stimuli on a simple dimension of preference, even when it is some intermediate level of a correlated dimension like sweetness that is most preferred. The same range-frequency compromise was also demonstrated for ratings of the pleasantness of various types of complex real-life events, encouraging generalized application to the understanding of happiness. These experiments provide the empirical basis for the broader theory of judgment, presented in the next chapter and incorporated into applications of the contextual theory of happiness throughout the remaining chapters.

6 The Range-Frequency Compromise in Judgment

The pleasantness of any particular experience is a judgment, determined by its place in a context of related experiences. Range-frequency theory was designed to further our understanding of how the contexts determine the judgments, not just hedonic but all types of dimensional judgments. The test of this understanding is how well the theory predicts category ratings in crucial experiments. This is the test that was applied to adaptation-level theory, the idea of an equal balance. Similar testing must be applied to any theory presuming to replace it.[1]

As described in Chapters 4 and 5, laboratory research that proved inconsistent with the theory of adaptation level led to a different explanation of contextual effects, expressed in terms of the range-frequency principles of judgment. Articulation of these principles was catalyzed by the peculiarly nonlinear relationships observed between category ratings and the numerical stimuli to which they were applied by experimental subjects (viz., categories shifting faster where stimuli are more densely packed, as in the figures presented in chapter 5). Here, I describe how these principles function in a predictive theory of judgment. The more technical aspects of the theory have been relegated to footnotes, but readers not wishing to go through the details of the theory might skip ahead to the summary at the end of this chapter.

---

[1]Theories are rarely deposed by negative instances alone (Kuhn, 1970). We tend to give up a theory only after finding an alternative that does the same good work without the embarrassment of contrary data or too many theoretical complications. In this case, the good work is to explain how judgments are determined by their contexts. Given the context, the theory must correctly predict the category rating elicited by the stimulus.

PRINCIPLES OF JUDGMENT

The Range Principle

This principle was first articulated by Volkmann (1951), a psychophysicist who foresaw its application to social judgments.[2] In essence, the range principle asserts that equal segments of the scale of judgment are assigned to equal segments of the contextual range. Expressed in terms of category ratings, *successive categories correspond to equal, successive subranges of the context.*

Insofar as the judgment of any particular stimulus conformed to this principle, that judgment would be determined solely in relation to the two endpoints of the contextual range. Thus, the skewing of the distribution of contextual stimuli would be irrelevant to the judgment. However, the research described in the last chapter showed that this principle cannot stand by itself: Although it explains the effects of independent manipulation of the endpoints, the range principle does not account for the effects of manipulating the relative frequencies and spacings of stimuli between the endpoints.

The Frequency Principle

The basic idea of the frequency principle is that each equal segment of the scale of judgment is assigned to the same number of contextual representations. For example, if fewer than one third of all contextual representations are below a particular stimulus, it falls in the bottom one third of the scale of judgment. If judgments were restricted to just three categories, this stimulus would elicit the bottom category. Thus, insofar as the context is representative of the stimuli, *each category corresponds to the same number of stimulus presentations.*

The frequency principle could also be stated in terms of category rather than stimulus frequencies: "The different categories are used with equal frequency," rather than, "each category is assigned to the same number of contextual stimuli." Although these alternative statements have sometimes been interpreted as equivalent, they do not seem so to me. Defining the frequency principle in terms of equal stimulus frequencies seems more directly tied to the notion of transmitting information, and it also seems more consistent with experimental research.[3]

---

[2]Upshaw (1969) also posited a range principle for judgment, attributing systematic deviations from it (as when contextual frequencies are skewed) to a response bias that distorts the report of subjective experience. Gravetter and Lockhead (1973) presented a range principle in which category ratings show statistical regression reflecting the less than perfect correlation between ratings and stimuli.

[3]To test between these two formulations of the frequency principle, squares of different size were alternated with different sizes of larger circles (Parducci et al., 1976). Because it would be much easier to establish independent contexts for circles and squares than to keep separate counts of the frequencies with which the same categories were used for circles and for squares, the demonstration that subjects could establish independent rating scales for circles and squares seems to favor the equalization of stimulus frequencies.

If judgments were determined solely by the frequency principle, the position of the stimulus relative to the contextual endpoints would be irrelevant. All that would matter would be the proportion of contextual representations below the stimulus being judged. But the research that independently manipulated the endpoints of the context (i.e., with median and mean held constant) showed this to be false. What the frequency principle does explain is the effect of varying the distribution of contextual values, for example, its skewing, when the endpoints are kept constant. As with the range principle, the frequency principle cannot stand alone.

The Range-Frequency Compromise

When contextual representations are distributed evenly over the range, judgments are equally consistent with both the range and frequency principles: In this case, both entail the same judgments. But when the stimuli are spaced unevenly or presented with unequal frequencies, the two principles entail different judgments. In these more typical cases, judgments reflect a compromise between the two: Each judgment falls between what it would have been as predicted from just the range principle and what it would have been as predicted from just the frequency principle. The judgment of any particular stimulus in a particular context is given by the following equation:

$$J = wR + (1 - w)F, \tag{1}$$

where J is the judgment, R is what this judgment would have been according to the range principle (its range value), F is what this same judgment would have been according to the frequency principle (its frequency value), and w is a weighting constant (between 0 and 1) that reflects the relative influence of range and frequency principles in determining the judgment.

The relative weighting of range and frequency values has typically been found to be fairly equal, that is, with w close to .5. However, a number of experimental conditions have been shown to either increase or reduce w. In general, the relative weighting of the range value is greater when stimuli are presented in a manner emphasizing their relationship to the endpoints of the contextual set, less when it is the relative frequencies or spacings of stimuli that are emphasized (e.g., Parducci & Marshall, 1961; Parducci & Wedell, 1986, Experiment 4C).[4]

---

[4]When a small set of stimuli are presented with unequal frequency, the relative weighting of the range value also seems to vary directly with the number of categories (the Category Effect), inversely with the number of stimuli (the Stimulus Effect). However, a more parsimonious theoretical account attributes both effects to systematic changes in the context for judgment, with weighting remaining constant at .5 (Parducci & Wedell, 1986). For example, when the context is limited to 12 representations, ratings on a three-category scale limit the number of contextual representations of any given stimulus to 12/3 = 4; with six categories, this limit is 12/6 = 2. The calculation of frequency values is performed using this limited, and thus more rectangular distribution of contextual representations. As reported in chapter 5, Haubensak (1992) and Fabre (described in Parducci & Fabre, 1995) have developed alternative explanations of the Category and Stimulus Effects.

From Judgments to Ratings

Equation 1 relates the judgment of a stimulus to the context in which the judgment is made. This judgment is assumed to be an internal, subjective experience, directly available to introspection but not publicly observable. Moreover, range and frequency values depend upon contextual representations that may not be directly observable. How can such a theory be verified?

As described in Chapter 5, experiments can be performed in situations so simple that that the context for judgment is probably an unbiased representation of the particular set of stimuli actually presented for judgment. Faith in the validity of this assumption hinges on how accurately the judgments are predicted from the set of stimuli actually presented. Such predictions require appropriate procedures for estimating range and frequency values and also for transforming internal judgments into overt category ratings.

The appropriate contextual representations of the stimuli are considered in the section entitled "Testing Range-Frequency Theory." Our first concern here is with the transformation of the internal judgment into the overt category rating expressing the judgment. The internal judgment is experienced as an attribute of a stimulus, such as its pleasantness. This is what we attempt to convey when we characterize the degree of pleasantness, either publicly to others or privately to ourselves. Our characterizations are typically expressed as category ratings, such as *wonderful*, *slightly disappointing*, or *very unpleasant*. A particular category rating is always one of an implied set of categories. When experimental subjects are allowed to express their judgments in terms of whatever verbal labels they wish, they have little difficulty generating their own sets of categories, sets in which some of the component categories may not even be used when rating the stimuli.[5] The fact that subjects permitted to generate their own categories follow the same principles of judgment as do subjects restricted to a prescribed set of categories encourages application of range-frequency theory to everyday judgments outside the laboratory.

Whether freely generated by the subject or rigidly prescribed by the experimenter, the verbal categories must later be transformed into numbers to permit more powerful quantitative tests of range-frequency theory. A simple linear equation,

$$C = bJ + a, \qquad (2)$$

describes how the judgment, J, can be transformed to a numerical category rating, C, with b representing the range of categories and a the value assigned to

---

[5]For example, if a subject used these four categories—*tiny*, *small*, *middle size*, and *large*, one would infer that his or her scale included a missing top category, such as *huge*. This assumption of implicit symmetry around the middle of the scale is justified by the accuracy of the predictions based upon it; ratings using these self-generated categories are just as predictable from range-frequency theory as are ratings restricted to a prescribed set of categories (see section on *open scales* in Parducci & Wedell, 1986, Experiment 1).

the lowest category.[6] The justification for this particular transformation is that it permits accurate numerical predictions of the category ratings. For example, suppose the predicted judgment of the size of a particular square were .75 (judgments being determined on a scale from 0 to 1). On a 5-point scale, ranging from 1—*Very Small* to 5—*Very Large*, its rating would be 4—*Large*, (which is three-fourths of the way up from the bottom category).

The Mean of All Judgments

The grand overall mean of hedonic judgments is the measure that most closely reflects the Utilitarian definition of happiness. Equation 1 and the definitions of its three variables permit an algebraic deduction of the general, abstract relationship between the frequency distribution of contextual stimuli and the mean of all the judgments of its component stimuli.[7] This crucial deduction shows that the mean of all judgments for a particular context is directly proportional to the difference between the mean and midpoint of that context, divided by its range: *the more negatively skewed the distribution of contextual stimuli, the greater the overall mean of the judgments of these stimuli.* This is the basis for asserting that happiness is a negatively skewed distribution (Parducci, 1968). It should be noted that this tongue-in-cheek dictum applies only when the context is an unbiased representation of the set of events actually experienced, as with number judging or with the simpler psychophysical experiments. It would not apply when the context is a biased representation of the events whose judgments are being averaged, as when representations of the more pleasant events drop more

---

[6]More specifically, the transformation is:

$$C_i = (n - 1)J_i + C_{min}, \tag{3}$$

where C_i is the category rating of Stimulus i, n is the number of categories, J_i is the judgment of stimulus i, and C_{min} is the number representing the lowest category in the scale. Categories are customarily identified by their ranks in the set of categories, namely, from 1 to n.

[7]The general logic of the deduction is that the mean of all the judgments is equal to the mean of all of the range and frequency values, weighted respectively by w and $(1 - w)$. If the stimulus values are scaled by their positions in the range, then their mean is also the mean of the range values. The mean of all the frequency values must always be .5, which is also equal to the midpoint of the range divided by the range. The weighted average of these two is then:

$$\bar{J} = .5 + w(\bar{S} - .5(S_{max} + S_{min}))/(S_{max} - S_{min}), \tag{4}$$

in which $\bar{J}$ is the mean of all the judgments on a scale from 0 to 1, $\bar{S}$ is the mean of all the contextual stimuli, and S_{max} and S_{min} are the two end-stimuli of the contextual range. Dropping the .5 and substituting the names for the descriptive statistics:

$$\text{Mean of all Judgments} = w(\text{Mean} - \text{Midpoint})/\text{Range}, \tag{5}$$

in which the mean, midpoint, and range on the right side of the equation refer to the distribution of stimulus values and the mean of all the judgments is expressed on a unitary scale from $-.5$ to $+.5$. This equation correlates almost perfectly, but negatively, with conventional measures of skewing.

quickly from the context. However, an overall mean judgment can be inferred using Equation 1 with range and frequency values calculated for whatever context is assumed.

Why the Range-Frequency Compromise?

"Why" questions about empirically verified principles seem to be asking for metaphysical or religious answers. But neither type of answer can add to the predictive utility of such principles. Without attempting an answer to the why question, I assume that range-frequency principles are built into the nervous system and that they do not have to be learned. When I collected ratings from children, even those as young as 3 or 4 years old seemed to be applying the range-frequency rules just like the university students typically used as experimental subjects. For example, after spreading blocks of varying size on a table, I have asked children to push the small blocks in one pile, the large blocks in the other. If a child had enough verbal mastery to follow this request, his or her dividing point between these two categories was higher when there were more of the larger blocks—showing that the frequency principle was already operating. Range-frequency effects were also found in chickens (Zoeke & Sarris, 1983), suggesting a more general neural basis.

Category Ratings as Communications.   Verbal categorizations are the way we ordinarily communicate our dimensional judgments, such as degrees of pleasantness: They are used to communicate our judgments to others and also to articulate the same judgments privately to ourselves. Consider the following thought experiment designed to illustrate the communicative character of category ratings. Two experimental subjects, undergraduates, are told to work as a team. They are shown, in random order, a series of squares that vary in size. Each successive square is sampled from a skewed frequency distribution of nine different sizes, with different relative frequencies (e.g., smaller sizes more frequent than larger sizes). Neither subject is allowed to say anything during this preview, after which one of the two is blindfolded. His or her team-mate, who continues seeing squares sampled from the same distribution, must describe each presentation aloud, using one of five verbal categories: *very small*, *small*, *medium*, *large*, or *very large*. The blindfolded subject must then guess which of the nine squares was presented. The closer the guess, the more points the team wins. The only information this blindfolded subject receives on each trial is the particular category selected by his or her teammate and then the change in the team's score (which reflects the accuracy of his own estimate of the rank of the stimulus in the set of nine).

What is the optimal strategy for gaining points? The most points may be won when "seeing" players use the verbal categories to describe how large or small the squares look to them and when their blindfolded team-mates respond by identifying the squares to which they themselves would have applied these partic-ular verbal categories. This assumes that category ratings, as typically used, are an efficient method of identifying particular stimuli in a known context of related stimuli (in this case, both seeing and blindfolded teammates presumably devel-oped the same context during the preview). It also assumes that ratings are an efficient method of minimizing the degree of error of identification.[8] The point of this thought experiment is to illustrate the communicative function of category ratings, particularly for efficient identification for others sharing the same con-text.

To understand how the range-frequency compromise facilitates correct identi-fications, consider first how the frequency principle is applied by skillful players of the parlor game, "20 Questions" (cf. Broadbent, 1958). In the game, one player thinks of a famous person, and the other player has 20 true-false questions with which to identify that person. For optimal efficiency, each question should be framed so that its answer reduces the context of possible persons by one half. For example, a good question might be, "Does this person's last name begin with one of the letters A through M?" It would be a poor strategy to start with a question that could eliminate only a small portion of the possibilities, such as, "Was this person born in the last 10 years?" If the game permitted questions with five alternative answers, each question should be framed so that its answer reduces the context of remaining possibilities by four-fifths; and a reasonable question might be, "With which of the following letters does this person's last name begin: A-E, F-J, K-O, P-T, or U-Z?" As in this game, category ratings most efficiently reduce the ambiguity about which of a known set of stimuli is being described when each category corresponds to the same proportion of the total set.[9]

Although the frequency principle is most efficient when the goal is exact identification, compromise with the range principle adds efficiency when degree of error also becomes important, as when points won in the thought experiment depend on how close the guessed size is to the size actually presented. If guesses in the thought experiment were governed solely by the range principle, the biggest error could be limited to the subrange corresponding to half a category, in this case, 1/10 of the range. This is more efficient than the frequency principle

---

[8]From five to nine categories are commonly believed sufficient for subjects to provide almost as sharp a discrimination as they possibly can between stimuli varying on a single physical dimension (Miller, 1956). However, my own recent research in collaboration with the Sarris laboratory at Frankfurt suggests that under certain conditions subjects may be capable of still finer discrimination. Using the Heller method of subcategorization, in which the subject first judges each stimulus with one of nine categories and then with a further subdivision within that category, we found that this subcategorization added significantly to the amount of information transmitted.

[9]This is the rule that transmits the most information in the Shannon/Weaver sense (Attneave, 1959, Garner, 1962).

insofar as there is a big penalty for *degree* of error.[10] Taken over a broad variety of situations, some emphasizing degree of accuracy, others absolute identification, the range-frequency compromise would seem to provide a generally efficient solution.

Category Pragmatics.   Some years ago, I conducted exploratory studies using the task described for this thought experiment. Although the experimental subjects mostly followed the range-frequency compromise, some engaged in additional pragmatics. For example, if the guesses by the blindfolded subject tended to be too low, the seeing partner would adjust his or her own ratings upward. Such efforts to change others' judgments seem most obvious in examples of advertising or political propaganda that employ superlatives when describing a product or policy. Because my primary interest is in understanding the judgments underlying happiness, I concentrate on situations that seem less likely to evoke the pragmatics of social influence and thus more likely to yield valid reports of subjective experiences, such as pleasure. Nevertheless, the likelihood of social pragmatics should be kept in mind when deciding how much credence to give self-avowals of happiness.

TESTING RANGE-FREQUENCY THEORY

The remainder of this chapter describes methods by which range and frequency principles can yield quantitative predictions for experimental tests. Although directed primarily to researchers interested in how the theory can be tested, specification of these methods gives a more precise articulation of the range and frequency principles and the compromise between them.

Calculating Frequency Values

Frequency values are considered first because they are normally calculated a priori, that is, without reference to experimental data. The frequency value for any particular stimulus is a numerical representation of what its judgment would have been if determined solely by the frequency principle. This is the value of F in Equation 1.

Counting Method.   Consider again the experiment on number judging in which 48 numbers were presented on the same page for ratings of numerical magnitude on a six-category scale. If the ratings had simply followed the frequency principles, the 48 numbers would have been divided equally between the six available categories. Thus, each

---

[10]This difference suggests that the relative weighting of range and frequency principles might vary with the system of payoffs, with whether points earned in the thought experiment depended on degree of error or only on correct identifications.

category would have been used 48/6 = 8 times; the first eight numbers on the page would have been rated 1—*Very Small*, the next eight 2—*Small*, and so on.

The same method can be employed in cases where a small set of stimulus values is presented with varying frequencies. For example, in the research using judgments of squares, one of the positively skewed stimulus sets consisted of five different sizes with frequencies of 10, 7, 4, 2, and 2, respectively, in each block of 25 presentations. When rated using five categories (assigned numerical values 1 through 5), the frequency principle would have each category used 25/5 = 5 times. Thus, one half of the 10 presentations of the smallest size are rated 1, the other half, 2—yielding a mean rating of 1.5. For the second size, five of its seven presentations are rated 3, the other two, 4—for a mean rating of $[(5 \times 3) + (2 \times 4)]/7 = 3.29$. For the third size, three of its four presentations are rated 4, the fourth, 5—for a mean rating of $[(3 \times 4) + (1 \times 5)]/4 = 4.25$. Both presentations of each of the two largest sizes are rated 5.

Percentile Ranks.   A more general procedure for calculating the frequency value of a stimulus (i.e., what its judgment would be according to just the frequency principle) is to rank the different contextual representations on the dimension of judgment and then to calculate the proportion of these representations that are below the stimulus being judged.[11] This is the procedure used to calculate the payoffs (representing different intensities of pleasure or pain) in the computerized happiness game described in chapters 8 and 9.

Thurstone Procedure.   The variability of judgment is a central concern of psychophysics, as it has been throughout a history that reaches back 150 years to Weber, through Fechner (1860) and Thurstone (1927), to the contemporary theory of signal detection (see Green & Swets, 1966). Many factors contribute to variability, including limits on the observer's powers of discrimination. In the idea of "discriminal process" developed by Thurstone, the same physical stimulus is assumed to have slightly different effects on different occasions, as though it were varying in magnitude. Other possible sources of variability reside in the process of judgment, including variability in the representations of past experiences, in the counting of their frequencies, and in transformation from internal judgment to overt category ratings. There may also be systematic differences between observers that contribute to the variability when judgments by different observers are combined—as is often done in the research reports of category ratings. One may thus think of many small factors contributing in relatively independent ways to the location of the boundaries (or limens) between categories.

To preserve this variability, an early model for range-frequency theory postulated a normal function, whose mean and standard deviation sufficed to describe the location of

---

[11]Actual calculations have used the following equation:

$$\mathrm{F}ic = (\mathrm{r}ic - 1)/(\mathrm{N}c - 1), \tag{6}$$

where Fic (the frequency value of Stimulus i in Context c) equals the difference between ric (its rank in the contextual set) and the lowest rank (viz., 1), divided by the difference between N, the highest rank (viz., the number of contextual representations) and 1. This equation gives the proportion of all contextual representations below the stimulus being rated. It therefore gives a value between 0 and 1. It is roughly equivalent to the conventional percentile rank (divided by 100).

each frequency limen (Parducci, 1965).[12] The advantage of this approach was that it permitted prediction of the complete stimulus-response matrix (i.e., the number of times each category was assigned to each stimulus). The disadvantage was that it complicated the exposition of the theory and drew attention away from my own primary interest in the measure of happiness: the mean judgment of each stimulus and hence the mean of all the judgments for each hedonic context. A more crucial consideration is that predictions using the simple counting method proved more accurate (Parducci & Perrett, 1971).

Calculating Range Values

How the range principle works is illustrated most simply by the experiment with ratings of numerical magnitude. Consider again the contextual set of numbers ranging from 100 to 1,000, rated using six categories. Insofar as the ratings follow just the range principle, each category must cover a subrange of 150, that is, $(1,000 - 100)/6$; all numbers between 100 and 250 (i.e., $100 + 150$) must be rated using the first category, 1—*very small*; the second category, 2—*small*) must be assigned to all numbers from 250 and 400; and so on. This produces a stepwise function relating range values to stimuli, with a sudden jump to the next category following each interval of 150. A smoother function can be obtained by calculating the range value for each stimulus as the proportion of the total range below that stimulus. Again, the range value (R in Equation 1) represents what the judgment would have been if subjects had simply followed the range principle.

With actual perceptual stimuli, the subranges cannot be assumed a priori (as was done with judgments of abstract numbers) but rather depend on the subjective scaling of the stimulus dimension. For simple psychophysical dimensions, this scaling has often been assumed to be logarithmic (as by Helson, 1964), which would mean that equal differences in range values correspond to equal ratios of physical values. For example, if the first subrange of lifted weights extended from 100 to 200 grams, the second would be from 200 to 400, the third from 400 to 800, and so on. But for other psychophysical dimensions, the scaling of equal subranges may be only quasilogarithmic; and for judgments of the sizes of squares, it is almost linear (Haubensak, 1982).

There is no simple physical measure to rescale for the more complex dimensions of everyday life, such as love or self-esteem. There may also be individual differences in the ordering of stimuli, as was found between subjects rating the pleasantness of different solutions of aspartime in lemonade. Thus, some more general method must be employed to characterize the position in the contextual range of each stimulus, sometimes for each subject. In the tradition of Thurstone (1927) and Anderson (1981), this is done by fitting the theory to the data: Assuming that the theory is valid and that the range value of each stimulus remains constant across contexts with the same endpoints, infer the particular range values that would make the obtained ratings most consistent with the predictions of

---

[12]To obtain predictions for the full matrix of stimuli and judgments, an iterative procedure was used to locate frequency limens (viz., where the divisions between categories would have been located in strict accordance with the frequency principle). In this case, the standard deviation of each limen's locations was set equal to the empirical standard deviation inferred from the data using the simplest Thurstone model (Case 5 in Torgerson, 1958). Tentative locations for the limens were shifted up and down until each category was assigned to the same number of stimuli (Parducci, 1965).

the theory.[13] Although using the actual ratings to infer the range values might seem to protect the theory against any possible negative instances, theoretical models are regularly infirmed by data treated in this way. Specific methods of scaling the stimuli are described in the following section.

Predicting the Ratings

As with any predictive theory, rules of correspondence must be established between the elements of the theory and observable events in the real world. Tests are clearest when the context for judgment is simply the set of stimuli presented for judgment, with ratings obtained from two or more contexts sharing the same endpoints but with different frequency distributions of intermediate values. In most such experimental tests, predictions are made for the mean of the ratings of a particular stimulus, averaged across its different presentations and the different subjects who rated it in a particular experimental condition. These mean ratings are first transformed linearly into hypothetical internal judgments (see footnote 6). Frequency values are then calculated a priori, as described previously, linearly transformed to a 0-to-1 scale, and substituted in Equation 7 to get an empirical estimate of the relative weighting of the range and frequency values.[14] This inferred value of w is then substituted in Equation 1 to infer the range value for each stimulus (averaging these estimates when the same stimulus occurs in more than one condition).[15] Substituting the inferred range value and the a priori frequency value into Equation 1 yields the inferred judgment for each stimulus in each condition. This is then linearly transformed into the predicted rating. Finally, these predictions are compared with the subjects' actual ratings to assess the goodness of fit.

Perhaps a better intuitive sense of the genuinely predictive power of the theory is obtained by using the range values inferred from one set of stimuli to predict the ratings of stimuli in other sets with the same endpoints. This was the procedure used in the most extensive of such explorations, judgments of the sizes of

---

[13]Birnbaum (1982) showed how this assumption of constancy, called scale convergence, is crucial for testing between different theoretical models (cf. Anderson, 1981).

[14]Substituting judgments and frequency values into Equation 1 for two different contexts, subtracting and transposing, yields:

$$(1 - w) = (J_{i1} - J_{i2})/(F_{i1} - F_{i2}), \tag{7}$$

where J_{i1} and J_{i2} are the judgments of Stimulus i in Contexts 1 and 2, and F_{i1} and F_{i2} are the frequency values of the same stimulus in these two contexts. This gives the relative weighting of the frequency principle, $(1 - w)$. A separate estimate of $(1 - w)$ can be calculated for each stimulus common to the two distributions. These different estimates are then averaged to obtain the best overall estimate. The judgments substituted in this equation should be as reliable as economically possible, usually taking means across the judgments made by many subjects. It is better not to include judgments of the two end-stimuli because even very small errors of unreliability could have a large effect on the estimate of w for judgments that are ordinarily so close for the two contexts.

[15]Best-fit range values have been inferred using ratings from all conditions with the same contextual endpoints (e.g., Parducci & Wedell, 1986); alternatively and more simply, range values for all conditions have been inferred from ratings of a single baseline condition (e.g., the rectangular distribution in Parducci & Perrett, 1971).

squares presented in some 20 different contextual sets (Parducci & Perrett, 1971). Figure 5.2 in the preceding chapter gives some sense of the accuracy of these predictions.

Such tests would hardly be possible in the absence of experimental control of the context for judgment. However, as described in chapter 3, the same theory can be used to infer a rough approximation to the contexts for judgments in more complex situations. This type of inference is crucial for applications of the contextual theory of happiness based on the range-frequency compromise in judgment.

SUMMARY

Range-frequency theory describes how judgments reflect a compromise between the range principle of assigning each category to an equal subrange of contextual stimuli and the frequency principle of assigning each of the available categories to the same number of contextual stimuli. These two principles are applied to the stimulus representations in the context for judgment: Each judgment is a weighted average of what it would have been following either just the range principle or just the frequency principle. A crucial deduction from the theory is that the mean of all judgments is proportional to the skewing of the frequency distribution of their context when this is an unbiased representation of the stimuli that are judged.

Procedures are described for estimating range and frequency values for each stimulus judged in a particular context and also for estimating the relative weighting of these values in determining the judgment. This internal judgment is transformed linearly for its overt expression as a category rating. These are the procedures that yielded the precise quantitative predictions of experimental data, both with respect to ratings of particular stimuli and to the overall mean of the ratings made in a particular context. Range-frequency theory also provides a basis for speculating about the contexts for particular experiences in everyday life, as when applying the contextual theory of happiness described in the next chapter.

7 The Contextual Theory of Happiness

The essential features of the theory have been presented in earlier chapters (and in Parducci, 1984b). Its central focus is happiness, defined as a theoretical summation across separate experiences of pleasure and pain. The theory identifies these hedonic experiences as judgments made on the dimension of personal preferences. As dimensional judgments, hedonic experiences follow the same range-frequency principles as do any other type of dimensional judgment. Thus, each hedonic experience is determined by its relationships to its own context for judgment, the relationships that determine the range-frequency compromise. It then follows that happiness is greater when the events, real or imaginary, that elicit hedonic judgments are concentrated near the upper endpoints of their respective contexts, regardless of the absolute levels of these events.

If this prescription for happiness seems abstract, it is because range-frequency principles do not specify the actual contexts for everyday judgments. For the simple perceptual judgments that range-frequency theory was developed to explain, it sufficed to treat the context as a representation of the particular set of stimuli that the experimenter presented for judgment: each stimulus enters the context at the time it is experienced. When this happens, the overall mean of the judgments is determined by the skewing of the frequency distribution of stimuli presented for judgment. The more general implication that *happiness is a negatively skewed distribution* thus applies most directly when the context is an unbiased representation of what is actually experienced.

The hedonic contexts of everyday life may not be so unbiased. Representations of some experiences may remain in the context much longer than others, and the contexts most important for happiness may also include representations of goals, fears, expectations and even imagined counterfactuals. In such cases, prescriptions for happiness depend upon the special assumptions that are made about the contexts for hedonic judgments. These may be considered as auxiliary hypotheses, not central to the theory but important for its application. Various possibilities for how the context is constituted were presented in chapter 3. Additional possibilities are discussed in this chapter and in those that follow.

As with any theory purporting to explain empirical phenomena, rules of correspondence are necessary to relate the concepts of the theory to observable features of the real world. This is done here in an intuitive fashion, using concrete examples of the effects of different conditions upon happiness. It is by these applications that the theory acquires meaning and that the reader can judge its usefulness.

But first, we must clarify a conceptual confusion that can impede understanding of the theory. This confusion is between the concept of pleasure used in this book and the concept of utility used in theories of expected utility and decision analysis. The two concepts are related in important ways, but they can yield very different prescriptions when treated normatively. Although the contextual theory of happiness is descriptive rather than normative, it does suggest certain types of choices if one should want to maximize pleasure or happiness—without implying that one should want to maximize them, either for oneself or for others.

PLEASURE VERSUS UTILITY

When one's income varies irregularly—depending upon the vagaries of the marketplace, the weather, or other unpredictable factors—the frequency distribution of recent earnings is likely to be a major part of the context for judging each paycheck. The ups and downs of income may be largely out of one's control, just as the sequence of stimuli selected by the experimenter is out of the subject's control. But in everyday life, we have at least some control. Consider the placing of bets at a racetrack. One can choose to bet on the favorites, winning frequently but never very much; or one can play the longshots, losing almost always but occasionally winning very large amounts. With enough information about the probability distribution of outcomes, decision theory tells us how to optimize our utilities, that is, what we prefer, which in this case is higher income from our wins and losses. With the same information, the contextual theory of happiness tells us how to optimize the pleasantness of our wins and losses.[1] Income does not correlate very highly with pleasure unless the different levels of income are experienced in the same hedonic context.

---

[1]This distinction was the subject of an illuminating chapter by Kahneman and Varey (1991), in which they discuss differences between *preference utility* and *experienced utility* (here called *pleasure*). Tversky and Griffin (1991) demonstrate that subjects give different answers to questions about these two kinds of utility.

Skewed Distributions

Presented with alternative distributions of earnings, descriptive versions of expected utility theory assert that people choose the distribution with the highest
expected subjective value.[2] Insofar as people prefer more money to less, they
choose that alternative whose distribution of expected earnings has the higher
mean. The contextual theory of happiness implies that people indeed experience
more pleasure with the higher mean income when the alternative distributions of
earnings share the same endpoints: For any given pair of contextual endpoints,
the mean of all hedonic experiences (pleasantness judgments) is proportional to
the mean of all of the experienced earnings.[3] However, when the endpoints are
not the same for two distributions of incomes, the one with a higher mean may
actually yield less pleasure. As an example of this reversal, consider the following two distributions of commissions we might earn as a sales clerk: Distribution
N, a negatively skewed distribution in which we earn $5 per hour on 90% of our
working days but earn nothing on the remaining 10%, and Distribution P, a
positively-skewed distribution in which we earn $15 per hour on 10% of our
working days and $10 per hour for the other 90%:

		x	x	
		x	x	
		x	x	
(N)		x	x	(P)
		x	x	
		x	x	
		x	x	
		x	x	
x	x	x	x	
$0	$5	$10	$15/hour	

The mean income is more than twice as high for P as for N ($10.50 per hour
vs. $4.50 per hour); and other things being equal, who would not choose Distri-
bution P? However, if our pleasures from income were determined solely by the
range-frequency compromise operating on the context of our own earnings, our
average pleasantness rating on a 9-point scale would be only 3.6 for the positively skewed distribution but a much higher 6.4 for the negatively skewed

---

[2]Indeed, the values are inferred from the choices so that the theory can only be infirmed by
inconsistencies of choice. This is a sophisticated variant upon the psychological hedonism discussed
in chapter 1.

[3]This assumes that the context is representative of the actual incomes, scaled by their range values
(see chapter 6).

distribution.[4] Realizing that it yields the greater income, most people would choose the positively skewed distribution—even though they would actually be less satisfied with these earnings than they would be with the lower earnings coming in the negatively skewed distribution.[5]

Contextual Effects upon Choices

Although economists usually assume that utilities are constant, that preferences do not change, this is of course an oversimplification (cf., Schoemaker, 1982, who also concludes that most of the empirical evidence is difficult to reconcile with the principle of maximizing expected utilities). Even in a short experimental session in the laboratory, utilities are subject to the same contextual effects that determine category ratings. For example, Zaidel (1971) found the usual range-frequency effects of contextual skewing when utilities were measured using Raiffa's (1968) lottery method. Mellers and Cooke (in press) demonstrated systematic reversals of students' choices between apartments that varied both in rent and distance from the university: When the range of rents was narrow, cheaper apartments were preferred to closer ones; when the range of rents was wide, closer apartments were preferred to cheaper ones. These choice reversals were demonstrated to parallel the shifts in judgment produced by the same independent manipulation of contextual distributions of rents and distances. These studies suggest that our understanding of utilities and choices would be enhanced by greater attention to the effects of contextual distributions. Although the contextual theory of happiness is not itself a theory of choice behavior, it assumes that an underlying scale of preference (or utility) is what distinguishes hedonic judgments from other kinds of dimensional judgments.

IMPLICATIONS FOR HAPPINESS

Proportion of Ecstasy

A common misconception about the contextual theory of happiness is that it implies less ecstasy for negatively skewed distributions. The mistaken reasoning goes like this: For a positively skewed distribution, the upper end of the range occurs so rarely that it must be spectacular when it does occur; but for a negatively skewed distribution, events near the upper end of the range occur so

---

[4]This predicted difference was confirmed experimentally, using two distributions of monetary outcomes that were somewhat less skewed (Parducci, 1968; also described in chapter 5).

[5]My friend James B. MacQueen chided me that although this may be true for the immediate satisfactions from earnings, a more complete picture would have to include the satisfactions from the goods these earnings buy. These consummatory satisfactions would depend in the same way upon the skewing of their respective contexts for judgment.

frequently that they must come to seem not all that great. Although intuitively appealing, this is the reverse of what is actually implied by the range-frequency compromise.[6] Contrary to intuition, the theory predicts twice as many top ratings (e.g., *Marvelous!*) for the negatively skewed distribution of our hypothetical earnings as a sales clerk. It is true that the top earning in the negatively skewed distribution must often be experienced as less than marvelous and hence elicit lower ratings on average; but the frequency with which it actually seems marvelous (and is so rated) is still much greater than the total frequency of the top earning in the positively skewed distribution, even though that top will always be rated *marvelous*.

This implication of the contextual theory of happiness for ecstasy seems contrary to the admonitions of 19th-century Utilitarians and to a number of earlier philosophers. John Stuart Mill (1863) wrote that the happiness of the utilitarians consisted of modest pleasures, with avoidance of the extremes. Much earlier, Epictetus urged that when experiencing extreme pleasure with something, we should temper the pleasure by imagining its loss.[7] The contextual theory of happiness implies that a marked overall balance of pleasure over pain can only be achieved by an abundance of extreme pleasures or ecstasies. Indeed, these pleasures can more than make up for the negative effects they have on lesser experiences.

Choosing Unhappiness

Insofar as real-life contexts are representative of those events that are actually experienced, the greatest happiness goes with the contextual distribution that is skewed most negatively. But happiness is not what we choose when, as in the example from selling, a positively skewed distribution offers more money or more of whatever else we prefer. And our success-oriented culture encourages efforts to get more. If someone turns down a promotion, it is thought that this indicates a bad attitude. Feminist writers warn women not to be held back by their own "fear of success," urging them instead to "go for the gold!"

In the computerized happiness game described in the next chapter, this going for more is illustrated by the experiences of an hypothetical door-to-door salesperson whom the player can send to a neighborhood with less potential for income but that usually brings the expected modest return. Alternatively, the salesman can be sent to a more challenging neighborhood where his average income will be higher but where the highest commissions are rare. Players regularly send their hypothetical salesman to the neighborhood yielding the higher income—even when the payoffs or points in the game, representing the

---

[6]However, this mistaken intuition is consistent with the theory of adaptation level (chapter 4), and that may partially explain its attraction.

[7]The attribution to Epictetus is borrowed from Diener, Sandvik, and Pavot (1991).

salesman's pleasures with his daily commissions, average lower. Few players settle for greater pleasure when it comes from a more modest income.

This is the first problem illuminated by the implementation of the contextual theory of happiness as the computerized game. We regularly choose more in preference to less. We may, in some sense, realize that more does not necessarily mean happier. We may even say in wonderment, "although I am making more money, I seem to be enjoying it less." But it is rare to deliberately choose the lower-paying alternative. To do so would go against the immediate preferability of more to less when both are experienced in the same context, as they are at the time of choice. It would also be contrary to much of our training and to the basic assumption of expected utility theory, namely, that preference is revealed by choice.[8]

Training for Success.   We learn to strive for higher levels of success by the teachings of others and also by the immediate consequences of our own choices. Since childhood, we have been admonished to aim high so that we will achieve more. This may be sound advice, particularly when achievement is measured in absolute terms. One does not master the violin by setting modest goals; students are drilled as though in preparation for solo performances on the concert stage. Business executives are said to look for young people who aspire to replace them. But this is a motivational theory that concentrates on worldly success, not on happiness. Although some people are no doubt happier as a result of higher levels of achievement, there is little evidence that this is generally the case. It may sometimes be false, as when people who reach the "level of their own incompetence" feel frustrated when blocked from further advancement.[9]

Reinforcement and Punishment.   The habit of reaching for more is also reinforced by the immediate consequences of success. Each new object that we acquire, each promotion, each success, is immediately rewarding. We learn that getting more is pleasurable. The painful effects of getting more, the diminished satisfactions with what we will be experiencing more regularly, come only later—so that the causal connection between getting more and the subsequent dissatisfaction is much less obvious. One can see this in the computerized Happiness Game. When first attempting to sell in a wealthier neighborhood, the salesman tends to get high payoffs in satisfaction (*very satisfying*). This is because the new commissions are high in a context that includes his lower earnings from less affluent neighborhoods. However, as these earlier commissions drop out of the context, the new, higher commissions are all that remains. If the lower

---

[8]However, MacQueen pointed out to me that the *spirit* of expected utility theory, as presented by Savage (1950), encourages taking account of how the consequences of each choice would be experienced. In the present analysis, this taking account would have to include consideration of how the respective future contexts would affect the satisfactions from these consequences.

[9]This phenomenon was described in a popular book, *The Peter Principle* (Peter, 1969).

among these new commissions come most frequently, the new territory will then turn sour; the salesman becomes increasingly disappointed with most of his commissions, even though they are higher than what he had earned earlier. Players may come to realize that they have sent the salesman to an unsatisfying neighborhood; but if the salesman is then sent back to where earnings are lower, these must be disappointing until the higher incomes have dropped from the context. Players feel trapped but cannot see that the cause of this frustration is that the pleasure of any absolute level of income depends on the context in which it is now experienced.

I hope the reader will forgive me for returning to the example of windsurfing. Although probably seeming trivial to others, the pleasures and pains I derive from sailing, and particularly from windsurfing, should not be overlooked in any overall accounting of my happiness. Starting in the 1960s, I was among the first to windsurf. Sailing and even cruising on the original big board, the strength of the wind was not the important factor that it later came to be. I liked the way the board went faster with higher winds but not the way it became harder to manage, more tiring. Nevertheless, averaging the pleasures and pains across a wide variety of conditions, windsurfing seemed a truly wonderful sport.

Around 1980, windsurfing was revolutionized by the discovery that enhanced performance could be achieved with a smaller board, one too small to support the sailor's weight without the hydrodynamic lift of forward movement. Copying the younger sailors, I built a smaller board and with it discovered new thrills and challenges: Like most people who have sailed both large and small boards, I greatly preferred the small ones, their lightness and maneuverability, the opportunity to play in the waves, and above all, the greater speed. According to the popular notion of going for more, my balance of pleasure over pain should have improved in this important recreational domain of my life.

I fear that the truth is quite the reverse. The problem with the small board is that it requires very strong winds. In Hawaii, when the trade winds are blowing, a small board is perfection itself. But in Southern California where I live much of the year, the winds tend to be too light for the water-starts that get the sailor up onto the already moving board. Like so many of my fellow sailboarders, I find myself driving to distant beaches where the winds tend to be stronger, often to find that even there the wind is insufficient. Small board sailing can be absolutely breathtaking, but my experience with it is much more often spoiled by lack of wind. Interpreted in terms of the contextual theory of happiness, the distribution of my windsurfing experiences was transformed from negative to positive skewing—from happiness to unhappiness.

What I should do is give up my small board and restrict my sailing to the original windsurfer that was once so enjoyable because it was so well adapted to the distribution of winds where I sail. But it is easier to make the diagnosis than to follow this prescription: When I try to go back to the big board, it seems slow, tiring, a little boring. The contextual theory of happiness tells me that it must continue to be so until the exhilarating experiences with the small board have dropped from my context, lowering the upper endpoint of the range. However, the theory does not specify how long this might take. Better not to have switched to the small board in the first place!

One might think this problem solvable by a compromise, that I should windsurf only when the wind is strong. But hope springs eternal, keeping the thrilling upper endpoint in my context for windsurfing. Because it seems to require some restriction of contextual range, my personal difficulty here seems a relatively benign case of a more general problem of adjusting to loss.[10]

When "Better" Is Really Better

The examples of the tug of war between success and happiness seem to counsel a lower level of aspiration, as though happiness actually varied inversely with achievement. But there is little reason to believe this to be true as a general rule. Consider one of our gravest social problems, unemployment. For many long-term unemployed, the frustrating search for work is depressing and demeaning. Although there may be better moments when there is the unrealistic hope for a job, or when earlier periods of employment are recalled, the distribution of events in this domain is likely to be positively skewed, with the awful feelings of rejection and hopelessness experienced most often. This is an unhappy balance. Now suppose that such a person eventually finds a regular job. Immediately, there is a flood of pleasure, continuing as long as the recent experiences of unemployment remain in the context. Everything seems perfect. In cases where the new distribution of incomes is negatively skewed, where the best comes relatively often, this domain will continue to be a happy one—even long after the bitter sense of being unemployable has dropped from the context.

"Moving up in the world" suggests increased power to control one's circumstances, to spend more time on preferred activities. Who doubts, for example, that it is better to be healthy than to be sick, to be well-fed than to be starving? But the enhanced freedom of choice is limited by insufficient knowledge of the fundamental conditions for happiness. It may also be limited by an inability or unwillingness to apply what knowledge is already available. Too often, we use our freedom to establish positively skewed patterns that work against long-term happiness.

Limitations on Happiness

If the hedonic contexts for everyday pleasures and pains were restricted to representations of recent experiences, as in a psychophysical experiment, the amount of happiness that could be achieved would be severely limited by the

---

[10]Adjustment to loss is analyzed in chapter 10.

frequency principle. Consider again the simple example of the negatively skewed distribution of our incomes as a sales clerk: One level of income occurs 90% of the time, a second and lower level occurs the remaining 10%. Applying range-frequency principles, the higher level is at the top of the range but its average rank in the distribution, that is, its frequency value, is only slightly above the median; the range-frequency compromise for this higher level yields an average judgment that is thus little more than three-fourths of the way up from 0 to 1, .78. Because the lower level is at the bottom of the range and below 90% of contextual representations, the range-frequency compromise places its judgment close to the bottom of the scale—0. The average of these two judgments, weighted for their relative frequencies, is only .70, which is between 6 and 7 on a 9-point scale (between *slightly satisfying* and *satisfying*). Because this upper limit of happiness is close to the average self-avowal of happiness obtained in surveys of adult Americans, it would seem that on the average we report ourselves just as happy as we could possibly be.

Would there really be happiness with such an extreme degree of skewing? Imagine prisoners fed the same meal every day, except that on 10% of the days they are not fed at all. Within the constraints of a psychophysical life, a life in which pleasures and pains are experienced in a context representing only the recent past events of the same type (in this case recent meals and fasts), this regime would be close to the happiest imaginable! Then why does it seem so dismal? We are repelled by the contemplation of such a monotonous diet because our own patterns of eating include so much more variety. However, the meals would not seem monotonous to these hypothetical prisoners, at least not according to the psychophysical analogy. The frequency principle implies that minuscule differences between successive meals, meals that would seem identical in the context of our own varied diet, would loom large to the prisoners. In Solzhenitsyn's (1963) *One Day in the Life of Ivan Denisovitch*, his prisoner-hero (a *yek* in the Gulag Archipelago) was thrilled to find a piece of solid potato in the soup. The slightest variation in quantity or quality, or perhaps even subtle variations in the internal state of the prisoners' digestive systems, would come to elicit pleasures that varied between the middle and top of the scale of judgment, with the prisoners' ratings varying from scarcely above *just so-so* to *absolutely wonderful*. Because their meal days come nine times more often than their days without food, their overall balance for this important domain would be halfway between *slightly pleasant* and *pleasant* (as in the formally-identical example of incomes from selling). These prisoners might reasonably question whether they were not as happy with their prison meals as they would have been with a normal pattern of eating, just as Solzhenitsyn's *yek* eventually questioned whether his life in the gulag was not just as happy as his life would have been back in his village.

The importance of other factors becomes apparent when real-life considerations are brought into the example. One prisoner on such a regime might spend his or her time in delightful anticipation of the next meal, another might live in dread of the day on which there will be no food at all. It is not just the actual meals or their absence that must be considered but also the anticipations and the dreads. In the contextual theory of happiness, these are conceptualized as imaginary events, although sometimes just as intense and real in their experienced pleasures and pains as the actual meals and fasts. And insofar as pleasures from these imaginary experiences occupy more of the prisoners' time than do the pleasures from actual eating, they make a greater direct contribution to their happiness.

Although anticipations can replace some of the actual eating experiences in the context for judgment, they are still subject to the same rules and limitations: Unless the extreme lower endpoint is experienced at least occasionally, it will eventually drop from the context, reducing the pleasantness of everything else. So one cannot have a completely happy life by simply concentrating one's attention upon pleasant daydreams. Insofar as the context is representative of recent experiences, even the best melange of delightful anticipations and actual meals cannot pull the overall average up as high as *satisfying* (i,.e., as high as 7 on a 9-point rating scale). However, as demonstrated in later chapters, there are other assumptions about the context that imply a much greater potential for happiness.

PROBLEMS APPLYING THE THEORY

Testability

Range-frequency theory was developed to explain how the context determines the judgment of any particular stimulus. When it is applied to the prediction of category ratings in carefully controlled experiments, the theory is directly testable by the public operations of science. The evidence waits only for a better theory to come along, one that will do a better job of predicting category ratings.[11] It is when such a theory is used to explain subjective experience, as is the contextual theory of happiness, that there is a question about whether or not it can be tested scientifically. How can we be sure that subjective experiences of pleasure or pain are reflected so directly by overt category ratings? My answer is simply to appeal to the reader's own experience (Parducci, 1982, 1990). Suppose that you were trying to describe the pleasantness of what you were experiencing but that your verbal rating came out too high or too low. Would not you then

---

[11]One technical possibility for such broader explanation is the associative theory developed by Haubensak (1992) and discussed here (chapter 5, especially footnote 7). Another is MacQueen's (1966) *K-Mean Model*, which assumes that categories are used so as to minimize the average variance of those stimuli assigned to them. Although much simpler than range-frequency theory, the K-Mean Model does surprisingly well at predicting some of the range-frequency effects upon category ratings.

simply revise your rating, lowering or raising it for a more accurate description of your actual experience?

Any application of the contextual theory of happiness to everyday life outside the laboratory requires special assumptions about the relevant hedonic contexts. Because these assumptions are speculative, applications that depend on them must also be speculative. One general problem is that the hedonic contexts of everyday life may not be representative of recent past experiences. Although guided by how contexts are established in simple experiments, attempts at broader implications encourage a variety of additional assumptions. We first consider ways in which the context may be systematically biased in its representations of past experiences and how this bias would effect the possibilities for happiness. Other practical considerations are concerned with the problem of how we can identify the contexts for everyday experiences of pleasure and pain and how we can control them.

Unrepresentative Contexts

Selective Dropping From the Context.   Time heals. Bad experiences eventually drop out of the context, as do good experiences; but it makes a big difference for happiness whether or not the good experiences drop out more quickly than do the bad. The contextual theory suggests that recovery from a disappointment, such as an unrequited love, depends on the dropping out of the upper, most preferred end of the contextual range. This upper endpoint might represent an earlier anticipation of love. Its dropping from the context would enhance the pleasantness of whatever is experienced in the truncated context. This enhancement would be supported by a longer retention of the worst of the context, perhaps a painful rejection. Popular advice is to reduce the pain by finding a new love. This may be impossible while the old love remains in the context, as though any new love were being subjected to invidious comparisons. However, the psychophysically generated assumption that there is a fixed limit on the size of the context supports the idea of flooding it with new experiences to drive out the old. An example is provided by the popular advice to "go find another," that "there are other fish in the pond."

The contextual theory of happiness does not specify the conditions in which representations drop from the context. The problem is that with the exception of certain simple laboratory experiments, the context is known only by inference. In most real-life applications to happiness, one knows how one feels about something but not the context on which the feeling depends. Working backward from experienced pleasures and pains, range-frequency principles can be used as tools for speculation about the composition of any particular hedonic context. But to change how one feels, to make particular conditions more enjoyable or at least less painful, one must change the contexts in which they are experienced. For example, speculating that it is the contextual representation of a lost love that is keeping one unhappy, different methods can be tried for removing this upper-endpoint from the context. None are likely to work as long as there is perceived likelihood of regaining the lost love, for any such pleasurable anticipation tends to keep the lost love in the context. The ability to drop such high points would be a powerful tool for happiness. More generally, any natural difference between the rates at which good or bad experiences drop from the context would be a crucial determinant of the limits upon happiness.

Imaginary Events.   Anticipations, memories, and fantasies may constitute the majority of hedonic experiences and the most numerous components of many hedonic contexts. Although some contexts may include both imaginary and real experiences, certain well-segregated contexts seem restricted to imaginary experiences. Fairy tales for children (often horror stories) may elicit such contexts, with little effect on how the real world is experienced. Such seems the case for much of television, including the popular dramatic series devoured by adults the world over.

Assuming that most of our pleasures and pains are elicited by daydreams, anticipations and memories, the workings of the imagination must be a major concern in most applications of the contextual theory of happiness. The simplest assumption is that the pleasantness of any imagined event is determined by its place in some context, just as for real-world events. Whether such a context was restricted to events that were imaginary or whether it also included representations of events that had actually happened, the contextual theory of happiness assumes that the pleasures of the imagination are governed by the same range-frequency principles that explain the results of laboratory experiments.

Pleasures and pains elicited by the imagination contribute to the overall level of happiness along with the pleasures and pains elicited by the real world of physical events. The relative contribution of real and imaginary experiences is determined by their respective frequencies and durations and also by their effects as context for other hedonic experiences. In the case of a delicious memory, such as an unforgettable lovers' tryst, the real event that is remembered may have occurred only once; but each reliving of it in our imaginations contributes directly to our happiness. However, its unconscious representation in the context for other hedonic judgments, perhaps in the context for other, more forgettable trysts, works in the opposite direction. Thus, the original event can work toward raising but also toward lowering our happiness.[12]

The goals or plans we have for the future seem particularly important for our happiness: goals can become major parts of our hedonic contexts, just as re-

---

[12]These dual, opposed effects were labeled *endowment* and *contrast* by Tversky and Griffin (1991) who demonstrated shifts in their relative contribution to an overall judgment, depending on the similarity or relatedness between earlier and present events (see also Strack, Schwarz, and Gschneidinger, 1985, for an interpretation of endowment in terms of mood).

peated presentations of a particular experimental stimulus result (but only up to a point) in its more frequent representation in the context for psychophysical judgments. Setting unrealistically high goals or subgoals in some particular domain, such as our work, reduces the pleasures of actual performance in that domain. And yet, the pleasures of anticipating success may outweigh the painful disappointment with what actually happens.[13]

Evoked Contexts.   Certain experiences might evoke contextual representations of events that have never actually occurred and perhaps have never even been imagined (see chap. 3; cf. Kahneman & Miller, 1986). A contextual counterfactual influences the judgment of any event experienced in its context, just as if the counterfactual represented an event that had actually been experienced. Our earlier experimental example was the counterfactual of losing $200 being evoked contextually by the real experience of winning $200, thereby lessening the pain of a real loss of $100 (Marsh & Parducci, 1978).

It seems more likely that the evocation of a contextual counterfactual requires at least a fleeting experience of pleasure or pain, akin to the painful disappointment that would have been experienced from a real loss of $200. The more frequently or longer that this imaginary counterfactual is experienced, the greater its direct contribution to the sum total of happiness. This direct contribution would be counterbalanced by its contextual effects on hedonic judgments of other events, particularly if its representation defined the endpoint of a context. As a new, more extreme lower endpoint, it would enhance the pleasantness of anything else experienced in the same context. Counterfactuals that extend their contextual ranges upward, perhaps the fantasy of winning a lottery or a Nobel Prize, would have the opposite effect.

Contextual elements of this type, even if they have been imagined with pleasure or pain only at some time in the distant past, could greatly expand the theoretical possibilities for happiness. Range-frequency principles would still operate, but they would operate on an expanded context that included events that were not now being judged in the same context.[14]

Identifying Contexts

Attempts to apply the contextual theory of happiness seem less daringly risky when attention is restricted to those nonlaboratory situations that most closely resemble, in the simplicity of their apparent conditions, the basic experiments through which range-frequency principles were developed. These are situations in which the context for judgment, the set of events whose representation would

---

[13]Using expanded versions of the computerized game, chapter 9 illustrates the implications for happiness of specific assumptions about how imaginary experience are represented contextually.

[14]Implications of this possibility are explored in chapters 9, 10, and 11.

be sufficient to predict the category ratings, can be identified with recent experiences. Applying the theory seems most straightforward for simple sensory domains. The pleasantness of a given temperature, for example, is experienced in a context representing the more recent temperatures, just as in a psychophysical experiment. But even here contextual considerations may extend beyond recent experiences, including representations of other temperatures from the distant past (as described in chapter 3). The 80-degree day in summer reminds us of other summer days: We might say that it is unpleasantly warm but not for this time of year or in comparison with a more typical summer; and if, after a series of days in the 70's, this 80-degree day does not feel unpleasantly warm, it may be that the much hotter days of other, more typical summers are represented in the context determining their pleasantness—even when we were not consciously recalling or thinking about those other summers.

Another difference that complicates generalization from simple laboratory experiments is that imaginary experiences elicit many of our everyday hedonic judgments. Just thinking about swimming in the winter ocean may evoke shivers, a momentarily unpleasant sense of cold. If such an imaginary experience were to enter the context for an early summer swim, the ocean might actually feel warm; water of the same temperature would feel unpleasantly cold later in the summer when the context would be more representative of recent summer swims.

The windsurfing example illustrates how difficult it can be to identify the hedonic contexts of everyday life. In the psychophysical experiments, the context represents the set of stimuli selected by the experimenter, but what is the context for windsurfing? It would be too simple to assume that it is restricted just to recent windsurfing experiences. What of the other experiences associated with the sport—the escape from work, the pleasurable anticipations of strong wind and high speeds, the good fellowship on the beach? These must also be represented, both in the context for windsurfing and in the overall balance of its pleasures and pains. If these related experiences were included, the skewing might change for the better, perhaps even to a happy overall balance.[15]

Averaging Across Domains

Insofar as the concern is with the happiness of a whole life averaged across the different domains of hedonic experience (such as work, recreation, eating, and social relations), there is the problem of identifying these domains and their relative contributions to happiness. How much pleasure can be sacrificed in

---

[15]A psychological hedonist would claim that I would not continue windsurfing unless I believed that its pleasures outbalanced its pains. Such a claim seems inherently untestable and therefore empirically empty, just like the other appealing but deceptive explanations in terms of psychological hedonism.

painful pursuit of career to enhance the pleasantness of one's recreations?[16] In direct application of the Utilitarian definition of happiness, the contextual theory weights the average for each domain by the summed duration of its component hedonic experiences.

There are higher-level contexts that subsume the contexts representing momentary events. When one evaluates the afternoon's adventure as a whole, related activities (such as the escape from work, driving to the beach, and talking to fellow sailors) may all be combined with the actual sailing to form an overall impression. In this case, the context for evaluating the overall impression would consist of other overall impressions, especially those of other windsurfing afternoons. People often concentrate on such integrated impressions when thinking about happiness. But the resulting overall judgment, pleasant or painful, might be experienced so infrequently as to be overwhelmed by the many separate pleasures and pains experienced in the course of any particular afternoon; the occasional overall judgment would then contribute very little to the hypothetical computation of an overall mean, the contextual theory's measure of happiness.[17]

Most of the serious research on happiness has concentrated on these grander, overall judgments of much bigger chunks of a life, perhaps covering recent weeks or months. Although correlating modestly with the overall balance of separate pleasures and pains for the same periods, these self-avowals of happiness may be momentarily satisfying in themselves. It feels good to be able to say that your life has been very happy. Even for people without any clear conception of what they mean by a happy life, this brief warm glow makes its own momentary contribution to their overall happiness. This may be part of a more general tendency toward positive thinking that could add to happiness whenever it was manifested. However, the habit of thinking positively could instead promote unhappiness if such pleasant moments were represented in other contexts. For example, awareness of one's lack of progress might be much more painful when experienced in a context that included representations of unrealistically positive self-assessments.

Choosing or Controlling Contexts

For practical considerations of happiness, the most crucial problem is one of control—not just of our life events, real or imaginary, but also of the contexts in which they are experienced. The possibilities for control are speculative: We do

---

[16]On the basis of 15 years of research on random time sampling of momentary pleasures, Csikszentmihalyi (1993) reported that people actually tend to get more pleasure from their work than from their recreations.

[17]The time scale for judgment remains a problem. My friend Chuck Turner described introspecting oscillations between pleasure and pain that are almost instantaneous. However, the pleasures and pains of experiences that are not so introspectively directed may last many seconds or minutes. For expository purposes, it is convenient to average across these, speaking of the pleasure of an activity or even of an entire working day (as in the computerized happiness game).

not know to what degree we might acquire such control or even already possess it. Some of the mechanisms for control might be determined by our genes, with different possibilities for different people. Certain lucky ones may be born to be happy. Happy people seem more often to be making positive assessments, but it does not follow that others would also be happier if they expressed themselves more positively.[18]

The general problem of establishing rules of correspondence between theory and the real world, in this case of identifying and controlling the contexts of everyday life, are not peculiar to the contextual theory of happiness. Analogous difficulties confront any theory of social science, whether in psychology, sociology, or economics. To apply such theories requires more information than we can ever have, and thus, a host of special assumptions. Many of these are not made explicitly, instead developing as a kind of specialized folklore that seems natural to those who apply them. The further development of the contextual theory of happiness in the chapters that follow is an attempt, by considering various practical applications, to make more explicit the assumptions underlying any particular assertion about the conditions for happiness.

SUMMARY

The contextual theory of happiness combines range-frequency principles with the assumption that pleasures and pains are judgments. It then follows that happiness, defined as the mean of all hedonic judgments, is greater when the events that elicit such judgments are concentrated near the upper endpoints of their respective contexts, regardless of the absolute levels of these events. In applying the theory, focus shifts from external events to imaginary experiences, to anticipations, goals, memories, fantasies, and counterfactuals, and to how these can function in contexts that are unrepresentative of recent hedonic experiences. These considerations enlarge the possibilities for happiness beyond the limitations implied by the psychophysical analogy.

Although the negatively skewed distributions of events, real or imaginary, are the most conducive to happiness and also to ecstasy (which is a frequent component of real happiness), people often choose a positively skewed distribution when its absolute levels are higher. Thus, the contextual theory of happiness differs from the theory of expected utility so popular in economics and decision analysis. The same range-frequency effects of context were demonstrated for the

---

[18]Myers (1992), in an engaging and thoughtful use of the survey literature, diagnosed a set of correlated behavioral traits, such as extroversion and optimism, that go with self-avowals of happiness. Although people who manifest these traits are also rated happier by others, it is an open question whether or not attempting to acquire these traits enhances happiness. Indeed, Myers also suggested acquiring a sense of one's own mortality, a different route to happiness closer to what is advocated at the end of chapter 11.

utilities implied by choices, but normative utility theory often seems to prescribe choices that are less conducive to happiness.[19] The tug-of-war that sometimes occurs between success and happiness is obscured by the immediate pleasures of success. Applications of the contextual theory of happiness require specific assumptions about hedonic contexts, their identification and possible control.

---

[19]In a book emphasizing psychological factors in economic behavior, the economist Scitovsky (1976/1982) asserted that the notion of maximizing expected utilities "set back by generations all scientific inquiry into consumer behavior, for it seemed to rule out—as a logical impossibility—any conflict between what man chooses to get and what will best satisfy him" (p. 4). This was cited, with apparent approval, by Schoemaker (1982).

III APPLYING THE THEORY

8 The Happiness Game: Simplest Version

The ideas thus far presented have been incorporated into a game played with a computer. Each feature of the game corresponds to a feature of the contextual theory of happiness, so that the game provides a sharper and more concrete conception of what the theory is about. The game also provides concrete illustrations of how the theory might work out in practice. Because the game attempts to simulate the consequences for happiness of different everyday-life choices, its limitations are readily apparent. One can see ways in which the theory oversimplifies life, leaving out what may seem most important. The game is thus a stimulus for thinking about the more elaborate contextual considerations that seem crucial to happiness.

Because the game has proven so difficult for players to master, it also raises provocative questions about what we ordinarily learn from our everyday hedonic experiences. Insofar as the game embodies basic principles of judgment, it illustrates how difficult it would be to master them from uncontrolled observations of life. The game has proven to be a poor teacher of these principles, but this ineptitude provides important lessons for the psychology of happiness.

General Features of the Game

Imagine that you are seated at the terminal of a personal computer, looking at the screen while it gives a bit of background information. It asks you to take control of the life of a young male salesperson who has been averaging less than $50 a day in commissions. He occasionally earns as much as $100, and if more ambitious could make $200 or more in a single day. The choice is now yours to set goals for him. In choosing appropriate goals, you are to operate as an altruistic psychologist, with the objective of making him happy.

On each trial, you establish a *goal* or objective for how much you want him to try to make that day. You are warned that although ambition in selling is generally rewarded with increased income, the disparities between his actual attainments and his aspirations are likely to be greater the higher his goal. After you type in a goal, the computer tells you what happened that day, how much this hypothetical salesman actually earned, and (most important for a theory of happiness) how he felt about it. The computer makes this estimate of how satisfying this particular day's earnings would be by applying a range-frequency analysis to the salesman's recent pattern of earnings. Thus, on each play of the game, the achieved level of satisfaction depends not just on how much is earned but also on the place of this earning in the context of recent earnings, a context largely established by the goals you have chosen.

For example, if at the beginning of play you chose for the salesman to try to make $50, the computer might tell you that he actually made the $50 and found it *satisfying* (or perhaps only *slightly satisfying*). This would add a certain number of points to your cumulative score. On any given play, you can make as many as 500 points when the commission is *very very satisfying*, but you can also lose up to 500 points when the commission is *very very disappointing* (as if one day the salesman scarcely makes anything after a run of profitable days).

The computer gives this numerical score in points, negative or positive, points won or points lost. It also averages this payoff with all earlier payoffs. The resulting cumulative average, the mean of all numerical payoffs, is the game's measure of happiness. This measure is not in itself sensitive to how long you play or to how many trials you can squeeze in during a given period of time. Thus, this simple version of the game is not concerned with how fully the salesman lives, in the sense of how great a proportion of his time is hedonically enriched.

Your objective as a player is to drive the cumulative average payoff as high as you can. . . .that is, to create a pattern of commissions that gives this imaginary salesman as much happiness as possible. There is no standard stopping-point. However, because most players lose more points than they gain, keeping the cumulative average on the positive side is something of a triumph. To understand how players typically set the stage for unhappiness, consider how each payoff (or score representing satisfaction) is determined.

Computing the Amount of Satisfaction

The Context for Judgment.   When the player begins choosing goals for the novice salesman, the computer already contains an hypothetical record of the salesman's earnings from his 10 most recent days of selling, as though the salesman's personal context for selling included only the commissions from these last 10 days. Consider the following example:

$35 $55 $20 $50 $60 $50 $30 $60 $55 $45.

If the player then chooses to go for $50 and makes it, this $50 becomes a part of the salesman's immediate context for judgment, and the contextual representation of the $35 earned on the 10th day back drops out. The context in which this new $50 is experienced thus becomes:

$55 $20 $50 $60 $50 $30 $60 $55 $45 *$50*.

Given this particular context, how satisfying was it to have earned a commission of $50?

Range-Frequency Determination of Payoffs. The structure of the game is a simple reversal of the psychophysical experiments on which its principles of judgment are based. In the usual experiment, stimuli (such as different odors sniffed from bottles) are selected by the experimenter who presents them successively to the experimental subject under instructions to rate the pleasantness of each presentation. Control of the context rests completely with the experimenter, and it is the subject who makes the judgments. In the computer game, however, the subject (player) controls the context by setting goals that establish the distribution of commissions, and it is the experimenter (computer) that calculates how satisfying a particular commission is in the context of recent commissions. The computer is programmed to derive this judgment from range-frequency theory.[1]

The computer first calculates the location of the $50 outcome in the range of outcomes for the last 10 trials. Because $50 is three-quarters of the way between $20 (the lowest commission in the context) and $60 (the highest), this range value is .75. The computer also calculates the proportion of the commissions in the context falling below $50. Counting one half of those tied with $50, this comes to .44.[2]

Taking the mean of these range and frequency values (i.e., weighting them equally), the computer obtains a range-frequency compromise of $(.75 + .44)/2 = .60$ which, when linearly transformed to the scale from -500 to $+500$, yields

---

[1]For this, my first serious effort at computer simulation, I was generously encouraged and taught to program in LISP by a friend, David Knapp, who is a computer scientist.

[2]The computer counts the number of contextual stimuli (called *outcomes*) below the outcome whose frequency value is being evaluated and adds 1 for the evaluated outcome and .5 for each additional outcome tied with it; this sum represents the rank, r, of this outcome in the context; the frequency value (between 0 and 1) is then computed using the equation presented in footnote 11 of chapter 6.

a score of $+100$ (the numerical equivalent of *Slightly Satisfying*). This is what you, as the player, might then see on the screen:

> You set $50 as your goal for the day, and selling door-to-door in this relatively easy neighborhood you earned $50.

> Outcome = $50
> Payoff = $+100$
> Slightly Satisfying
> Cumulative Average = $+100$

Suppose that on the next play you set a higher goal, $100, but that the salesman actually earns only $70. This value is added to the updated context, and the 10th outcome back ($55) drops out. The new context, used by the computer to calculate how satisfying this $70 would be, is then:

$20 $50 $60 $50 $30 $60 $55 $45 $50 *$70*.

The printout might read:

> You went for a $100 commission, and you almost made it!

> Outcome = $50
> Payoff = $+500$
> Very, Very Satisfying
> Cumulative Average = $+300$

Because the $70 constitutes the upper endpoint of the context, with respect both to range and frequency, its payoff in points is the maximum possible—which raises the cumulative average to $(100 + 500)/2 = 300$.

Encouraged, you may again set the goal at $100. Suppose that this time the outcome is only $50, updating the context to:

$50 $60 $50 $30 $60 $55 $45 $50 $70 *$50*.

The $20 has dropped out so that $50 is now half way between the new lower endpoint, $30, and the upper endpoint, $70—yielding a range value of .5. Taking ties into account, 40% of contextual values are below this $50—yielding a frequency value of .40. The range-frequency compromise, $(.50 + .40)/2 = .45$, which transforms to -50 on the payoff scale from -500 to $+500$ (close to the lower boundary of the middle category of the 9-point verbal scale). The message from the computer might now read:

You made some good sales in this prosperous neighborhood, but most people were not at home. Your net commission was only $50.

> Outcome = $50
> Payoff = −50
> Indifferent
> Cumulative Average = 183

Note that earning the same $50 was *slightly satisfying* (+100) on the first trial but is now at the low end of *Indifferent* (−50). This loss in satisfaction partially reflects the drop in frequency value but mostly the larger drop in range value due to the raising of both the lower endpoint (20 to 30) and upper endpoint (60 to 70) of the contextual range.

Despite instructions emphasizing the relationship to recent earnings, a novice player might well be puzzled that the same $50 is now less satisfying. Even after becoming accustomed to getting different payoffs for the same outcome, the typical player has a difficult time trying to increase the young salesman's happiness (as measured by the cumulative average payoff). Thus, the game illustrates a common dilemma: We know how to make more money but not how to get more enjoyment from the money that we make.

Determining Outcomes

How did the computer determine on this particular trial that the salesman would earn only one half of the $100 you set as his goal? Built into the computer program are rules for converting the player's choices to outcomes in accordance with preconceived probabilities. For example, when the player selects $100 as the goal for a particular trial, the probability of earning a commission close to $100 is .3, with the same probability of earning considerably more (up to $200), and a .4 probability of earning much less (around $50). Thus, the salesman's earnings on those trials for which the player sets a goal of $100 are (in the long run) fairly evenly distributed across a range of from $50 to $200 but with earnings below the goal coming somewhat more frequently than those above the goal. Staying at this level of goal or ambition means that the frequency distribution of recent earnings tends to have a slight positive skewing so that the balance of satisfaction, represented by the cumulative average payoff, tips slightly to the negative (−22 on the scale from −500 to +500).

In programming this feature of the game, it was assumed that higher goals would produce higher commissions: Commissions tend to be higher when the player sets a goal at $100 than when he goes for only $50, and higher yet when he goes for $200. However, achievement on any particular play is usually below the goal selected by the player, farther below when the goal is higher. For each goal, there is a probability distribution of actual earnings. The different earnings are thus predictable in the long run—for example, that the salesman will actually make close to $100 in commissions on only 30% of those days for which $100 was the selected goal, but the computer's random-number generator ensures that it is impossible to know exactly when a $100 day will occur. The assumed relationship between ambition and achievement is not an intrinsic part of the contextual theory of happiness. Rather, it is a special assumption, reflecting common-sense notions about how ambition affects achievement. As in life, the player quickly acquires a general idea of the likely distribution of earnings for each of the five levels of goal. A sophisticated player could use this knowledge to select and stick to the goal that establishes the most negatively skewed distribution of earnings and hence the highest possible cumulative average payoff in satisfaction (not necessarily in dollars earned). However, most players never learn to use this knowledge of the distribution of outcomes. Even though doing well by repeatedly setting a goal of $50, with a negatively-skewed distribution of outcomes yielding a .20 probability of making only about $25 but a .80 probability of making close to the $50, most players periodically gravitate to higher goals that yield more money but in less-satisfying, positively-skewed distributions.

A crucial decision when programming the game was to establish a modest correlation between the level of goal and the skewing of outcomes. For example, even at the lowest level of choice, when the salesman did not aspire to any income at all on a particular day (e.g., the goal being just to distribute brochures or free samples), he would occasionally sell something; these unexpected commissions would be rare enough to skew the distribution of outcomes in the positive direction, tipping the overall consequences of this low level of ambition toward unhappiness. In a more sophisticated version of the game, such days might enhance the sales on other days or might even be enjoyable because they foster gratifying anticipations of future sales. However, it was assumed that the distribution of consequences would be skewed more positively when goals were higher because such a beginning salesman would be less likely to fulfill the higher goals. One can imagine him sometimes scoring a dramatic sale, but most days would fall short of the higher levels. This seems consistent with the pyramid-like character of competitive situations: Even an inexperienced or ungifted salesman could fulfill a goal that was sufficiently low; but although this same salesman would probably earn more if he aimed higher, his best days would be relatively rare. Only the very best salesmen can regularly sell at the highest level.

Although the game illustrates some of the consequences of these particular assumptions about life's contingencies, it cannot demonstrate their validity. We can use the game to rule out assumptions only when their consequences seem extraordinarily unlikely. The most important consequence for happiness of the assumptions built into this simple version of the game is that it is the skewing of the distribution of outcomes, rather than their absolute levels, that determines the overall balance of happiness. This is the major implication of the contextual theory of happiness.

Experience with hundreds of players shows that it is easier to learn these distributions of material outcomes (sizes of commissions) than to learn the relationship between contextual skewing and overall satisfaction. Certainly, the relationship between choice of goal and dollars earned is much more overt: Players always know precisely what choice was made on a given trial and what was its outcome (in dollars). Their grasp of the context in which the outcome is experienced, the last 10 outcomes, is less precise and may not even be consciously articulated.

In some versions of the game, the player is shown the context for each successive outcome (as in the numerical examples). This relieves the burden upon memory, but it still leaves the player with the problem of figuring out the range-frequency rules—in particular that the happiest contexts are those in which most of the outcomes are near the top of the contextual range, however low this top may be. In the section that discusses the difficulty of play, it is argued that the recognition of this range-frequency implication is thwarted by the pattern of immediate reinforcements.

The computer might have been programmed to give the cumulative income in addition to the cumulative average of the points (representing happiness). Indeed, a friend suggested that a bell should ring for any unusually large commission. But this additional information might actually make the game more difficult, encouraging the player to maximize income rather than happiness. This already seems to be a powerful tendency of choice, in life as in the game.

Independence of Contexts from Different Domains?

There is more to life than selling. Even in this simplest version of the Happiness Game, players are allowed to choose between work and recreation. They are told that the salesman is an experienced windsurfer (why that sport?). On each trial, the player can choose to let the salesman go windsurfing instead of trying to sell. The game's instructions state that it is easier to achieve a high cumulative average (more pleasure than pain) while windsurfing but that after too many days away from work the salesman will start to worry about the lost income.

Each time the player sends the salesman out sailing, the computer consults the recent record and, on a probabilistic basis, determines whether or not there has been too little work. If so, the player will receive a message like this:

> You chose to go sailing again, but aren't you overdoing it? All you could think about while sailing was that you were not making any money. Shape up!

$$\text{Payoff} = -400 \text{ (of selling)}$$
"Very Very Depressing."

Note that although the player sent the salesman out to sail, the computer threw him back into the domain of work—meaning that, though sailing, the salesman's mind was nevertheless on work. And because he was thinking about his lost earnings, the thoughts were depressing. This -400 would pull down the cumulative average payoff (not shown).

Do these negative thoughts become part of the context for sailing or the context for selling? The computer was programmed to classify them by domain: Because they are about not making any money, they enter the context for selling as if it had been a day of selling without any commissions (Outcome = $0). When the player elects to go back to selling, the context of commissions will include this $0 day. Unless such days were already frequent, keeping this extreme lower endpoint within the context by suffering it on every 10th trial would enhance the net pleasure from selling.

Because windsurfing is generally more satisfying than selling in the game (if not in life), players tend to send their salesman off to sail, forcing him to work just enough to avoid bad thoughts while sailing. In other respects, the game treats the domain of sailing in the same way it treats the domain of selling. On each play, there is a choice between different levels of sailing—for example, between a quiet lake near home and more dramatic conditions in the ocean. Each choice evokes a pre-determined probability distribution of possible outcomes, conditions for sailing that vary on the salesman's scale of preference. Some choices prove to be more "satisfying" than others, and players can optimize their cumulative averages by sending the salesman to sail where the conditions are most often near the top of the current range of contextual events (however low this top might be).

When adding this additional domain to the game, a decision had to be made about whether a bad day at work would enhance the satisfaction from the next day's sailing. It is commonly believed that the opposite happens in real life: After a reprimand at work, the employee may "take it out" on the family at home. In such cases, the employee may be still at work psychologically, as when, after too much sailing, the salesman dwells on the fact that he is not selling. The game was programmed to put work and play in independent contexts so that the level of achievement at work has no effect on the amount of satisfaction derived from sailing—or vice versa.

It would be conceptually simpler to combine the events that occur in different domains into a single, all-inclusive context, ordered by preference. But this seems contrary to experience and also to empirical evidence for independence between people's overall assessments of different important domains of their lives.[3] There is also experimental evidence that people can partially control

---

[3]This research (Gutek et al., 1983) confirmed the usual finding that objective conditions do not correlate highly with self-avowals of happiness; however, it did find a high correlation between *changes* in objective conditions and the same self-avowals. For example, the quality of one's neighborhood did not correlate with how satisfied one reported being with it; however, a recent move to a better neighborhood was a good predictor of high satisfaction with the new neighborhood. This is a striking example of relational determination, too often neglected in surveys of happiness.

whether or not different psychophysical domains are independent.[4] The computer might be programmed to give the player some control over the independence of the contexts. For example, the player could have the hypothetical salesman compare sailing with going to work. But should the player be allowed to pick which selling experiences enter the salesman's immediate context for sailing, perhaps turning him into a Polyanna, deliberately recalling the worst aspects of his work in the hope that his sailing would thereby become more enjoyable? In that case, would such painful memories more than counterbalance the added pleasures?

Avoiding these more debatable possibilities, the game adds a second recreational domain which does share its context with sailing. On each trial, the salesman can be sent out to sell, to sail, or to *socialize*. If the choice is to socialize, the choice is then between different hypothetical levels of this domain—to have the salesman stay home alone in his apartment, have him get up early and bicycle with his buddies, see his regular girlfriend with whom he has a stormy relationship, ask out a new date, and so on. As with selling and sailing, pre-determined rules (again somewhat arbitrary) establish the probability of different outcomes for each choice in the social domain. But the outcomes for socializing go into the same context as the outcomes for sailing, as though the salesman compared his social activities with his sailing—lumping them all in one inclusive recreational context in which the different outcomes of each are ordered with respect to an intuitively assumed scale of preference.

Pleasures and pains are averaged across all three domains in computing the cumulative average payoff. This is consistent with the definition of happiness as the sum or average of all pleasures and pains. A happy day at work contributes neither more nor less to the cumulative average payoff in the game than does a happy day of recreation. However, hedonic experiences may be largely absent from a long day at work, yet they may occupy much more of a day devoted to an intense social relationship. Use of a day as the unit of time is thus a crude oversimplification. So, too, with the assumption that the whole day is lived in one domain, although one could both work and play on the same day. In thinking about happiness outside the game, pleasures and pains experienced during any particular day should be weighted for their separate durations, regardless of the different domains in which they are experienced.

Preference Scaling of the Outcomes

Although the essence of the relativistic determination of pleasure is most readily illustrated using different amounts of money as outcomes, most of life's experiences do not come with numbers attached to them. Even the preference values of

---

[4]In one large-scale study (Parducci et al., 1976), our subjects rated the sizes of circles and squares presented on alternative trials: When the subjects were told to establish independent scales for each shape, ratings of squares were not affected by the sizes of the circles; however, when told to ignore shape, ratings of squares did depend on the sizes of the circles.

the salesman's commissions would be inadequately represented by their dollar amounts; realistically, they must often include other meanings affecting their place in his context of earnings. A $100 commission would be higher on the scale of preference when it is a sign of future sales than when it is clearly the customer's last purchase. The same $100 is better when the salesman is short of funds. It is better on days when the commissions earned by colleagues are lower. And it can also be better when it sets the salesman to thinking about what that $100 might buy.

Because the game is only illustrative, it would be confusing to bring in too many of these qualitative factors affecting the preference values of the outcomes, their positions in the contextual range. Therefore, the game merely suggests what some of these factors might be, as in the following outcome:

> Your $200 commission seemed like $100 when the other salesman from your office reported his $300-day.

The computer then treats this outcome as though it were only $100 when computing the satisfaction it brings.

If, in the social domain, the player has chosen to have the salesman stay home alone, the following imaginary outcome might have a subjective value as high or higher than the real thing:

> Getting carried away just imagining a night alone with that cute waitress!

Or the relationships between elements of the situation might make what would ordinarily be a modest level of sailing equivalent to a much higher level:

> After waiting an hour for the wind, a light breeze finally filled in.

As with any other outcome, each of these was assigned a number to represent its value as an outcome—that is, its relative position on a scale of preference. The range-frequency values were then calculated in the context of the preference values of the 10 most recent outcomes, just as the $50 day in the example was compared with other days characterized by other earnings. The principle concern is to explore the relational character of the payoff rather than the determinants of its position on the salesman's scale of preference.

Each outcome in the game is treated as a stimulus, represented by its own specified numerical value on this scale of preference. Defining the stimulus is one of the most fundamental goals of scientific psychology, and only in the case of the simplest psychophysical stimuli do the physical determinants of the stimulus value seem clear. Indeed, the stimulus value is not itself directly available to consciousness, instead serving as an hypothetical abstraction useful for developing and testing psychological theories (cf. Anderson, 1981).

Just as stimuli are assigned numbers when scaled psychologically, possible outcomes are assigned numbers when programming the game. In principle, any outcome's position on a scale of preference can be represented numerically. But even when outcomes come in numerical form, like amounts of money, these numbers must be transformed to represent the psychological differences in preference. The psychological transformation of monetary value has often been assumed to be logarithmic, as posited by Bernoulli in the 18th century. This suggests that dollar outcomes in the game should be rescaled logarithmically. In offering the player a choice of different goals with respect to income, the choices were separated by equal ratios rather than equal differences—$25, $50, $100, $200. This geometric progression was violated for Level 1, which was set at $0 for convenience of presentation; and similarly, it was for simplicity of exposition that commissions in dollars (rather than their transformed stimulus values) were used in the examples of how the computer calculates the payoffs or degrees of satisfaction. People know that Bernoulli was close to the truth, that a $1 discount on a $10 item is in some sense psychologically equivalent to a $10 discount on a $100 item—a 10% discount in both cases; however, we often forget to take this kind of relativity into account when thinking about happiness. For example we may forget how distressing the loss of a dime can be for a streetperson whose total cash on hand may be less than a dollar.

For each domain in the game, the different levels of outcome represent a scaling by preference, assuming that the salesman himself would always choose a higher level in preference to a lower one. The characterization of these levels is strictly illustrative, not being based on any deep knowledge of what such a fellow would actually prefer. For example, it was assumed that he would prefer to be getting along well with his sometimes girlfriend, rather than quarreling with her, that he would rather go partying with her than bicycling with his buddies, and that staying home alone would be his least-preferred choice. Given world enough and time, this preference scale could be discovered empirically from the choices made by real young men when actually confronted with such alternatives.

The contexts produced by the player's successive choices each consist of the 10 most recent of these pre-scaled outcomes. Given their assumed preference-scale values, the computer uses range-frequency theory to derive the implications for happiness. Consider, as a concrete example, the consequences of choosing to have the salesman go windsurfing on the light-wind lake near where he lives. This is the lowest level of sailing. Presumably, he would have low expectations and would not make this choice himself unless there were at least some wind. And if there were no experiences of more exciting conditions in his context for sailing, even this light wind could be exhilarating. In the game, some variety was programmed into the outcomes for even this restricted choice: The wind can drop to nothing before he even gets out on the water, another boat can sail right past him so that he feels he is going too slowly, and so on. The subjective value of each of these outcomes (on the scale of supposed preferences) is used to calculate its position in the contextual range. If the player always sent the salesman to sail in the light-wind conditions close to home, he would learn that sailing conditions from the top half of the range of outcomes occur four times more frequently than those from the bottom half; and the cumulative average payoff would be as high as possible in this simple version of the game, though still only at the happier end of *neutral*.

If, instead, the player elects to send the salesman to a distant beach where wind and waves tend to be much more exciting, the range of sailing experiences would be broader. The player might think that tearing down the faces of giant waves, carving exciting bottom turns, and making the board jump over the crest on the way back out would guarantee true happiness in this domain. However, in deference to reality, outcomes programmed for this choice also include such horrors as broken masts and having to swim the board in when the wind suddenly drops. Because such lesser outcomes occur on 60% of the days, they bring down the cumulative average payoff for continued choice of the distant beach, so that it is actually lower than the average for the quiet lake near home.

This would surely seem counterintuitive to experienced windsurfers who would consider it self-evident that a 20-knot day at the ocean is preferable to a 10-knot day on a lake. And so it would be if both were experienced within the same context. What is crucial to the game is that the player is constructing the context. And if the player repeatedly chooses what the salesman would most prefer, the resulting context may be skewed less negatively than if a more modest goal had been chosen. Windsurfers might still object (as in last chapter's account of my own difficulties) that once the delights of ocean surf had been savored, it would be impossible to be content to sail a big board on a quiet lake: When the game assumes that representations of past experiences drop out after only 10 trials, it seems to be going against common sense. Other versions, to be considered shortly, keep such extreme experiences more permanently in the context.

The problem of scaling the outcomes for each of the three domains is much like the traditional problem of scaling psychophysical stimuli. Indeed, the outcomes are conceived as stimuli, mostly external events that can be scaled on the dimension of preference. Thus, within an hedonic context, the representation of each outcome reflects the degree to which it is preferred to other outcomes in the same context. This determines its range value. However, its pleasantness also depends on the proportion of all representation in the context to which it is preferred, the hedonic judgment reflecting the range-frequency compromise.

Imaginary Outcomes

Many of our most intense experiences seem purely imaginary, perhaps not even evoked by specific external events. Such private thoughts are treated in the game just like objective outcomes. In the example of the salesman thinking about not selling while he is out sailing, this outcome is scaled as though he had tried to sell but failed—as an external event at a low level of preference in the context for selling. But there might be whole domains in which everything is imaginary, relatively unaffected by external events. Private religious experiences might fall into such a domain. Consider the Carthusian monk, living in silent isolation, perhaps attempting to achieve a union with God. Sometimes he may experience a mystical closeness, an ecstatic sense of fulfillment; other times he may feel forsaken by God or contemptuous of his own religiosity; but most of his religious experiences would fall between the two extremes. Although none of these might seem tied directly to external events, there is no particular problem in ordering them with respect to the monk's preferences or to the satisfactions they evoke when in the same context. The monk might even have different goals in this respect, deciding one day to just say his prayers and do his work, another day to strive with all his concentration to become closer to God. Creating the respective distributions of outcomes for these different levels of aspiration or goal might seem even more arbitrary than for the domains actually programmed, and certainly more awkward to describe. However, such a domain could have been programmed for the game just like the dollar-based domain of selling, and the same principles of judgment would apply.

Many of us believe that it is in our own, purely imaginary worlds that we experience most of our pleasures and pains. Such experiences need not be religious in character. Plato's inner core of happiness might have been based on abstract thoughts about the nature of "the good," Donatello's on imagined beauty. Our private thoughts in domains of the imagination may have little to do with what we are actually accomplishing. We have some control of our imaginations but not complete control: When burdened by terrible thoughts we try to switch them to something better, that we prefer and will find reassuringly pleasant; but unpleasant thoughts often sneak back to overwhelm us, in spite of our most determined efforts to banish them. If we could achieve more complete control over such thoughts, we would be in a better position to improve the overall hedonic balance of our lives. There should be in the Happiness Game domains that the salesman lives entirely in his imagination, domains in which these imaginary experiences are also scaled with respect to his presumed preferences.

Size of Context

In the simplest version of the game, the context is restricted to just the last 10 outcomes. This restriction was suggested by experiments demonstrating that the context in psychophysical experiments could represent as few as the last 10 stimuli (Wedell, 1984).[5] However, the same experiments also suggested that the

---

[5]In Wedell's (1984) research on the effects of reversing the skewing of the distribution of stimuli, the rate of readjustment suggested that the context could represent between 10 and 20 stimulus presentations.

context could represent as many as the last 20 stimuli. Suppose that the game were modified to incorporate this larger context: would this increase the cumulative average payoff?

The answer is only slightly encouraging. Basing the range-frequency compromise on a larger context of the last 20 outcomes raises the cumulative average payoff for the best pattern from $+50$ to $+70$, from a high *Neutral* to the lower side of *Slightly Satisfying*. This increase in the game's measure of happiness seems due to the mathematical fact that with smaller samples infrequent outcomes are less likely to be represented at all (Parducci, 1992b). For the best pattern, the probability of any particular outcome being from the lower half of the contextual range is only .20, and the randomly sampled contexts for more than 10% of the trials do not include any outcomes from the lower half of the possible range of outcomes. This lowers the range values and resulting payoffs for these trials. The cumulative average payoff would of course be higher if the context always included the entire range of the distribution being sampled.

Although the cumulative average payoff for the best pattern of outcomes is increased by increasing the size of the context from the last 10 to the last 20 outcomes, stretching the context to include the last 30 items has little additional effect. This is because with samples as large as 20 the infrequent outcomes are already represented on all but 1% of the trials.[6] Thus, the size of the context is not a major factor when the distribution from which outcomes are sampled remains constant—when the player is not switching from one level of goal to another. The contexts established by outcomes in the game are more representative of the overall distribution of outcomes for a particular choice than the emphasis on only the most recent outcomes might suggest.[7]

Strategy for Play

The most successful strategy for any particular domain is to search among the possible goals for the one whose pursuit yields the most negatively skewed distribution of outcomes. For selling, this would be the distribution yielded by a goal of $50, with commissions evenly distributed over the bottom half of the range on 20% of the trials, over the top half on 80%. However, sticking with this

---

[6]Tests for 5-, 10-, 20-, and 30-outcome contexts found the probability of anything from the bottom half of the range of outcomes not being represented at all in the context for any particular trial was .33, .11, .01 and .002, respectively. However, increasing the number of contextual items beyond 10 has little effect on the cumulative average payoff for the much more realistic test distribution (described in chapter 9) in which there are relatively few outcomes at either extreme.

[7]On the other hand, the random sampling of outcomes utilized in the game precludes some of the correlation that might be expected between outcomes for the same choice on successive occasions in real life. This correlation would reduce the proportion of trials having the lowest possible outcome in the immediate context—a discouraging limitation on the possibilities for happiness.

happiest pattern of selling yields a cumulative average payoff of only $+50$ (corresponding to the high end of *indifferent*). Such a modest level of happiness may discourage optimistic players, encouraging them to pursue other strategies.

If players had complete control over the salesman's earnings, each successive commission could be higher than any earned before. But because each commission would, in its turn, already provide the highest satisfaction, this would not quite fit the famous formula that (according to Bartlett, 1982, p. 684) is inscribed in Coue's sanitarium at Nancy, "Every day, in every way, I am getting better and better." Moreover, a constant succession of highs is no more possible in the game than in life, there being only a limited set of choices or goals, and even these not often attained. Another optimal but unrealistic strategy would be to have the salesman earn no commission at all on exactly every 10th trial. If this were possible, $0 would always be in the context; and the cumulative average payoff for sticking with the $50 goal for all other trials would rise from $+50$ to almost $+90$ (from *Indifferent* to *Slightly Satisfying*). Even this modest level of happiness would depend on never allowing the $0 to drop from the context. In real life, deliberate $0 days would be unlikely to enter the context for selling, being represented instead in some other domain, such as planning for future, where they would not affect the happiness gained from selling.

Why does the game seem limited to such a low level of happiness? Perhaps the arbitrary stipulation of the distribution of outcomes for each choice of goal is too pessimistic, the negative skewing of these distributions being less extreme than that afforded the happiest lives in the real world. However, in the optimal patterns that yield the best of the game's returns, outcomes from the top half of the range are four times more likely than outcomes from the bottom half of the range. Contexts may be this skewed for basic biological domains, such as eating, drinking, sex, and the creature comforts; but although crucial for survival and happiness, biological domains hardly encompass the totality of our hedonic experiences. For the other domains occupying many of our waking moments, including those of work and recreation exemplified by the game, the most reasonable distributions of outcomes might not even be skewed as negatively as this 20–80 distribution. Consequently, their cumulative average payoffs would be proportionally lower, with sometimes an unhappy surplus of pain over pleasure.

Difficulty of Play

Most players make choices that condemn the hypothetical salesman to a negative cumulative average payoff, that is, to unhappiness. Whereas players improve with practice in most games, they tend to get worse in the Happiness Game. At first, all seems to go swimmingly well, with very high payoffs. Then things begin to fall apart, the cumulative average sinking progressively deeper into the negative. This downturn seems sufficiently striking to examine its possible lessons for the difficulty of mastering the grander happiness game of life.

Typically, the player begins cautiously, setting a goal of $50 which, as explained in the instructions, is just slightly more than what this inexperienced salesman averaged before the altruistic player took charge of his goals. If the player kept him at this modest level of aspiration, the outcomes would continue to average only slightly below $50, with a cumulative average payoff only a slightly positive +50.

Although setting the goal at $50 is actually the best choice for this domain, players try to attain a higher cumulative average payoff. After a few trials, they raise the salesman's goal to $100 or even to $200. This is rewarded by higher commissions and, what is more important in the game if not in life, by immediate pleasure (i.e., by higher payoffs). In the earlier example where the player firsts shifts the goal up to $100, earning $70 proves *very, very satisfying*. Getting this big payoff encourages the player to go for more, to set higher goals. But higher goals are less likely to be achieved: On most high-goal trials, the commissions fall well below the goal. As in the same example, it is not very satisfying to earn only $50 after having so recently earned $70. The upward extension of the range, abetted by the eventual dropping from the context of the lower endpoint of the previous distribution of outcomes, lowers the payoffs for most of the outcomes that the higher goal produces.

The occasional elation derived from a $100 commission may keep the player aiming high, in spite of this drop in cumulative average payoff. The drop reflects the shift to the more positive skewing of outcomes programmed for the goal of $100. Even when bitter experience should teach that going for higher commissions lowers the cumulative average payoff, players rarely return permanently to the modest goal that would yield the most happiness in the long run.

Consider what happens when the player does give up on higher commissions, dropping down to the previous goal of $50. At the time of this downward shift, the context is likely to include some large commissions resulting from the player's more recent choice of a higher goal. For example, if the player had regularly chosen $100 as a goal,[8] a typical sequence of the 10 most recent earnings might be:

$90 $200 $50 $180 $50 $45 $55 $220 $110 $100.

The $50 or $60, the best the salesman can earn when his goal is only $50, will be disappointing as long as the much higher values remain in the context. It will take 8 trials for the representation of $220 to drop out, 10 trials before $50 can be close to the top of the range. Few players subject their hypothetical salesman to such a long succession of disappointments. If a player did wait out the losing streak, the average of the payoffs would eventually turn positive. However, any

---

[8]Remember that the scale of preference on which range values are computed equates the difference between $50 and $100 to the difference between $100 and $200 (equal differences in preference corresponding to equal physical ratios).

resurgence of ambition would extend the context upwards, ensuring that the salesman will again become dissatisfied with most of his earnings.

A more elaborate version of the game (presented at the beginning of the next chapter) allows the two extreme values of any context to remain beyond the customary 10 trials. This greater retention of past endpoints increases the difficulty of the game for the player. Grasping the long-term effects of shifting from one goal to another is hard enough when it takes just 10 trials before an endpoint can drop out, almost impossible when that endpoint is still operating after hundreds of trials in which the outcome it represents has not occurred. In life, we often make conscious comparisons with events from the distant past. Thus, we might say of a particularly good wine that although great, it is still not as good as our very first glass of Pouilly-Fuissé. The question is whether we can experience delight with what we now have—even though we know we once had something better. Although we can still clearly remember a great experience from the distant past, it may no longer be part of the context determining current hedonic experiences.[9]

To summarize these difficulties of winning in the game, what seems most important is that the player gets immediate reward for shifting to a higher goal and immediate punishment for shifting to a lower goal. The pain of the higher goal comes only later, as does the pleasure of the lower goal. All of this works against the strategy that would maximize overall satisfaction. Insofar as this feature of the game mimics what often happens in everyday life, we seem trapped by the contingencies of reinforcement and punishment. Whenever we experience some new success, whether it is getting a promotion, winning the mate of our dreams, or overcoming some previously intimidating obstacle, it is likely to establish a new upper endpoint for that particular context. This upward extension reduces the satisfaction from our more common, everyday experiences. We cannot see this because the new success is so immediately gratifying, the subsequent dissatisfactions so delayed.

This may be easiest to recognize in our marketplace experiences. When we buy a new car, the resulting satisfaction is immediate and its source is obvious. The inevitable dissatisfactions as the car ages, the loss of novelty and approving attention, the added burden of the monthly payments when income drops, the need for costly repairs, invidious comparisons with newer models—these dissatisfactions tend to come later. It is thus difficult to accurately assess the overall effects upon happiness of the initial purchase.

There is another feature of the game that works against its mastery, a feature intrinsic to our everyday experiences. This is the correlation between payoff and outcome *within any given context*. For any given trial or within any given pair of

---

[9]Alternatively, there may be a separate context restricted to just the best wines one has experienced, wines that would not otherwise be represented in the context determining our pleasure from more ordinary wines.

contextual endpoints, the payoff is always higher for a more preferred outcome: The salesman is more pleased when his commission is bigger, when the wind is stronger, and when he is getting along better with his girlfriend. Because this is the normal relationship between pleasure and outcome in everyday life, players come to the game expecting to find it. And they do! They find it even when the context changes, as when the outcome that was high in the previous context is low in the new context. Players can see that although the payoff for this outcome has dropped, the higher among the outcomes in the new context now yield the higher of the new payoffs. This obscures the cause of the overall drop in payoff that occurs when the highest of the outcomes in the new context is coming less frequently. The often false inference that the choice yielding higher average income must also yield higher average pleasure is thus derived from the close relationship between income and satisfaction within any particular context.

When first developing the game, I hoped that it might prove useful for teaching students how to apply range-frequency principles. But in spite of the game's gross oversimplification of life, college students do not learn the best strategies by playing the game. The most successful players, those who attain the highest cumulative average payoffs, are professional colleagues who already have some grasp of the contextual theory of happiness underlying the game. My conclusion is that if life were really like the game, we could never master the principles of happiness from uncontrolled observations of life. Basic understanding is more likely to be advanced through controlled experiments.

Empirical Tests

When I have described the game at scholarly meetings of psychophysicists, usually someone in the audience has suggested that I use it to test the contextual theory of happiness experimentally. My reaction to such suggestions has been predictably skeptical. The attraction of psychophysics is its simplicity and consequent possibilities for experimental control of the context for judgment. However, in the game it is the players who, by their trial-by-trial choices of goals, determine outcomes and thus the context. The experimenter would have little control of the context. Furthermore, the efforts to characterize the outcomes as complex events of selling, sailing or socializing, might be expected to evoke extra-experimental contexts from the player's own life that would hopelessly confound the results. As in any research that is poorly controlled, the door would be opened to a plethora of alternative interpretations.

One unusually sophisticated psychologist, Echtibar Dzhafarov, was more specific in his recommendation: Insofar as the underlying assumptions are correct, players of the game should be able to predict the amount of pleasure that would be elicited by each of the successive outcomes; their own judgments should thus correspond to the game's payoffs. In spite of my fear of complexity, I made a modest attempt to follow Dzhafarov's suggestion, using myself and several undergraduate volunteers as experimental subjects. To simplify the analysis of the results, play was restricted to the selling domain. Instead of being given the payoff (from -500 to $+500$), the subject was asked on each trial to use a 9-point scale to rate how satisfied the "salesman" would have been with his earnings for that day. Thus, each trial began with the subject choosing one of five levels of goal, then seeing a computer display of the consequent outcome in dollars earned, and finally typing in his or her own hedonic rating of that outcome. The game's computer-generated estimates of pleasures (the usual payoffs) were never displayed. The instructions also required staying with each choice of goal for at least 30 trials before switching to another goal. At the end of 1 hour of these ratings, the subject was allowed to move freely through the five levels of goal, without having to stay with any particular level.

To ensure a more powerful test of contextual effects, commissions between $30 and $39 were programmed to come frequently for each level of choice. However, these test outcomes would be near the top of the range of outcomes ($10 to $39) when the choice was Level 1, near the bottom of the range of outcomes ($30 to $59) when the choice was Level 5. The payoffs for the $30 to $39 test outcomes were thus very positive after continued play on Level 1, very negative after continued play on Level 5.

For all subjects, and no more for myself than for the undergraduates who knew nothing of the underlying theory, the test outcomes ($30 to $39) were rated very much higher for Level 1 than for Level 5. Indeed, there was no overlap between these ratings, always *satisfying* or higher for Level 1, overwhelmingly negative (e.g., *dissatisfying*) for Level 5.[10]

Although these results seem to confirm the particular application of the contextual theory embodied in this simple version of the game, there must be much more to the influence of goals than their effects on the distribution of outcomes. The everyday observation that it is disappointing to fall short of one's goals suggests that the goal may itself be part of the context determining one's pleasure. This notion is explored in the next chapter, describing more realistic versions of the game.

Lessons

Perhaps the most striking lesson to be drawn from the computerized happiness game is its difficulty for players. Given the game's egregious oversimplifications, the extreme difficulty of mastery suggests the impossibility of understand-

---

[10] The influence of the goal in this test may have gone considerably beyond its effect upon the distribution of earnings. Even at the end of the experimental session when subjects roamed freely between levels of choice, judgments of the common outcomes varied inversely with the level of goal. This suggests an alternative interpretation. Suppose that the subject thought of the goal as determining the number of hours worked on that day. In this case, $39 in commissions would be interpreted as a higher hourly rate after a choice of a low goal than after choice of a higher, more ambitious goal. If so, the simple-minded notion that more is better would suffice to explain the inverse relationship between judgments and goals.

ing happiness by simply observing the ups and downs of everyday life. Insofar as the game models underlying principles of happiness, we could never learn these principles from uncontrolled observations of life in all its complexity. Analysis of the rewards and punishments the player receives in the game suggests that similar processes in everyday life must often lead us into the wrong choices for happiness. Within any context, it is always more pleasant to get more of what we prefer, and this encourages reaching for more—even when the reaching can turn happiness into unhappiness by extending the context upward. Furthermore, it is difficult to return to less preferred conditions—even when the return would eventually bring increased happiness.

Recognition of the game's oversimplification of the contexts for everyday hedonic experiences encourages exploration of more lifelike assumptions about these hedonic contexts. For example, a minor change in the game permits exploration of the consequences of endpoints enduring longer than intermediate representations in the context. An alternative possibility pins the durability of any contextual representation upon how satisfying it was when actually experienced. The role of the goal is still another candidate for further exploration. In this simplest version of the game, the goal determined what outcomes would be experienced but was not itself represented as part of the context. If it were, the pleasantness of outcomes surpassing this chosen level of aspiration would be enhanced. However, higher goals might be experienced as satisfying in themselves. This kind of speculation is encouraged by a disappointing consequence of the simplest form of the Happiness Game: Regardless of what strategy the player adopts, the resulting happiness never sums up to much more than the high end of neutral, neither satisfying nor dissatisfying. Surely life offers possibilities for something better than this only slightly positive balance.

The next chapter describes richer versions of the game. Elaborated rules for what gets into the context are systematically explored to determine their implications for happiness. Particular attention is given to factors, such as imaginary experiences, that could increase the overall level of happiness.

SUMMARY

The computerized Happiness Game illustrates how the contextual theory of happiness works out in concrete situations. Players construct their own hedonic contexts by selecting goals for the outcomes they will experience. The pleasantness of each experience is determined by its place in a context of recent experiences in the same domain, such as different degrees of success at work or in recreational activities. The object of play is to maximize pleasure rather than income or social success. Players have surprising difficulty mastering the game, apparently because they are mislead by the immediate pleasures of earning more money or experiencing preferred recreational activities, without appreciating how this extends the context upward. Even when the context is simply the 10 most recent experiences, its effects upon pleasure are too difficult for most players to grasp. If life were really like this game, we could never discover the secrets of happiness by observing life in all its complexity. A disturbing implication of this simple "last 10" version of the game is that its limited possibilities for happiness seem perilously close to the even balance that the theory rejects.

9 Optimistic Versions of the Happiness Game

With its discouraging limit on the possibilities for happiness, the simplest version of the game may seem an exercise in pessimism. Even if the player employs the best of strategies, the cumulative-average payoff can reach only +50 on the scale from −500 to +500. This might seem to imply a degree of balance between pleasure and pain almost as disappointing as the even balance implied by the theory adaptation level. It would be ironic if the upper limit to happiness suggested by this application of range-frequency principles were really so close to that of the theory they were designed to replace.

My students groan when they hear they cannot average much above +50 in this simplest version of the game: Can life really be so limited? Some of them might be comparing it with the constant high they imagine to be somehow attainable. However, I find the possibility of averaging +50 at least promising, perhaps because I was imprinted so early on the notion of an equal balance. Whether an overall balance of +50 seems happy or not depends, like all dimensional judgments, on the context in which it is evaluated. In a context that includes the entire range of pleasures and pains, from −500 to +500, +50 might well seem *neutral*. But in a context of more realistic possibilities, restricted to averages between −100 and +100, a cumulative average of +50 could indeed be happy. Is it possible that the rosy self-avowals of happiness, obtained so regularly in polls on the quality of life, are made in such a restricted context?

This cumulative average of +50 is not an absolute upper limit for the contextual theory of happiness, only the limit for the particular contextual assumptions embodied in the simplest version of the game. The best of the game's frequency distributions of outcomes could have been skewed much more negatively, which would have yielded a proportionately higher average. For example, if all but one of the outcomes were at the top of the range and that one stayed in the context in spite of occurring only rarely, the theoretical average would approach $+250$.[1] However, with the context restricted to the last 10 outcomes, any outcome below the top of the range would drop from the context whenever it had not occurred since the 10th trial back—reducing the skewing and hence the cumulative average payoff. Even if this lowest outcome occurred on every 10th trial, the average would drop to $+140$.

Experimental research suggested that the contexts for simple psychophysical judgments are restricted to the most recent presentations. The simplest version of the game then tells us that when the contexts for everyday pleasures and pains are also restricted to the most recent experiences, the overall balance of happiness cannot be very positive. However, it seems unlikely that contexts are so restricted for real-life judgments. Range-frequency principles do not in themselves identify the context, only what the judgments must be for any particular context.

The contextual theory of happiness assumes that the contexts for everyday pleasures and pains include goals and fantasies, memories and anticipations, and even counterfactuals that can weigh more heavily on the balance of happiness than do those objective physical events to which we respond hedonically. These imaginary events may occur with greater relative frequency and remain in their contexts much longer than do simple psychophysical stimuli. Also, the contexts most important for happiness may represent a biased sampling of such experiences. The present chapter explores how these possibilities could raise the upper limit imposed by the simplest version of the game.

Method of Exploration

The overall balance of happiness was derived by computer simulation for various elaborated versions of the game based on different assumptions about what gets into the context determining the payoffs. The range-frequency principles built into the simplest version of the game were applied to the new contexts generated by each of these new versions. However, the exposition shifts from the viewpoint of a player of the game to that of a researcher studying the implications of these different contextual assumptions, as revealed by the game's computer simulations.

Overview of Tests.   The implications of each new version of the Happiness Game are investigated by assessing what it does to the cumulative-average pay-

---

[1]If almost all outcomes were at the top of the contextual range, the mean of all range values would approach 1.0; but because frequency values must average to .5, the range-frequency compromise must be close to .75 and the cumulative average payoff close to three fourths of the way up from -500 to $+500$—close to $+250$. This would be brought down by any additional experience of a lower outcome.

off, the game's measure of happiness. These tests are restricted to those contextual possibilities that seem most optimistic without being completely unrealistic. Often, the tests yield a happier balance of pleasure over pain.

The testing of each new possibility employs only two different distributions of expected outcomes. The first is the 20–80 distribution described already as the happiest of the different distributions used in the simplest version of the game. The second is a more continuous distribution, selected to be more representative of frequency distributions found in nature. In separate tests, the computer was programmed to randomly sample 1,000 successive outcomes from each of these two distributions, calculating the 1,000 successive payoffs and the cumulative average payoff for each.[2] It is as though a player chose Level 3 of selling (viz., a goal of $50) for 1,000 consecutive trials in the simplest version of the game. However, the objective here is to discover the implications of each new hypothesis about what gets included in the context for judgment. Because these implications are often not intuitively self-evident, the algebraic discipline of the computerized simulation ensures that one has drawn the correct implications for happiness as measured by the cumulative average of the payoffs. And because each new contextual hypothesis must be programmed for the computer, it must be phrased more precisely than is our everyday discourse about the relativity of judgment and happiness.

The Distribution of Outcomes.   As described in chapter 8, the simplest version of the Happiness Game utilized 15 different frequency distributions of outcomes, one for each of five levels of goal for each of three domains. For the most negatively skewed of these distributions (the one yielding a cumulative average payoff of +50), each outcome was selected from the bottom half of the range of outcomes on a random 20% of the trials, from the top half on the remaining 80%. Thus an outcome from the bottom 10th of the possible range of the 20–80 distribution is to be expected for only 4% of the trials, from the top 10th for 16%. as shown in Table 9.1.[3]

The dramatic shift in frequencies at the midpoint of this 20–80 distribution seems unrepresentative of everyday distributions of events. The distributions of values that we can most easily measure (like daily temperatures, people's heights, or incomes) are much smoother, with no abrupt shifts in frequency, and with lower frequencies near the endpoints. Therefore, a smoother test distribution was selected as more representative of the continuous distributions typically found in nature, with lower relative frequencies of outcomes near each endpoint. Selection of a particular outcome was random within each successive 10th of the range; but these different 10ths were sampled with varying probabilities, corre-

[2]A more detailed description of how these tests were performed and also of their results may be found in Parducci (1992b).

[3]The numerical values of the outcomes represent their positions on a preference scale.

TABLE 9.1
Percent of Outcomes (OC) in Each 10th of the Range

OC:	0-9	10-19	20-29	30-39	40-49	50-59	60-69	70-79	80-89	90-99
20-80:	4	4	4	4	4	16	16	16	16	16
Test:	1	1	7	7	10	15	22	25	10	2

sponding to the percentages shown in Table 9.1 for this test distribution: Bottom and top 10ths of the range are both much less frequent (only 1% and 2%, respectively), and the degree of negative skewing is reduced by almost one-third from that of the 20–80 distribution. As implied by range-frequency principles, the cumulative average payoff is also almost one-third lower—+35 in place of +50. Separate 1,000-trial simulations were run for each of these two distributions of outcomes to assess the effects of different hypotheses about how outcomes are represented in the context. The conclusions from these tests are similar enough for the two distributions that, unless otherwise noted, results are reported only for the test distribution.

Retention of Endpoints

Several different lines of psychophysical research suggest that endpoints are retained longer in the context than are intermediate values. First, psychophysical ratings do not shift as a function of the number of trials since the last presentation of an endpoint, for example, 10 versus 20 versus 30 trials (Wedell, 1984). Second, after a sudden restriction of the range of the distribution from which the psychophysical stimuli are sampled, hundreds of presentations may be necessary before judgments readjust to the restricted range (Parducci, 1956). Wedell's transfer research kept endpoints constant so that its evidence for a context composed of just the 10 to 20 most recent stimuli was concerned only with frequency effects, not with the possible persistence of contextual endpoints.[4] Our everyday judgments sometimes continue to be affected by an extreme experience long after intermediate experiences, occurring more recently, have ceased to have any effect. Therefore, it is possible that the extreme outcomes are more enduring in their effects than are the intermediate outcomes.

As a concrete test of the implications of this possibility for happiness, the computer was programmed to save any new endpoint of the context for 30 trials, unless it were replaced sooner by a more extreme endpoint. This increased the

---

[4]Wedell's (1984) research compared the effects of different numbers of trials with a skewed distribution upon the rate of postshift adjustment to another distribution skewed in the opposite direction.

TABLE 9.2
Percent Use of Categories

Categories:	1	2	3	4	5	6	7	8	9
Context:									
Last 10	14	7	8	9	11	12	10	13	15
Last 20	9	6	9	12	14	13	12	12	13
Last 10 + 30-Trial endpoints	6	7	1	11	13	14	17	13	8
Last 10 + 0 and 99	1	7	11	13	15	17	17	13	5

size of the context on which the range-frequency determination of payoffs was based to 12 (last 10 trials plus 2 endpoints). With this greater retention of endpoints, the cumulative average payoff for the test distribution increases from +35 to +50—by 43%.[5] This is almost as high as the +51 obtained when range values were determined by the two most extreme of the possible endpoints, 0 and 99, even though these may never have been sampled.

Besides raising the cumulative average payoff, retention of the endpoints would reduce the overabundance of extreme payoffs, positive or negative, that can be a surprising feature of the simplest, last-10 version of the Happiness Game. Using the test distribution of outcomes, restricting the context to the last 10 simulates a life lived at the extremes of pleasure and pain, with 29% of all hedonic experience corresponding to one or the other of the extreme categories, either *very, very dissatisfying* or *very, very satisfying*.[6] Retention of the endpoints for 30 trials reduces this overuse of the two extreme categories to a total of 14%; adding 0 and 99 (the most extreme of the possible outcomes) to the context for every trial produces a further reduction to 6%, as detailed in Table 9.2.

Whether or not this reduction in the percent of intense pleasures and pains seems a good thing might depend on one's view of life. If life seems a vale of tears, one can be consoled that there would have been even more misery without these enduring endpoints. However, if life seems dominated by pleasures, it would be discouraging to think of how much more pleasure one could be having without these constant dampeners.

There may be no simple answer to the question of how long extreme experiences from the past can continue to influence one's present hedonic experiences: We may always be affected by some great loss, as of a loved one, yet adapt completely to a different climate or to a different level of salt intake after only a few weeks or months. Certainly, we sometimes remember, with great clarity, traumatic events from the distant past. The question is whether, apart from the pain suffered while recalling them, they continue to affect our current pleasures.

[5]The corresponding increase for the 20–80 distribution is from +50 to +70, that is, by 40%.
[6]This is even higher for the 20–80 distribution for which about one third of all of the payoffs are either in the top one ninth or bottom one ninth of the range of payoffs.

Goals and Other Imaginary Experiences

Why do some of us persist in bringing home briefcases filled with more work than we ever actually accomplish? One answer is that the bulging briefcase is an expression of ambition, motivating us to greater accomplishment than we could achieve with goals that are more modestly realistic. This possibility was built directly into the simplest version of the Happiness Game as a positive correlation between goals and outcomes, with the player's selection of a goal for each trial determining the probability distribution of outcomes. For example, higher goals resulted in higher income, if not greater happiness.

Another explanation of the bulging briefcase, only partially incorporated into the simplest version of the game, is that it is intrinsically satisfying to imagine all the work we are going to accomplish. Anticipatory pleasure may be a major hedonic consequence of ambition. It was represented by some of the game's outcomes, as in the following example:

> Just imagining that you could clear $100 today was as enjoyable as actually making that much.

The computer treated this outcome as if the day's commissions were actually $100, even though the salesman may have earned much less. Consequently, the imaginary $100 takes the place of real earnings in the distribution of outcomes, a distribution that may seem reasonable for his actual commissions but not sufficiently concentrated toward the top of the range to reflect his anticipations of success. Many of us believe ourselves happy even in domains where our achievements fall far short of our goals.

To explore the implications of these imagined successes, an elaborated version of the game made them the actual outcomes for a random one half of the trials. There is, of course, no evidence that exactly half of all hedonic experiences are imaginary anticipations of success. For people who emphasize their private experiences, one half might seem a gross underrepresentation; others might think they experience little of such escapism. Taken as simply illustrative, programming the proportion at an arbitrary one half provides a reference point for assessing the direction and possible magnitudes of the effects upon happiness of recurring anticipatory experiences that are high in an hedonic context.

Representation of high anticipations was accomplished by adding a second distribution of outcomes, varying randomly from 70 to 99, sampled as the actual outcome for a random one half of all trials. Thus, the combined distribution of outcomes, one half being the test distribution of real-world outcomes, the other being the 70–99 distribution of high anticipations, tended to be much more packed in the top one-third of the range (with 0 and 99 as additional fixed endpoints for computing the range values), as shown in Table 9.3.

TABLE 9.3
Distribution of Outcomes (OC):
Real (R) or Real Plus Imaginary (R + I)

OC:	0-9	10-19	20-29	30-39	40-49	50-59	60-69	70-79	80-89	90-99
R%	1	1	7	7	10	15	22	25	10	2
(R + I)%	.5	.5	3.5	3.5	5	7.5	11	28.5	22	18

The resulting cumulative average payoff is a very much higher +119 (*slightly satisfying*), more than double the +51 obtained without these imaginary experiences.

Table 9.4 presents the relative frequencies with which different rating categories would occur to produce this +119 average.

Almost one half of the payoffs correspond to either 7—*satisfying*, 8—*very satisfying*, or 9—*very, very satisfying*! With the exception of the biological domains, eating, drinking, sex, and the creature comforts, can there be a non-imaginary domain where the majority of experiences would be rated so highly?

If it seems unrealistic to assume that one half of all our hedonic experiences are pleasurable daydreams of success, consider that many of our fantasies might be memories of, or slight embroideries upon, real past successes—and thus not purely imaginary in origin. Reading and television may also take us into fantasy worlds that can be pleasing even when portraying the misfortunes of others ("How much luckier I am than that poor chap!"). Sometimes the distinction between imaginary and real experiences may be blurred, as with fantasizing during sexual experiences. Imaginary experiences may often be realistic anticipations of events that in fact occur (almost three eighths of the real outcomes in the test distribution fell between 70 and 99). The 50% represents one half of just the hedonic experiences: If less than 2% of all experiences were hedonic, these pleasing anticipations would then be fewer than 1% of all experiences.

The representation of goals as imaginary experiences does not seem such a big step away from some of the stimuli actually studied in laboratory research. Telling the experimental subject to imagine a greatly preferred stimulus lowers

TABLE 9.4
Percent Use of Categories

Categories:	1	2	3	4	5	6	7	8	9
R + I (endpoints 0, 99)	2	5	8	11	14	15	15	15	16

TABLE 9.5
Distribution of Outcomes (OC):
Real (R) or Real and Imaginary (R + I)

OC:	0-9	10-19	20-29	30-39	40-49	50-59	60-69	70-79	80-89	90-99
R%	1	1	7	7	10	15	22	25	10	2
(R + I)%	17.5	17.5	19.5	3.5	5	7.5	11	12.5	5	1

the ratings of those stimuli actually presented.[7] Such experiments seemed to argue for setting lower goals. However, when goals were treated as outcomes actually experienced in the imagination, computer simulation demonstrated just the reverse—although payoffs for any given outcome were lowered by higher goals, the cumulative average payoff was raised! This is another example of how deceptive our intuitions and even our retrospective accounting of such experiences can be; *we are painfully aware of falling short of our goals, but we do not ordinarily appreciate that such disappointments can be outweighed by the pleasant anticipations of success.*

In everyday life, not all anticipations would be high relative to the distribution of real outcomes. Frequent anticipations of failure, insofar as they are low in the context, must lower the balance of happiness. This is because such anticipations reduce the negative skewing or change it to positive skewing. Consider Table 9.5, in which one half of the outcomes are imaginary, randomly distributed between 0 and 29.

Although the slight positive skewing of the combined distribution, R + I, would raise the payoffs for real outcomes, the prevalence of so many imaginary experiences near the bottom of the range produces a negative cumulative average payoff, −68 (with almost one half of the payoffs corresponding to the three lowest categories).

In general, representing the goal as a frequent imaginary experience implies that (other things like the distribution of real outcomes being equal) higher goals lead to greater happiness. This seems to contradict the obvious implication of judgmental relativism that if one expects less, one is more satisfied with what one gets. The contradiction is only apparent. Lower goals do increase the satisfaction with actual achievement (i.e., payoffs on trials with real outcomes); but if the depressing anticipations of failure or of regretting that one is so lacking in ambition are averaged in, the balance of happiness becomes more negative. This is an implication that is easily missed in attempts to apply range-frequency principles. When the context is representative of all events that are experienced,

---

[7]See McGarvey (1943), Dermer et al. (1979), and other anchoring research of this type, particularly in the literature of experimental social psychology.

real or imagined, its skewing is the crucial factor determining the overall average of the judgments.

Treatment of the goal as an imaginary outcome need not divest it of its role in determining the skewing of real outcomes. Insofar as the salesman almost always comes close to the level of commissions he aspires to when his goals are low, the distribution of his actual commissions is likely to be more negatively skewed than if his goals were higher. At least, this was the assumption when programming different distributions of outcomes for the simplest version of the game. Unfortunately, insofar as higher goals increase the positive skewing of the real outcomes, the negative skewing of the combined distribution produced by inclusion of imaginary successes would be reduced. This would tend to equalize the overall balance between satisfaction and dissatisfaction. Thus, the +119 average obtained by adding the high anticipations to the standard test distribution may be unrealistically high.

Is the 70–99 distribution a reasonable representation of our anticipations of success? Insofar as we learn from experience, we come to expect what is in effect the average of our actual experiences. Adding frequencies (in this case, expectations or imagined outcomes) at the mean of the distribution has no effect upon its skewing. By analogy to a teeter-totter on which the distribution of outcomes is represented as a set of weights balanced on a weightless plank, any disproportionate amount of weight at one end of the plank can be balanced by locating the fulcrum closer to that end. The position of the fulcrum when the plank is evenly balanced represents the mean position of the weights. Additional weight placed at the fulcrum does not upset the balance. So it is with imagined outcomes: To the degree that they correspond to the mean (expected range value) of the real outcomes, the overall balance of happiness is not affected.[8] To tip the balance further toward happiness, anticipations of success must be unrealistically high!

The skeptic might object that unrealistic expectations constitute a prescription for unhappiness, warning of the debilitating consequences that must result from substituting imaginary success for the real thing, such as accomplishing less in the real world. However, accomplishing less does not necessarily mean unhappiness—which would come only if the combined distribution of unrealistically high anticipations and the more lowly accomplishments were positively skewed. The contextual theory of happiness encourages a different skepticism. The usual assumption of utility theorists is that more is better, that people must be happier with more because they so regularly chose more in preference to less. The game illustrates how the reverse may sometimes be true.

---

[8]When the context is an unbiased representation of the distribution of outcomes and the fulcrum is located at the midpoint of this distribution, the mean of all judgments is proportional to the tipping moment of the weighted plank (i.e., to its tendency to tip).

Daydreams Rather Than Goals

Daydreams are often unrelated to real goals or ambitions. Insofar as this imaginary life functions like the fairy story, forming a separate domain that does not enter the context of real-world experiences, one might expect the pleasures of daydreaming to be dependent upon a context composed only of daydreams. Free from the constraints of reality, it might be possible to control one's daydreams so that the best among them come relatively often. Alternatively, the distributions for an imaginary hedonic domain might tend naturally to be negatively skewed. These private worlds of the imagination might thus be happy in themselves, with little effect on anything else. Their contribution to overall happiness would then depend on their frequency or duration as compared with hedonic experiences of the real world.

How happy might such an imaginary domain be, in itself? As already reported, the combination of 50% high anticipations and 50% test outcomes yielded a cumulative average payoff of +119. Perhaps with greater control of the imagination, a context representing purely imaginary experiences might be skewed much more negatively. Consider the J-shaped distribution of Table 9.6, perhaps possible for a domain lived entirely in the imagination.

In the 1,000-trial test simulation for this distribution, the cumulative average payoff was +193 *(satisfying)* when the contextual endpoints were fixed at 0 and 99, +107 *(slightly satisfying)* when the context was restricted to simply the last 10 outcomes. It is important to note that even a domain consisting entirely of imaginary experiences cannot be all highs; as with any distribution of stimuli, such a domain elicits the whole sweep of hedonic experiences from agony to ecstasy, their cumulative average depending on the skewing of the distribution of imaginary experiences.

Imagining the Worst

Another way in which imaginary experiences can increase the negative skewing of a context is by establishing a lower endpoint that is much more extreme than any so far considered. In life, this might come from imagining something much worse than anything one has ever actually experienced. For example, a mother

TABLE 9.6
J-Shaped Distribution of Imaginary Events

OC:	0-9	10-19	20-29	30-39	40-49	50-59	60-69	70-79	80-89	90-99
%:	1	1	1	1	1	1	1	3	20	70

might imagine the death of her child, this desperate fear being evoked by a lifethreatening illness or by the actual death of someone else's child. The imagined loss would be so much worse than anything the mother has actually experienced that the downward extension could double the contextual range. To test the implications of this possibility, permanent endpoints were fixed at -99 and $+99$, otherwise using the usual test distribution (0 to $+99$). This produced a cumulative average payoff of $+150$, approximately three times greater than if the endpoints had been fixed at 0 and 99. The cumulative average is even higher when only the lower endpoint is permanent. For example, with the lower endpoint fixed at -99 and the upper endpoint set to the highest of the last 30 outcomes so that it rarely reached $+99$, the cumulative average payoff was $+170$, with only 14% of payoffs on the negative side and none in either of the bottom two categories of the 9-point scale.

This impressive gain in happiness could only be achieved if the lower endpoint occurred very infrequently. For example, the mother might experience such a moment of fleeting terror only once or twice while her child was growing up. However, if she morbidly dwelled on the awful possibility of losing her child, the number of truly dreadful experiences would pull down her sum total of happiness. Unlike anticipatory experiences of future success, frequent anticipations of the worst can have only negative effects on happiness.

Systematic Dropping of Pleasant Outcomes

How much control do we have over our hedonic contexts in everyday life? We can sometimes banish bad thoughts by admonishing ourselves: "Don't think about that now!" But often, in spite of our efforts, the same dreadful scenarios keep replaying in our imagination. Even when we do succeed in shaking off discouraging thoughts, fears, or memories, they may still remain in the contexts determining our pleasures and pains, just like some real-world events that we can no longer remember. Any increased retention of the contextual representations of bad experiences would increase the pleasantness of events experienced in hedonic contexts and hence the overall level of happiness.

Perhaps the Happiness Game would be closer to life if the player were allowed additional control of the context of outcomes. In the simplest version of the game, any such control rests only in choosing different domains of activity (selling, sailing, or social) and levels of goal (1 to 5); and even this control is limited by the need to earn money, as when the computer reports that the salesman cannot help thinking about the money he is not making, with the implication that he was not working enough. Otherwise, choice of a particular domain and level determines the probability distribution of outcomes and, as a consequence, the contexts that determine the payoffs.

Suppose the salesman could drop the more satisfying of his recent earnings from the context: "I know that yesterday I cleared more than $200 in commissions, but I am not going to let that affect how I feel about earning only $100 today!" If we had this kind of contextual control, our opportunities for happiness would be much greater. However, if this opportunity were introduced into the Happiness Game, it is the painful outcomes that most players would try to keep out of the context. Contrary to their deepest intuitions, this would actually reduce the cumulative average payoff. To ensure a more positive cumulative average, it is the happy events (those yielding the more positive payoffs) that should be kept out of the context.

In one test simulation, the probability of an outcome being dropped immediately from the context was programmed to vary inversely with the payoff it elicited; happy outcomes were more likely to be dropped, unhappy ones to be retained.[9] This ensured that the context for judgment would be skewed more positively than if, as in the simplest version of the game, it represented the last 10 outcomes regardless of their payoffs. Although positive skewing is ordinarily a prescription for unhappiness, it has the opposite effect in this case because the actual outcomes tend to be high relative to those lesser outcomes that are more likely to be represented in the context. With endpoints fixed at 0 and 99 and frequency values determined by the last 10 of those outcomes that had not been dropped, this selective retention of unhappy outcomes more than doubled the cumulative average payoff, from +51 to a *slightly satisfying* +113. If the 70–99 fantasies of success were added as the outcomes for one half of the trials, this measure of happiness would rise to a *satisfying* +205!

Because +205 is the highest cumulative average obtained for any version of the game,[10] the plausibility of this kind of selective dropping of happy outcomes deserves special consideration. Table 9.8 shows how often would each of 9 hedonic catego ries would be used, for these last two versions of the game.

With almost one third of all hedonic experiences in the highest category, *very, very satisfying*, the combination of selective dropping and high imaginary goals yields too much ecstasy to be entirely credible for most domains of experience; but perhaps there is this proportion of the best in certain imaginary domains and

---

[9]This inverse relationship is specified by Table 9.7.

TABLE 9.7
Probability of Sampled Stimulus Remaining in Context

Payoff (PO):	PO > 300	301 > PO > 100	101 > PO > -99	-100 > PO > -299	-300 > PO
Probability:	.2	.4	.6	.8	1.0

The fixed lower endpoint is crucial to the +113 average obtained for this version; when there are no fixed endpoints, the cumulative average is only +47 (but still well above the +35 obtained without selective retention of disappointing outcomes).

[10]However, when endpoints are fixed at −99 and +99, the cumulative average payoff is an even higher +225.

TABLE 9.8
Percent Use of Categories

Categories:	1	2	3	4	5	6	7	8	9
Selective dropping (0 - 99)	3	7	8	9	11	13	18	18	13
Sel. drop. (0 - 99) + 50% (70 - 99)	2	4	5	7	8	9	17	17	31

in the very special domain of sexual experiences. This high proportion of ecstasy would have to occur much more generally, across most domains, to produce the overall level of happiness claimed by the average American ($+200$, or 7 on the 0-to-10 scale used in the Gallup polls).[11]

How reasonable is it that the worst of the past should have so much more influence than the best of the past? Tests of recall have provided mixed results— but with a tendency toward better recall of pleasant than of unpleasant experiences. Given the difference between the type of memory tapped by such tests and the *implicit memory* that better describes the role of past events in the context for judgment, the assumption of greater contextual retention of unpleasant experiences does not seem unlikely. However, the chief reason for invoking it is to raise the cumulative average payoff to the level that random samples of the U.S. population claim in their self-avowals of happiness.

SUMMARY

Computer simulations using elaborated versions of the game demonstrate how different assumptions about what gets into the context might tip the hedonic balance much further toward happiness. Although there is little effect of expanding the context to represent the most recent 20 or 30 experiences, greater retention of contextual endpoints can raise the upper limit of happiness by almost 50%—even while reducing the overemphasis on extreme pleasures and pains found with the simplest version of the game. This higher level of happiness is in turn more than doubled when fantasies of success are experienced as frequently as real-world events in the same hedonic context. Such imaginary triumphs do reduce the pleasantness of actual achievements, but this reduction is more than counterbalanced by the pleasures of anticipated success. A separate context for fantasies can be even more satisfying when there is an extraordinary concentration of experiences at the top of its range. An imagined tragedy that establishes

---

[11]As argued in earlier chapters, these self-avowals should not be taken without a healthy dose of skepticism.

an extreme but enduring lower endpoint can also substantially increase the over-all level of happiness, provided that it is experienced only rarely. However, the greatest happiness results when the more pleasant experiences drop more quickly from the context. This raises the overall measure to the level actually reported by the average American in surveys of happiness, a level for which almost one third of all hedonic experiences are *very, very satisfying*!

Readers should feel encouraged to consider other ideas about what gets into the context, possibilities that are more congruent with their own ideas about happiness. The computer simulations of the consequences of the different assumptions explored in this chapter do not force one to give up any particular idea. However, the computer's dependence on precise programming encourages a more precise specification of the possibilities. The next two chapters explore these possibilities further, with practical examples of their application to every-day life.

10 Real-World Strategies for Happiness

The implications of the contextual theory of happiness, illustrated quantitatively by the Happiness Game, may seem too abstract to be applied in everyday life. These formal implications are fleshed out in this chapter with illustrative examples, many drawn from personal experience. Interpretation of these examples is speculative in nature, as must always be the case with the psychology of everyday life. In particular, applications to real-life situations always involve auxiliary assumptions that can be rejected without rejecting the basic theory. For example, one of the more widely employed of such assumptions is that hedonic experiences occur primarily in the imagination. Another is that only a small proportion of all experiences are genuinely hedonic. However, the list of auxiliary assumptions is so long that it would be tedious to list them all (a rough count showed that some 70 have been proposed thus far, and there are almost twice that number in the remainder of this volume). Readers are advised to watch out for these assumptions, considering whether any direct evidence supports them and also either their intrinsic attractiveness or the attractiveness of their implications when combined with the rest of the theory.

The emphasis here is on real-world problems that seem particularly important for happiness. The theoretical balance of happiness for many of these examples would be altered substantially if account were taken of imaginary pleasures and pains. Contributions of imaginary experiences will be considered separately in chapter 11.

SUCCESS VERSUS HAPPINESS

Limits to Success

When success is pursued for its own sake, when we are always pushing to higher and higher levels, we must eventually arrive at the limits of our ability or good fortune. The structure of most competitive situations is intrinsically pyramidal. Just as there can be only a few concert soloists, only a few captains of industry, there can be only a few at the top of any field of competitive endeavor. For these few, the high ambition, the drive to succeed, and the holding up of successful models may seem perfectly realistic.

However, even the most successful often suffer from a sense of their own inadequacy. With their impossibly high standards, they have difficulty pleasing themselves. I remember a guest lecturer giving a perfectly brilliant performance in one of my graduate classes. Later, after his lecture, he confessed to me that he had considered telephoning in the middle of the previous night to cancel the lecture because he felt insufficiently prepared. Although sorry for having provided an occasion for his anxiety, I concluded that his night of personal suffering was justified by the sheer splendor of his performance and the intellectual satisfaction he gave some two dozen students.

Consider the much larger number of competitors who, as victims of the inexorable geometry of the pyramid, find themselves stuck at levels far below their aspirations. Even if they are likely to achieve more for having set such high goals, they are less likely to experience their actual achievements as adequate. At some point, they must lower their sights. This is not easy. Dropping the upper endpoint of the contextual range takes much longer than the upward extension of the range that can come with each new success. The resistance to restricting the contextual range reflects the tenacious fixation of contextual endpoints. This fundamental asymmetry is demonstrated by simple psychophysical experiments in which adjustment to extensions of the range of stimuli are immediate but adjustments to restrictions come slowly—if at all.[1] It is also supported by bitter experience. We adjust so quickly to a raise in pay that our swollen checking accounts can be quickly overdrawn; however, some people never adjust to a reduction in income.

The problem of unrealistic goals may seem more characteristic of the overly ambitious than of the average person working his or her way up the ladder of success. Most people seem to be realistic, fitting their aspirations to their talents. Although the contextual theory of happiness must seem misguided to those who measure happiness by the absolute level of success, they might consider the quite

---

[1]These experiments (e.g., Parducci, 1956) are consistent with range-frequency theory; adjustment to restriction of range can be very slow in psychophysical experiments (cf. Haubensak, 1992; Parducci, 1992a).

different attitude expressed in Terkel's (1972) almost condescending quotation from a postman:

> I'm doing a job that's my life ambition. When I was in school you said in the yearbook what you're most likely to be. I did say mailman . . . This is a profession that everyone has looked up to and respected. They always say, "Here comes the mailman"—pony express or something. This always brought a gleam to every-body's eye. Everyone likes to receive mail. I feel it is one of the most respected professions that is throughout the nation. You're doing a job for the public and a job for the country. (p. 271)

In his quasipopular book, *The Conquest of Happiness*, Russell (1930/1975) claimed that his gardener was the happiest person he knew. This gardener waged a constant battle against the rabbits who were always threatening to take over Russell's carrot patch. Although disaster frequently seemed imminent, the gardener always won out in the end. This fits Russell's belief that the process of overcoming obstacles is a crucial condition for happiness. But Russell possessed enormous intellectual abilities. In his philosophical work on the foundations of mathematics, he had the wisdom to set himself difficult problems that he could solve, not always easily but with sufficient skill to impress the best logicians.

At a more mundane level, there are features of some jobs that insure the progressive overcoming of obstacles emphasized by Russell. Many careers, like those in civil service, advance by seniority, so that at any given step on the career ladder the position is likely to be higher than it had been just a few years before. The accumulation of wealth and power in business sometimes follows the same orderly progression. If one's context represented only where one had been, not where one was going, this type of ascending sequence would yield more satisfaction than dissatisfaction. A similar ascension might be experienced in fields where knowledge or skills continue to grow. This is supposed to be one of the advantages of intellectual endeavor. If so, historians ought to be happier than mathematicians, for the bits and pieces of information crucial to the historian accumulate with age, whereas the mathematician is more likely to reach his apogee of creativity in his 20s. On the other hand, it may be easier for mathematicians to accept their subsequent decline in creativity because it is more readily apparent—historians can maintain unrealistic goals throughout their lives. Everyone who lives long enough must experience a decline in physical agility; but because this decline is so clearly inevitable, it is rarely a source of profound unhappiness.

Attitudes Toward Success

There is a tug of war between success and happiness: Attitudes that encourage one can be inimical to the other. To maximize happiness, one ought to stop the upward climb toward higher and higher levels of achievement at that step where the best of the context is experienced relatively often, whatever that best might be. Success would then be seen as instrumental, a means toward happiness rather than a substitute for happiness.

This may seem to suggest that one should pursue happiness, even at the expense of greater achievement. Einstein is said to have claimed that he would have been happier as a plumber. But if this were true, it still seems fitting (in the Aristotelian sense) that Einstein should have been the great theoretical physicist rather than just another among the hundreds of thousands of plumbers. His creative genius inspired the rest of us with awe, even when we could not understand his theory—in part because we could not understand it. Einstein's personal happiness seems a small thing beside the immensity of his intellectual achievements. For Utilitarians devoted to Bentham's (1789/1948) greatest happiness of the greatest number, the gain for the world would greatly overbalance Einstein's personal frustrations.[2]

In calculating this gain, many of us could include our enjoyment in reading about Einstein's intellectual achievements. Similarly, we take pleasure in the achievements of the best athletes, rather than suffering from our own comparative lack of talent. It is only perhaps a handful of other great physicists or great athletes that might experience pain from such comparisons. And yet, we may suffer empathicly when our favorite stars do not perform at their usual high levels. In this case, the great past performances that did not enter the context for judging ourselves did enter our context for judging these star performers.

Any sacrifice of personal happiness on the alter of achievement raises the question of choosing between what is personally gratifying and what is morally right. Cases like Einstein's may be the exceptions that prove the rule: Most run-of-the-mill achievements are thought to bring happiness to the achiever; if they do not, it would be hard to justify them as bringing happiness to others. What difference does it make if we have one more successful doctor, lawyer, businessman, or professor? A dozen others would have been ready to take their places, accomplishing just about as much.

One objection to this denigration of achievement is that the economic well-being of a society depends on its people being success-oriented. Invidious comparisons between the United States and either contemporary Japan or the former so-called communist states of Eastern Europe reinforce this notion that a society's attitude toward achievement may be an important factor in its economic success. One problem impeding Russia's shift to a market economy is the resentment directed toward new entrepreneurs, toward those who seem to be getting ahead on their own. But where is it written that Japanese are happier or Russians less happy than Americans?

---

[2]Einstein has sometimes been blamed for the atomic bomb, although his role in its development appears to have been only in advising President Franklin D. Roosevelt of its feasibility.

Antagonism toward success has perhaps always been a factor in American public education; but starting in the 1960s, parents and schools began to place even less emphasis on scholastic achievement and more on children being satisfied with themselves. This was the beginning of a well-documented decline in scores on standardized tests. Part of the justification for lowering educational standards was to open higher education to previously underrepresented segments of the population . The ultimate goal was for most young people to receive the credentials that bring prestige, enhanced self-esteem and, especially, economic rewards. But one of the consequences of the lowering of standards is that even the best students, the top 1% of the college-bound population, are achieving less,[3] with potentially disastrous effects on the general international competitiveness of the society. It would be reassuring to conclude that this was a small price to pay for the resulting increase in happiness. Indeed, if one believes the students' own reports of how they feel about their levels of academic performance, Americans are more self-satisfied in this domain than are students in other industrialized countries: Although performing less well, they nevertheless feel better about how well they are performing! But considering how many young people with academic credentials are either unemployed or underemployed (both in the United States and in Western Europe, where there has been a similar opening of higher education), one might conclude that after graduation it is the general level of frustration and sense of failure that increased, not overall satisfaction.[4]

There is another objection to the thesis that happiness is what counts, not achievement. Consider the higher career aspirations of contemporary women. Some feminists might argue that women should risk sacrificing their own happiness to pave the way for future generations, opening possibilities for careers that have traditionally been closed to women. This is a tempting argument, particularly if it is the strongest, most capable women that hear the message. Unfortunately, the goals established by the successful trailblazers often prove elusive: instead of the exciting promotion into higher management, the career is likely to be stalled at a lower position, with the resulting sense of not living up to one's aspirations. One problem is that there are relatively few of the exciting jobs for either gender; if there were more such jobs, most of them would not be judged exciting. Whether or not the frustration of failing to fulfill one's dreams can be

---

[3]As measured by the Scholastic Aptitude Test on which the entire distribution of scores has shifted downward over the past quarter century—not just the lower end of the distribution, as sometimes assumed (see Krech et al., 1982, chap. 15). Other factors have been blamed, especially the competition from television for the student's time (e.g., Wirtz, 1977).

[4]This was documented in Parducci (1976). An even more extreme case of the mismatch between goals and outcomes is described for Micronesia in chapter 12. The same frustration of goals is happening all over the world, even in the most prosperous of the industrialized countries where credentials have been devalued.

more than counterbalanced by the pleasures of dreaming is discussed in the next chapter.

Mistaken notions about conditions for unhappiness reflect an orientation toward absolute levels of achievement that ignores the relativity of judgment. Consider how we think about justice. Our principles of justice are absolute in character, and properly so; if we did not insist on absolute rights, they would be quickly eroded or compromised. But when we consider the *sense* of justice, the psychological state of feeling that things are fair, relational considerations become crucial. Children are ordered about by adults, in school and at home, often without their experiencing any sense of injustice; that is the way they and other children have always been treated. But as they grow into adulthood, similar incursions upon their liberty become insupportable. Nevertheless, tens of thousands of young Americans volunteer for military service each year, submitting to absolute authority as part of military discipline. During my own naval experience in World War II, my fellow sailors willingly endured all sorts of humiliations. Because everyone had to submit to authoritarian control, moral outrage was not widespread; as with other cases of relative deprivation (Crosby, 1972), the obvious impossibility of changing the situation may have lessened any sense of injustice.

Obstacles to change also lessen the outrage of people under the harshest of dictators whom people in democracies regard as unspeakably cruel and unjust. However, even the most totalitarian rule cannot preclude all sense of injustice. I remember an early escapee from Stalin's terror telling me that he was not bothered by the mansions in Beverly Hills but that in Moscow he had been bitter when those with the right connections moved into the new flats while his family was passed by. In this case, the sense of relative deprivation depended on the stated principles of the Soviet Union—equality and sharing of material wealth in accordance with need; unhappiness was caused by the violation of professed principles, by the disparity between what was supposed to be and what was, rather than by the absolute level of deprivation. The writings of Solzhenitsyn provide powerful examples of the resulting sense of injustice, apparently a dominant feature of his own conscious experience.

The relationship between objective success and happiness, like that between objective injustice and the psychological sense of injustice, is governed not by the absolute level of success but rather by the place of that level in a context of related experiences.[5] A level of achievement that falls below one's own standards

---

[5]The same relational analysis is applicable to campaigns against pornography. At any given time, the more extreme examples of sexual deviation from the current standards for sexual expression will seem offensively pornographic, regardless of their absolute characteristics: A century ago, exposure of a woman's ankle could seem shamelessly provocative; later the calf and then the thigh became the permissible limits. If a campaign against pornography suppresses the extreme examples, the most deviant of those that escape suppression become, in their turn, pornographic. And if this new worst is more prevalent, the campaign has inadvertently increased the total amount of pornography.

must be disappointing, regardless of how excellent it might be by the standards of others.

Love and Hate

It should be clear that the relational considerations applied here to pleasure and pain, or to the sense of justice, also apply to other dimensions that may be only moderately correlated with the hedonic dimension. For example, love and hate define one of the dimensions most heavily laden with feeling, usually with overwhelming hedonic components, and yet not simply reducible to pleasure and pain. The experience of love can produce the most intense pleasure; but, as many teenagers would testify, it can also be unbearably painful. Hatred for another person is often experienced as a crushing pain, perhaps with a sense of shame at having been mistreated or overpowered. However, we sometimes relish our hatreds, taking pleasure in our loathing for some detestable criminal or tyrant. As I write this, the United States (like much of the Western World) is recovering from a pleasurable binge of hatred for Saddam Hussein, the tyrannical ruler of Iraq. For many of us, it felt good to hate Saddam. He was said to be a torturer, a mass killer, a genocidal monster. No one reproached us for expressing our hatred, and for most people any concomitant pain would have been due to empathy for Saddam's victims.

Quite apart from pleasure and pain, one can ask the pragmatic question of how the sum total of love can be maximized. The simple range-frequency answer is that the distribution of events on the love-hate dimension should be skewed as negatively as possible: Whatever its absolute character, the worst of these would be experienced as hate and the much more frequent best would be experienced as love. The sum total of love is maximized when the lower endpoint of the contextual range is as far as possible below the great bulk of experiences.

This relational conception of love is at odds with the religious ideal of absolute love, the saint that experiences only love for others, never hate. The distinction should be drawn between the psychological experience of love or hate and the particular overt behavior by which love or hate is expressed. A saint might always behave in loving ways, even though this behavior sometimes masked private feelings of indifference or even of hate. Perhaps it would be a better world if only the love were expressed. However, the psychological necessity for an occasional experience of hate should be recognized. Insofar as we thought about Saddam only rarely, hating him may have reduced the total amount of hate we experienced. Our tolerance for other rulers was enhanced: with Saddam anchoring the extreme lower endpoint of this context, lesser tyrants seemed almost benign.

When the spirit of pacifism and love for one's enemies was a frequently articulated ideal on American college campuses during the 1960s and early 1970s, I heard a psychiatrist from a University clinic describe student patients who were suffering insupportable guilt about their hatred for those they were supposed to love. Marchers in peace protests might find themselves detesting those who taunted or physically abused them. Their consequent feelings of guilt seem based on the mistaken belief that one can regularly experience love without, at least occasionally, experiencing hate.

In marriage, in relationships with one's children, or in any other intensely loving relationship, occasional hatred may even have to be directed toward the loved one.[6] This depends on whether the relevant context represents only experiences with the loved one, or whether it also includes experiences with other people who can serve as the psychologically requisite targets. Love might be strongest when a couple is united as a team against the outside world. But if the two were to live in complete isolation from others, as on a desert island, the worst moments of their relationship would evoke intense hatred. This may be a problem with honeymoons where the deliberate isolation can restrict the context to just each other and where unrealistic expectations of a completely loving idyll diminish the love that would otherwise be experienced.

Instrumental Domains

A common justification for aspiring to higher levels of achievement is that although the hard work on the way up may not be intrinsically satisfying, it enhances future satisfaction. Thus a parent may admonish: "Do your algebra or you will never get into medical school!" Neither the algebra nor the later training in medicine are considered worthwhile in themselves, only as necessary hurdles that make possible a securely prosperous life. But where is the evidence that doctors are happier than plumbers or even that they feel more affluent? In a provocative joke, a housewife complains to her plumber about his exorbitant bill: "That's higher than what my husband charges, and he's a brain surgeon!" to which the plumber replies, "I know, lady, I used to be a brain surgeon myself!" Plumbers may not really charge more than brain surgeons, but they may be more satisfied with their incomes. Medical doctors, finding it easy to borrow money, can slip into a lifestyle in which they must constantly fight off their creditors. The long hours worked by some doctors may reflect a sense of economic "need," a perceived lack of money.

Studying to become a doctor is perhaps not representative of the more general value of sacrificing for the future. Figuratively speaking, we all chop firewood in the summer to ensure being warm in the winter. This seems indisputably rational: accept a little suffering now so as to avoid a great deal of suffering later!

The payoff need not be in the distant future but in another domain of one's

---

[6]Spinoza (1677/1994), although asserting a close psychological connection between love and hate in his *Ethics*, deduced a rather different account of their relationship.

present life, as in the trade-off between work and family. In the computerized Happiness Game, the player must not allow the hypothetical salesman to avoid work too often, for then other domains will be spoiled by unhappy thoughts about not making enough money. Most players find an optimal balance between these domains, having their salesman work just enough so that his recreational activities can yield their greater balances of pleasure.

One ought not to accept uncritically this arbitrary assumption that work yields less satisfaction than play. Indeed, as cited in chapter 7, Csikszentmihalyi (1993) found that people are more likely to report themselves satisfied when they are at work. I have a friend who made a fortune manufacturing and selling shoes. Eventually, his factory was bought out. He continues to sell shoes to stores but at a level of financial remuneration so small (in comparison with his accumulated wealth) that the money can hardly be a motivating factor. "Why don't you simply give up selling," I asked him. "Why not play more tennis and golf or even go back to your old dream of studying history?" He could not articulate an answer; but it seems likely that he truly loves selling shoes, enjoys his own prowess in this highly competitive field, and fears he would become bored were he to give it up. He may be exceptional only in that his great personal wealth leads one to question his motives for working. Others who think they are working only for money might also be gaining considerable satisfaction from their work.

Another possibility, one that might suggest itself to the sociobiologically inclined, is that we are descended from food gatherers whose survival depended on building up stores of food even when they were not hungry. Thus, we might have been naturally selected for the genes that keep us pursuing the necessities of life when continued pursuit is no longer necessary for survival. Without giving much credit to this sort of "explanation,"[7] one can nevertheless agree that lots of people pursue their work for its own sake. The work may also be an escape from boredom. Some relatively prosperous mothers, after their children are in school, take jobs that pay too little to cover the additional expenses of clothing and transportation occasioned by working. Their employment may not be particularly fulfilling in itself, but it gets them away from what they experience as the boredom of an empty house, perhaps also restoring a sense of purpose to their lives and winning respect from their friends.

Whatever the overall balance of satisfaction with work, one hard statistic must not be overlooked: Most jobs require 40 hours of work each week. When the time spent traveling to and from the job is added, and also the time spent thinking about work-related problems during off-hours, the total may often exceed 60

---

[7]The problem with such "explanations" is that they have no predictive power and are thus not really explanatory in a scientific sense. Consider what might falsify sociobiological explanations: Suppose we find people who refuse to save for the future—would this prove the theory wrong? This sort of objection was developed by the preeminent philosopher of science, Popper (1959), who established the criterion of *falsifiability* for measuring explanatory power.

hours a week. This could mean that the majority of waking hours are devoted largely to this one domain. Consequently, if the overall balance of satisfaction with work is unhappy, life as a whole is likely to be unhappy—unless satisfactions greatly overbalance dissatisfactions in the other domains that occupy fewer waking hours. This suggests that one should be careful about settling for unhappiness at work just to support other, happier domains.

But fortunately for the survival of the species, providing for one's children is almost universally seen to justify enormous sacrifices in other domains. Family pleasures loom very very large, such as the joy of feeling a child's arms around one's neck, of knowing that you signify security and love for this helpless little sample of perfection. Among my happier memories are of our family dinners, sitting surrounded by five young faces and their doting mother. However, the pains of parenthood, the anxiety when a child is injured or seriously ill, or later when one's own values are rejected by offspring trying to find their own ways—these are all too common sources of misery. And because children's pleasures and pains can be so contagiously intense, one's own happiness sometimes seems remarkably dependent upon them.

WHEN THE BALANCE IS POSITIVE

When life seems good, it is a time for self-congratulation. Consider the domains concerned with the fulfillment of basic bodily needs: eating, drinking, sex, the creature comforts. In each of these, life usually marches to the beat of a happy drummer. At least in industrialized countries, the great majority can eat when hungry and escape environmental discomforts. It may not be practicable to have all of the sexual experiences desired, but most manage to arrange their lives so that the best of sex comes satisfyingly often—and there is always the happy realm of sexual fantasy.

Earlier chapters proffered several interpretations of why these biological domains seem so happy. One interpretation centers on the presence of a natural *optimum*, a best state, beyond which improvement was scarcely imaginable (Klusky, 1990; Parducci, 1989). Thus, the optimum cannot be diminished by comparison with anything better. Perhaps the simplest example is temperature: Inside an office or home, a level close to 72 degrees (22 C) is close to the ideal for most lightly-dressed people, higher is too warm and lower becomes chilly or requires heavier clothing. However, our pleasure in this optimum comes mostly from sudden change, coming in out of the cold in winter or out of the heat in summer. Constant temperatures give neither pleasure nor pain, and so we are rarely conscious of temperature.

In my own experience, pleasure from creature comforts is most likely during outdoor adventures. For example, on the beach after windsurfing, sitting inactively with the wind blowing on my damp wetsuit, I become aware that I am shivering and unpleasantly cold. Up to that point, my pleasure or pain came from other sources. After being cold, getting under a hot shower produces genuine pleasure. Camping is another occasion for suffering from heat or cold, but then it affords the pleasures of getting back to the optimum, as by finding shade, starting a campfire, or crawling into a warm sleeping bag. The difference between happy and unhappy camping adventures is not in whether all discomfort and pain have been avoided—but rather in the proportion of conscious experiences relatively close to the optimum. This means that short intervals of real deprivation, as far below the optimum as is supportable, provide the springboard for an euphoric sense of comfort. This kind of euphoria is most likely to be experienced when conditions suddenly improve. The overall balance will be a happy one only insofar as the worst does not endure but is quickly replaced by something closer to the optimum which will be satisfying only as long as the context continues to include the miserable conditions. This suggests a positive hedonic value for an asceticism limited to occasional deprivations. When asceticism gets out of hand, with extended periods of deprivation, the hedonic balance is likely to become negative. Then only the joys of anticipation and memory, the imaginative events stimulated by deprivation, can tip the balance back toward happiness.[8]

With eating, our natural cycle of hunger and satiation follows a biological rhythm that can control our hedonic swings. Sometimes we suffer genuine pangs of hunger, unpleasant except insofar as they evoke anticipations of eating. Experienced hosts know that their guests will find the meal more satisfying if they come to the table hungry. But should a host force the guests to suffer first, delaying the meal until they feel unpleasantly famished? This tactic might work if there were pleasant diversions to mask the hunger, such as outdoor activities, tennis, skiing, or hiking, in which the physical effort, perhaps the struggle to get back home, would be in a different domain from eating. Arriving at the table, the guests suddenly realize that they are famished; but their pangs of hunger are quickly overwhelmed by pleasant anticipations as the food appears. For a favorable balance of pleasure over pain in this domain, it would be a mistake to eat compulsively, to eat so much and so often that there is never real hunger and never real pleasure. Reading, television, or engrossing conversation while eating divert our attention from the food, stealing away this potential pleasure; but these diversions are sometimes more gratifying than the actual eating.

Another interpretation of the pleasures of eating rests on the assumption of systematic downward drifts in the context. This assumption is encouraged in this case by the sense that we forget how good certain foods can be, as though their remembered values had fallen. Most of us learn that even these favorites taste better after a longer period without them.

---

[8]Camping, backpacking, and some of the other rugged outdoor challenges probably generate the great preponderance of their pleasures within this world of the imagination, the concern of the next chapter.

Whatever the interpretation of why basic biological domains like eating are usually much more pleasurable than painful, one should be able to increase one's sum total of happiness by ensuring that these domains are experienced more often—and thus living more fully. However, the pleasures of the table have been affronted by changing standards of bodily weight, the fashion toward slenderness and beliefs about health that make many of us feel guilty after consuming highly caloric foods. People periodically follow painful crash diets, quickly losing much of the weight they intended to lose but then slowly increasing their intake and weight until they decide to diet again. Whatever the consequences for health, this periodically ascending series might be good for the overall balance of satisfaction with eating.[9] However, as is so often the case with practical applications of abstract theory, this one is confounded by other factors. Dieters would cite the remorse and self-contempt they experience when straying from their diets or when finally realizing that they have regained all of the weight they had so firmly resolved to keep off. To the degree that the pains of remorse outweigh the pleasures of eating, the overall balance in this domain becomes negative. In this case, fashion and popular notions about health seem particularly pernicious in getting people to change what would otherwise be a happy domain.[10]

More generally, we are winners in these bodily domains, and winners tend to stick with their successful patterns of play. It is when we imagine that there is something more, that "the sex is better on the other side of the street," that we risk making things worse. This can destroy a happy pattern by extending the contextual range upward to include exciting events that can be experienced only rarely—not to speak of the unhappiness it could bring to others, as in the breakup of a family.

One misconception in such cases is that we can experience an ecstasy greater than anything experienced before. Another is that we can experience continuous highs. Both misconceptions afflict people attracted to drugs. And both may contribute to the high rate of divorce, as when a couple says, "we do love each other and always will, but we are separating because we think there should be more to life." This reminds me of a man who had previously been a professor in Hawaii. He had loved the islands, the climate, the luaus, the easy way of life. But at the same time, he had fretted that his scientific achievements were not getting sufficient recognition from the rest of the academic world. After transferring to a major mainland university, he confided to me: "What a fool I was! Now, I would swim all the way to Hawaii if it could get me my old job back."

Although most of us share a good and realistic attitude toward the fulfillment

---

[9]The greater cumulative average payoff for periodically ascending series was derived algebraically from range-frequency principles and then demonstrated experimentally for ratings of odors (Parducci, 1973).

[10]See Tiger (1992) for an insightful discussion of how contemporary customs of eating and dieting could reflect genetic traits evolved through natural selection.

of our basic physiological needs, we have more difficulty in other domains. Particularly in our careers, we regularly reach for more, extending the contextual range. A typical major decision involves the choice of jobs or whether to accept a promotion to a different position. The promotion usually brings higher income and status, just what we thought we were working for. The contextual theory of happiness suggests that we will all too quickly adapt to the higher income, that after only a month or two we will cease to feel affluent. Instead, we will compare our income with the new "needs" generated by the promotion, associating with new colleagues who are paid more, perhaps having to match their more expensive lifestyle.

With respect to happiness, less emphasis should be placed on the absolute gain in income and status, more on how we are likely to feel about such matters in the new contexts in which they will be experienced. The same prescription holds for the nature of the new duties. Will our sense of competency be affected by the change? Will we feel better fitted to what we are doing, or will we feel under stress to perform at a level just beyond our capacities? This calls for realism. It should be easier to adopt a realistic attitude if one begins with the assumption that an "advance," although immediately gratifying, is not necessarily an hedonic improvement, that the "better" job may yield less satisfaction in the long run. Such realism should be easier to adopt when one is already content with one's situation. However, the same considerations apply when one is less than content.

In the academic worlds of teaching and research, there is a special kind of advancement that involves almost a new career. This is the promotion to administration. High school teachers become principals. University professors become deans. Researchers in industry move into management. The new duties and responsibilities are usually very different from the old ones, so that the teaching or research skills that led to the promotion become less important. New skills are needed and sometimes also different basic goals and values. Previously happy at teaching or research, there must be many new administrators who find themselves less happy. It should be possible to return gracefully to the former position; but for some, such a return would be an admission of failure; and if the goals appropriate to administration have been internalized, the return might prove extraordinarily painful. Better not to have made the inappropriate move in the first place!

Even when a major change does bring increased happiness, there can be a problem of unrealistic notions about how much happiness is possible. In the Happiness Game, the pattern that yields an overall average of $+50$ on the scale from -500 to $+500$ is too neutral for some players who may mistakenly believe that, by finding the right pattern of play, they could do much better. If life is like the game, they will not do a great deal better in their own lives, either. A more realistic appreciation of the limits of happiness would encourage sticking with what is already close to the best possible overall balance.

A similar error may be the belief that something is basically wrong when one is experiencing occasional extreme lows, for example, between -400 and -500 in the Happiness Game. But the worst of any context is extremely painful. This agony can be completely avoided only if there could be a lower contextual endpoint that was never actually experienced, perhaps a counterfactual that is only a theoretical possibility. We naturally try to avoid whatever would be worst. But if we did succeed in completely escaping the particular conditions that seemed least supportable, the worst of what was left would be experienced with the same misery and, in some cases, with much greater frequency. Such an escape would constitute a Pyrrhic victory, indeed.

We each have our psychological techniques for dampening the duration of our worst experiences. By intellectualizing them, adopting an analytic attitude toward them, reminding ourselves that "this, too, shall pass," we reduce the suffering. However, there is a serious danger of applying such techniques too broadly: When something wonderful happens, we should not dampen the pleasure by reminding ourselves of its inevitable brevity or by fearful anticipation of subsequent letdowns. In a television interview conducted long after he had resigned from the Presidency, Nixon confessed to suffering from this tendency. When questioned about the common impression that he was too stiff, too restrained in his emotions, Nixon responded that it was perhaps true, citing as an example his reaction to Kissinger's enthusiasm after a minor triumph in the Middle East: Kissinger was dancing a little jig around the oval office, but Nixon could not share his delight, knowing that this triumph was unlikely to last, that it was just paving the way for future disappointment.[11] Whatever the political justification for Nixon's analysis of this particular triumph, his own attitude would not be conducive to happiness if applied so broadly as to dampen the delights of success. Mathematically, ecstasies and euphoria must be major contributors to any powerful balance of pleasure over pain. Pleasures should be dampened only when to do so would prevent the establishment of a new and rare endpoint that would otherwise diminish the pleasure of events experienced much more frequently.

Increasing the relative *importance* of a happy domain should improve the overall balance. As in the Utilitarian conception of happiness adopted for the contextual theory, greater importance is determined solely by greater frequency or duration of experience. In the Happiness Game, this means choosing as often as possible a domain in which the player has found a good overall balance, recreation rather than work. And even a happy domain can be made still happier by increasing the proportion of its experiences that are genuinely hedonic. Counting nonhedonic experiences as zeros in the hypothetical calculation of happiness makes sense of the prescription to "live more fully."

---

[11]Paraphrase from memory of Nixon's interview with Robert Frost.

However, there is another meaning to living more fully that makes much less sense—the emphasis upon breadth of experience, sought for its own sake. Although adventures that prove truly awful can improve the overall balance if they are sufficiently rare, extending the range upward reduces the average level of happiness unless the new upper endpoint can be experienced with high relative frequency. For example, a once-in-a-lifetime vacation at a spectacular but distant ski resort would decrease the pleasure from the modest local skiing, although this might be balanced by pleasant memories and anticipations of going back again. A horrendous wipe-out would increase the pleasure of successful ski runs, although these might be spoiled by anticipation of injury.

Fear of boredom can be at the heart of the quest for new experiences. But this, too, seems based on a false assumption, namely that everything must seem the same when the contextual range is narrow. Instead, narrowing the range actually improves discrimination because the discriminability of any two events is inversely proportional to the range of the context in which they are experienced.[12] I once attended a travel lecture by a man who had homesteaded in an isolated valley of the Brooks Range in northern Alaska. He reported that when first settling there, he could watch the caribou for only a few minutes before becoming bored; after years in the wilderness, he would watch them for hours, fascinated by their differences in behavior. This is like the Micronesian's contextual adaptation to the narrow range of equatorial temperatures, so that 80 degrees seems cold to them and 90 degrees hot.

In summary, the prescriptions for people who are already happy suggest caution about rocking the boat in the hope of becoming still happier. There are limits to happiness, although perhaps not so restricted as the simplest version of the Happiness Game implies. The most positive balances often occur in basic biological domains where a natural optimum can be approached with great regularity. In other, more problematic domains, the great danger is that by reaching for more we can actually make things worse. It is the relational rather than the absolute level of outcomes that determine our happiness: the overall balance will be higher when we concentrate on those domains where the best comes relatively often and the worst only rarely—whatever that best and worst might be.

WHEN THE BALANCE IS NEGATIVE

Making Matters Worse

One needs no rule for determining whether one is miserable, even if the misery is concentrated in a single domain, such as work. It is when the balance is only slightly negative that there is doubt and also the danger of making matters worse

---

[12]At least in psychophysics, where such assertions can be experimentally tested (Braida & Durlach, 1972; Parducci & Perrett, 1971).

by transforming the mildly negative to the intolerably bad. I remember asking a former *refusednik* from the Soviet Union how it had felt living under that total-itarian regime. He described his frustration at having to watch his nonJewish colleagues getting promoted ahead of him at the research institute, aggravating but bearable. The big change came when he finally made the decision to leave. Suddenly, the injustice of the Soviet system became unbearable. He recalled the long wait for his exit visa as "an almost continuous low, one long -10!" The momentous act of applying to leave had made psychologically real what had only been a remote possibility: At last he would gain recognition for his scientific accomplishments. His contextual range suddenly extended so far upward that his daily life as a *refusednik*, bad enough by his earlier standards, sank relatively closer to the lower end of this context. When he was eventually permitted to emigrate, his objective situation became very much better but not much happier. Where other Soviet Jews in his field of research had gone to the United States, he had chosen to go to Israel. I met him when he was visiting one of their well-equipped laboratories in California. He expressed bitterness that Soviet immi-grants here were receiving so much more technical support than he could get as an immigrant in Israel. These invidious comparisons were spoiling what he had hoped would be a marvelous new life.

It seems to me that this unfortunate man had traded one form of slavery for another. As Thoreau (1854/1973) wrote, "It is hard to have a southern overseer; it is worse to have a northern one, but worst of all when you are the slave-driver of yourself" (p. 7).[13] We each can be a slave to the unfavorable comparisons that we ourselves make, to contextual possibilities that breed a sense of entrapment.

Although this former *refusednik* may actually have been happier in the Soviet Union (at least during the period before applying for his exit visa), he denied ever having considered returning there. He preferred being a free citizen of Israel to being a victim of anti-Semitism in the Soviet Union. What he had failed to anticipate is that he would be comparing his opportunities for research in Israel not just with his former lack of support but also with the greater support he could have been receiving in the United States.

In less dramatic ways, we each run the risk of unforeseen contextual changes resulting from our carefully calculated decisions. The choice of a career, of a mate, of having children, of a move to a new location—each brings important changes in its own context. One might think that these changes would tend to be for the better. However, there is an important factor favoring disappointment: We are more likely to undertake major changes when we expect them to prove very much for the better; because such expectations are so high, they are more easily disappointed. As long as the better world we had anticipated remains as the extreme upper endpoint of the new, expanded context, we are likely to suffer. The new situation may indeed be better than the old one, but the balance of

---

[13]The final chapter of this book applies the contextual theory of happiness to Thoreau's life as he described it in *Walden*.

happiness may actually be worse if it carries with it the baggage of unrealistic expectations.

Improving a Negative Balance

When one is extremely unhappy, too many of one's hedonic experiences are occurring close to the lower endpoints of their respective contexts, too few close to their upper endpoints. It is easy to identify the miseries, harder to get rid of them. We have each developed our own techniques for "tuning out" bad thoughts and escaping from bad situations.

When the best in the context is coming infrequently, this upper endpoint is not so easily identified. One must ask which among the possibilities would one truly enjoy. Is it some hoped-for success, the return of one's health, or of a lost love? The cure can take either of two directions: (a) letting go of this upper endpoint, or (b) changing one's life so that events close to this upper endpoint are experienced more often, perhaps by actually achieving some goal. Apart from the pleasures of anticipation (considered in the next chapter), the choice between these two directions should be governed by reality. What is the likelihood of actually letting go? What is the likelihood of achieving one's goal? Either route, if successful, would reduce the unhappiness, and either could shift the balance from unhappiness to happiness.

Letting Go. Time is said to be the great healer. As one comes to accept that the inflated hopes or expectations cannot be fulfilled, they drop from the context. The best of what remains becomes the upper endpoint of the newly restricted range, with a more positive overall balance. Letting go of unrealistic dreams or expectations is thus one route to happiness. But it is hard to let go as long as achievement of the desired conditions remains a possibility. The former *refused-nik* could not give up the unfavorable social comparisons as long as there remained a possibility of emigrating again, this time to the United States. So, too, with unpublished poets. Perhaps if all printing presses were to be closed down, their lives would be free of the dream that keeps them dissatisfied with not being published; they might then experience more of the intrinsic pleasures of creating poems, unburdened by any lack of recognition or "fulfillment."[14]

The loss of a loved one, perhaps life's cruelest grief, presents a particularly difficult challenge. The ritual of the traditional funeral is said to be an aid to recognizing that the loss is permanent, that the loved one will never return. This

---

[14]However, if their poems were published but unnoticed, the dissatisfaction might prove even greater. While remaining unpublished, poets can continue to anticipate the appreciation their poems will evoke. Barrow (1980) used the example of the unpublished poet to illustrate his claim that happiness requires the fulfillment of one's most crucial goals. Barrow's conception of happiness seems closer to Aristotle than to the strictly Utilitarian definition adopted here. His book provided a thoughtful review of philosophical writings on happiness, with emphasis on recent work.

recognition may be a necessary condition for letting go. We are temporarily ignoring pleasurable memories of the lost love. My mother-in-law, widowed in her 30s, was still dressing elegantly in her late 90s—in order, as she said, "to appear at her best on reuniting with her husband in heaven." Who can know whether these pleasurable anticipations balanced the suffering encouraged by not letting go? Or perhaps she had let go of this world, successfully segregating her hopes for the future world after death.

It may be even more difficult to accept the finality of a loss that comes not by death but by rejection, by infidelity, betrayal, or the realization that one's love is unrequited. In such cases, there is always a possibility, however unlikely, of winning the lost love back. This increases the difficulty of letting go.[15] The possibility of being loved again, sometimes greatly idealized, remains as the upper endpoint of a context in which the loss of love seems unendurable.

Letting go is difficult because it seems to mean giving up on happiness. One fears that life would be empty without the impossible dream. However, the fear is often misplaced: When this upper endpoint of the contextual range eventually drops from the context, the best of what remains becomes the new upper endpoint. As the best, it is experienced as very good, indeed: Insofar as events close to this new best are experienced with greater relative frequency, the proportion of ecstasy increases and the overall balance of satisfaction is improved. Figure 10.1 illustrates these relationships using the physical model of a teeter-totter.

This analysis seems implicit in the social philosophy of Ivan Illich, the liberation theologist, as when he criticized modern medical practice for establishing unrealistic hopes in third-world sufferers. Illich (1975) argued that patients are really on their own with most ailments, even in industrialized countries, and that most kinds of bodily suffering, including the aches and pains of aging, are made less supportable by the belief that somewhere there is a doctor with a cure. If people can accept the fact that no one else can help them, their sufferings actually lessen. The present analysis attributes this to a dropping of the unrealistic upper-endpoint representing hope for a cure. Illich concluded that although it is already too late for such a change in industrialized countries, we should try to spare Third-world peoples the misery resulting from unrealistic expectations of salvation from modern medicine.

Tuning Out.   One way of letting go is to banish an entire unhappy domain from one's life. For example, I used to get great pleasure from racing small sailing outriggers. Because this class was not very competitive, I was able to work my way up through the fleet until I was winning most of the races. As so

---

[15]I once described this psychology to a friend who had separated from his wife and children to escape from the Soviet Union (with little possibility of ever seeing them again) but who was still suffering from regret and guilt: "You would be happier if you could forget your family, fashioning a completely new life for yourself." He replied, quite properly, "Perhaps, but there are some things that are more important than happiness."

FIG. 10.1. Changes in the balance of happiness from letting go: Left balance tips slightly toward unhappiness because most experiences, represented as weights, are so far below upper end of contextual range, represented by plank; greater tipping of middle balance illustrates increased unhappiness commonly (but incorrectly) anticipated if upper-endpoint were dropped; right balance shows increase in happiness that would actually follow, for the same-sized plank now represents newly restricted range of experiences. Tipping moment proportional to skewing.

many do in their work or in other hierarchical domains, I then shifted to a more competitive type of sailboat, a developmental class of high performance catamarans raced primarily by the professional sailors who designed them. Starting in this new class, I was pleased whenever I did not finish last; but I expected to improve, as I had with the outrigger, and to become at least an occasional winner. It was not to be. If I improved at all, my competition must have improved just as rapidly. I became accustomed to finishing close to last, but it continued to be disappointing—for there always seemed to be the possibility of doing much better. Finally, with dissatisfaction predominating, I completely withdrew from racing. I have never missed it.

This kind of tuning out may be a workable alternative to success. Many students say that being graded is the worst part of college life. But one can tune out grades. As an undergraduate, I stuck determinedly to the principle of never picking up my grade reports. Years later, when I finally saw a transcript of my undergraduate record, I felt indignant with some of the low grades I had received; but these grades had not figured in my college experience at all. I had successfully eliminated what might otherwise have been an aggravating domain of my undergraduate years.

Another example, said to be experienced more often by women, is the discontent with one's own physical appearance. Current fashion sets a standard of slimness that few women can achieve.[16] In extreme cases, the effect may be threatening to survival, encouraging the self-induced starvation called anorexia nervosa. It would be difficult to resist the whole culture by tuning out this frustrating domain, as by avoiding people who openly value slimness. However,

---

[16]In the early 1980s, 80% of the coeds at the University of California, Los Angeles, confessed in a student poll to being disgusted by the sight of their own bodies. Now, some 10 years later, polls continue to report similar self-depreciation in this particular domain.

I once met a young woman who had, at least temporarily, employed an extreme version of this very tactic. As a Peace Corps Volunteer, she was assigned to an isolated atoll in the Pacific. Although extremely overweight by American standards, she became a veritable goddess on this island where the ideal weight for feminine attractiveness was remarkably heavier. Sadly, in contemporary societies of affluence, too many people become completely absorbed in losing weight— even joining programs designed to motivate them to diet. Given the discouraging long-term results of such efforts, the programs would be more useful if they helped people tune this domain right out of their lives.

Succeeding.   Letting go and tuning out suggest failure. Although they may often be the easiest way to deal with unhappiness, sometimes a more optimistic alternative is to try to increase the relative frequency of what is already at the top of the contextual range. I could have stuck with competitive sailing, people unhappy with their weight can go on diets, those disappointed in their career advancements can try harder. The popular advice to the abandoned lover is to find someone else, someone even better. Such ambitions do get fulfilled, sometimes.

To maximize the psychological sense of success, goals should be realistic. In the case of sailboat racing, my mistake was to shift to a racing class that was too competitive for my abilities. If I absolutely had to shift, it should have been to a fleet in which there was a better chance of again working my way up into the winners' bracket. Perpetual dieters can try to assess their natural weights, endeavoring to modify their eating and exercise to achieve not the ideal weights dictated by fashion but rather their own genetically programmed *set points.*[17]

Consider the interacting effects of the particular combination of genes with which a child is endowed and the particular social influences to which he or she happens to be exposed. The boy with an inherited gift for mathematics and a father in engineering or science is likely to be pushed toward that type of career. But regardless of career objectives, there are always crucial decisions to be made, such as choice of schooling. Having taught at one of the most intellectually elite of private colleges and also at several public universities of varying academic standards, I am impressed by the extraordinary differences between the intellectual demands these schools placed on their students. A level of performance that would be more than adequate at one school would be failing at another. Occasionally when focusing my lectures on the brightest of my honor students, my concern drifts to the lesser achievers in the same classroom, wondering whether they would have been happier in a less demanding environ-

---

[17]The extraordinary similarity in weight of identical twins, although separated at birth and raised in different environments with different attitudes toward weight, testifies to the overwhelming importance of hereditary factors (Bouchard et al., 1990).

ment.[18] Perhaps they would even have learned more in classes without the competition from those truly exceptional students who set the standards for honors classes. This is the irony of the concern over the standardized testing used to select between applicants for admission to college. Many high school students pay for special tutoring designed to enhance their scores on these aptitude tests. How unfortunate it would be if this tutoring really enabled them to overachieve on the test, hiding their actual lack of preparation, and thus dooming them to a program in which they are likely to become mired in mediocrity!

College students have to choose between different fields of study. Sometimes the choice is governed by interest and preparation, but too often the decisive factor is a mistaken notion about the best road to success. For example, when in the early 1980s the Master's Degree in Business Administration (the MBA) opened doors to high income careers in finance, undergraduates flocked to departments of economics, believing this major would facilitate their admission to an MBA program. Efforts by professors and counselors to convince undergraduates that business schools did not favor economics majors proved unavailing. Perhaps there should have been more sympathy when the high-paying positions on Wall Street suddenly evaporated, for to adjust to the harsh reality of unemployment in a context of financial success must be an unhappiness similar to a loss of love or health.[19]

In the world of business, as in academia, there should be a good match between the candidate and the demands of the position. Unfortunately, there is rarely sufficient information to make the best decision, either from the standpoint of employer or employee. The claim here is for a more realistic assessment of the future contexts in which the good and bad of the career will be experienced. For example, when considering future income, it is not the absolute level that should dominate the choice but rather the place that income is likely to have in the context in which it will be experienced. When the high average incomes in professions like law or medicine or investment banking are compared with the dizzying heights of income possible in such fields, it can be understood why the resulting sense of affluence may be diminished—perhaps even far below what would have been experienced in a lower paying field, such as civil service or teaching.

SUMMARY

Concrete examples illustrate the application of the contextual theory of happiness to everyday problems. Beginning with the tug-of-war between success and happiness, the emphasis is on separating concepts often assumed to be inseparably

---

[18]Marsh, in his work on the big fish in the small pond (e.g., Marsh & Parker, 1984) demonstrated how the scholastic context determines students' perceptions of their own abilities and achievements.

[19]*The Bonfire of the Vanities* (Wolfe, 1987) presented a humorously poignant account of a successful Wall Street bond salesman who loses his job as a result of his own imprudence. The novel showed how this loss of career was much more traumatic because his commissions had been so high.

correlated. Just as with justice or love, happiness depends not on absolute levels of preference, but rather on relational considerations, such as the direction of movement on the ladder of success. Stress was placed on the dangers of sacrificing happiness in one domain to promote it in another and also of seeking an unrealistically high level of happiness when life is already good. Increasing the amount of time devoted to the happier domains is one practical way to improve the overall balance of pleasure over pain. An unhappy balance can be improved by letting go of an upper endpoint that is experienced too infrequently or by tuning out a frequently experienced lower endpoint or even an entire unhappy domain. A more optimistic alternative is to work toward goals that are eminently achievable, remembering that the pleasure of any achievement depends upon the context in which it is experienced.

11

The Imagination as the Theater for Happiness

THE ROLE OF THE IMAGINATION

The contextual theory of happiness focuses attention on how pleasures of the imagination could substantially increase the overall balance of pleasure over pain. For example, anticipations of success occurred on one half of the trials in one of the elaborated versions of the computerized Happiness Game. Although reducing the pleasantness of actual earnings, the cumulative average payoff more than doubled when pleasures of anticipation were averaged in. This enhancement of overall happiness could have been even greater if, instead of entering the contexts for actual earnings, these anticipations had been experienced in their own separate contexts restricted just to imaginary events. Insofar as we have greater control over imaginary than over real-world events, we can more easily establish with them the negative skewing conducive to happiness.

Examining my own life, the great bulk of pleasures and pains seem to occur in my private world of anticipations, memories, and fantasies. This is probably true for most people. Ruminating about happiness, Mark Twain (1962a) wrote:

> What a wee little part of a person's life are his acts and his words! His real life is led in his head, and is known to none but himself. (p. 111)

Leo Tolstoy, so good at getting into the heads of other people, has his fictional characters in *War and Peace* experience the great bulk of their pleasures and pains in their imaginations.[1]

---

[1]However, none of his adults seem particularly happy. Tolstoy grants happiness primarily to children! In another testimonial to the role of imaginary thoughts in happiness, Powys (1935) wrote in his *Art of Happiness*:

> The more we consider this matter of the mind's control—of even its partial control—over its thoughts, the more we are compelled to recognize that these thoughts are intimately associated with the fact of our being happy or unhappy.

I have tried to get friends to estimate what percentage of their own hedonic experiences are purely imaginary. Just phrasing the question creates confusing difficulties, as when trying to explain that a crucial characteristic of one's own imaginary experiences is that they cannot be experienced directly by anyone else. This informal survey produced an average estimate of around 80%. However the range of individual estimates of the percentage of pleasures and pains occurring in their imaginations varied all the way from 0% to 100%! The estimate of 0 was given me by a French psychiatrist who asserted that only a psychotic would live any important part of his life in the imagination. The highest estimate came from a mystically inclined author of a book on Buddhism, reflecting her idealist meta-physics in which all experiences are imaginary—whether hedonic or not. Readers who try to make their own estimates are likely to agree that one cannot be very confident about them. With this caveat, my own impression is that *for most people the great majority of hedonic experiences occur in the realm of the imagination.*

One friend speculated that the role of her imaginary experiences increased as she grew older. Especially while suffering through a long illness, her pleasures had come mainly from recalling earlier experiences. However, it seems to me that the hedonic experiences of children are just as likely to occur in the imagination. From the age of 12, I delivered newspapers on my bicycle each day after school. Sometimes, returning home with an empty sack, I would anxiously wonder where I had left all the papers. The actual deliveries had become largely automatic, my mind being completely absorbed in fantasies, imaginary scenarios based on the day's news, on the history I was learning at school, or on a make-believe sport performed by teams of professional athletes on motorized bicycles. These fanta-sies were certainly more evocative of pleasure than were the 7 miles of suburban streets over which I pedaled each afternoon. This type of daydreaming is not restricted to childhood. Now, while driving, I may suddenly be called back to reality by my wife who asks, "What are you grinning about?" My facial expression reveals to her that I am immersed in a private world, unrelated to the objective events of the moment. Perhaps I am reliving some amusing experience from the past. Perhaps I am fantasizing some future triumph. But often my imaginary hedonic experiences have only the most tenuous relationships with anything that has happened or will ever happen: They seem most likely to occur in repetitive situations that do not demand close attention to the external world (driving may not be the safest setting for this type of activity), and they seem to be encouraged by mild physical exercise, as when strolling or bicycling at a lazy, undemanding pace that does not shift my attention to the rigors of physical exertion. Priestley (1937) described a visit in the 1930s to a kind of sweatshop in England where young women repeated the same dressmaking operations throughout the working day. When Priestly asked why the tasks could not be varied to reduce the tedium, the manager pointed to the pinups of movie stars on the walls, asserting that the women preferred repetitive operations that freed their minds for daydreaming![2]

---

[2]Described in *Self-selected Essays.*

In the hypothetical tabulation of the overall balance of happiness, the pleasures and pains of imaginary events must be averaged in with those of events in the real world. Insofar as the hedonic experiences of the imagination are more frequent and include the most intense pleasures or pains, their influence on the overall average must be considerable. If one really has more control over these private scenarios, a wiser shaping of one's imagination would be the most practical way to happiness.

POSSIBILITIES FOR CONTROL

Marcus Aurelius, the Stoic philosopher who became Emperor of Rome, wrote: "We each can think what we wilt."[3] Certainly, we each know that we have considerable control of our imaginations. In our choice of reading, for example, we establish whether this imaginary world is going to be calmly philosophical or full of exciting physical adventures. In my own recreational reading of fiction, I return repeatedly to the same books.[4] Knowing what I am getting allows me greater control of my own imagination. Television viewers are immersed in a quasi-real, albeit two-dimensional world created by the imaginations of others. Insofar as viewers are stimulated to construct, later, their own scenarios, their control may be largely in choosing those programs that provide this stimulation. However, because television programs are designed to discourage switching to other stations, they bombard us with everchanging (limbic) stimulation, effectively interfering with our own fantasizing. Most such fantasies occur later, as when children emulate what they have seen on television. However, the decline in academic test scores may be due, in part, to the inhibition of creative thought while actually viewing the programs, an inhibition that generalizes to other activities, such as reading and problem solving, that require more perseverance with a single topic.

We do have at least some control of the purely imaginary scenarios we construct for ourselves: we can create magnificent triumphs for ourselves, and we can usually terminate those scenarios that are steeped in failure. However, we cannot always escape from depressing or awful thoughts that seem to intrude of their own accord. Lack of control is clearest for nighttime dreaming and also for the hypnogogic state intermediate between sleep and waking. Years ago, I corresponded with a firm believer in the notion that pleasures and pains *must* be exactly balanced, regardless of what happens. In response to my experimental results demonstrating that negatively skewed distributions increased the overall mean rating of pleasantness, he replied that in that case painful dreams while sleeping would exactly balance the surplus pleasure of waking life! Although his belief in an equal balance was as completely a priori as mine once had been, it

---

[3]Quoted by Pater (1934/1963).

[4]Rereading too many times both Dostoevsky's *The Brothers Karamazov* and *The Idiot*, both of which have the power to reach into my soul.

would be interesting to know if there were indeed a correlation between the pleasantness of waking life and the unpleasantness of dreams.

As constructors of happy scenarios, we should not aspire to Utopias so unrealistically hopeful that all is sweetness and light. Insofar as our pleasures of the imagination are not experienced in real-life contexts, they depend on contexts that represent imaginary events: Daydreams experienced solely in a context of other daydreams cannot make much of a positive contribution to overall happiness unless the context also includes an occasional painful experience. For the same reason, I doubt that we could ever isolate certain wonderful events from more normal activities, preserving them from adaptation and preventing them from diminishing our pleasure from lesser events. For example, it has been proposed that there could be special holiday feasts that would not be compared with anything else—events that would not evoke or be part of any context.[5] But a basic implication of the contextual theory of happiness is that events are pleasant if and only if they occupy the more preferred positions in an hedonic context. With only themselves as context, the same events would be neutral, neither pleasant nor unpleasant. When experienced in some more varied context, they must diminish the pleasantness of lesser events experienced in the same context. This seems part of the reason why birthdays and holidays, though so delightful for children who experience them in a context of normal days, can be disappointing for adults who are more likely to experience them in a context of other holidays. The same objection applies to any notion of establishing isolated imaginary events that would be extremely pleasant in themselves but would not diminish the pleasantness of other events, real or imaginary.

The arguments for establishing negatively skewed distributions of real-life events also apply to conceptually isolated, private experiences of the imagination. If we somehow manage to eliminate the "bad thoughts," the worst of those that remain become the new bad thoughts, as painful as the former worst. And if the skewing of the imaginary events is thereby reduced, the overall balance becomes more neutral.[6]

---

[5]The holiday example was proposed by Brickman and Campbell (1971) and cited by Kahneman and Varey (1991) as an optimistic possibility for escaping the "hedonic treadmill" of a perfectly even balance between pleasure and pain. Tversky and Griffin (1991) also argued for trying to isolate extremely pleasant events so that these would not reduce the pleasantness of lesser events.

[6]Concern for scientific control discourages the study of imaginary experiences because they are so much less constrained by the immediate physical environment. Nevertheless, experimental subjects have occasionally been asked to imagine stimuli that are never actually presented. Such research has demonstrated the expected contextual effect on hedonic judgments of asking subjects to imagine the most pleasant color they could think of (Hunt & Volkman, 1937) and on moral judgments of asking subjects to imagine something worse than those acts of behavior actually presented (e.g., Dermer et al., 1979; McGarvey, 1943). The stimuli for such research were often written descriptions of real-world events, that is, symbols that presumably stimulate the imagination. Research with this type of stimulus produces the usual range-frequency effects of context upon affect, in this case a context in which imaginary events are represented (e.g., Parducci, 1968; Wedell & Parducci, 1988). Experiments providing this type of test of range-frequency principles are reviewed in chapter 5.

Just as there is no need to seek misfortune in our interactions with the real world, there may be no need to invent imaginary misfortunes. The trick for happiness is to ensure that, whatever they might be, the worst of our fantasies occur only rarely, whereas the best occur with high frequency. Habitual anticipations of failure may be the most common mistake. When realistic, such fears can sometimes help us avoid failure in the real world; too often, they merely weight our overall balance of happiness toward the negative. Shakespeare's *Julius Ceasar* has the famous line: "Cowards die many times before their deaths; The valient never taste of death but once" (Barlett, 1982, p. 215). When such apprehensions predominate, we can attempt an active process of tuning out—either by trying to escape completely from that domain of experience or by concentrating on the possibilities for success.

Although daydreams are typically experienced in contexts of other daydreams, they may also enter the contexts of real-life experiences. For example, disappointment at falling short of a goal that has previously been achieved only in one's imagination suggests that the imagined achievement is part of the present context. However, we saw that this type of disappointment can be more than balanced by the pleasures of imagined success, doubling the overall happiness of experiences in the combined context of imaginary and real achievements.

Daydreaming Versus Escapism

If pleasant flights of the imagination can increase our sum total of happiness, why is such daydreaming denigrated as inconsistent with a realistic approach to life? It is said that daydreams are impractical. However, even the daydreams of children can have practical, real-world consequences. My paper-route fantasies sometimes served as self-organized reviews of the history I was learning in school. These many years later, I rehearse my lectures while driving to the campus, even responding to arguments or questions from imaginary students or colleagues. This can be an efficient method of preparation. More generally, the imagining of different possible solutions is a crucial step toward the solution of problems. But even if daydreams had no instrumental value for changing real-world events, their pleasures are important contributors to happiness.

This emphasis on the possible benefits of fantasy is in apparent conflict with the belief that daydreams are neurotic escapes from reality, as in the opinion of the French psychiatrist cited at the beginning of this chapter. Fear of such escapism may be another manifestation of the view that it is money that counts rather than the happiness that money can buy (or cannot buy!). The escape into fantasy may also be seen as a failure to deal with real problems, a failure that makes the problems worse, with consequent unhappiness. Such concerns argue for greater control of one's fantasies, making them useful in dealing with real-world problems. However, in assigning this instrumental role to the imagination we should remember that its intrinsic pleasures may play a bigger role in happiness than do any real-world outcomes the imagination might facilitate.

Perhaps just because we cannot know what other people are imagining, we tend to talk about daydreaming in terms of those objectively observable events that stimulate the imagination, like the reading aloud of fairy tales to young children. Although enjoyed for their own sake, fairy tales may also provide the more enduring benefit of encouraging children to make up their own stories. Do shepherd children, who can still be seen tending flocks in third-world countries, make their own isolation more pleasant by fantasizing stories for themselves, even if they have never been read to or told stories made up by others?[7]

Living Fully

If relatively few of our experiences are hedonic and those that are hedonic are lived mostly in the imagination, increasing the role of the imagination would seem an important method for increasing happiness. This depends on whether, for the theoretical measure of happiness, the algebraic total of all pleasures and pains is divided by the *total* duration of time in question, perhaps more than 100 hours per week, or whether it is divided by only the summed durations of those experiences that are genuinely hedonic, perhaps only several hours per week. In our considerations of happiness in everyday life, we are typically concerned with the total duration. The more hedonic experience we can cram in the better—even if the average pleasantness of the hedonic experience is not affected. Happiness would be enhanced by living more fully. However, living more fully does not necessarily mean sleeping less, being more conscious, doing more things. Living more fully requires more pleasures and pains, more of the kinds of adventures that are experienced hedonically. If pleasures and pains are experienced primarily in the imagination, a fuller life means living more in the imagination. Adventures in the real world contribute to this measure of happiness primarily by stimulating memories, anticipations, and fantasies.

Stimulating the Imagination

As adults, reading to ourselves can be a major stimulus for fantasy. Hemingway's boyhood stories catalyzed vividly aesthetic daydreams for me, particularly when visiting the North Woods country of Michigan in which these stories are set. Similarly, Tolstoy's description in *The Cossacks* (1887) of the solitary hunter pushing through the thick brush by the river, by stimulating a vision of myself as a rugged outdoorsman, added pleasurable romance to my experiences with similar outdoor obstacles that I would otherwise have found disagreeable.

---

[7]This is intended as a rhetorical question, but it has sometimes been claimed, no doubt falsely, that there was little experience of romantic love before the later Middle Ages when the troubadours began to sing its praises. However, the Greeks wrote of romantic love 1500 years earlier (e.g., Plato's *Symposium*, 360BC).

The stereotypic presentations of love in contemporary romance novels are supposed to stimulate the imaginations of their mostly female readers. The more frankly erotic literature, written mostly for men, is designed to stimulate sexual fantasies. But the enormous individual differences in sexual interests means that what is erotic for some readers may be comical or even disgusting for others. Do sexual fantasies diminish the pleasure from traditional sexual activities? This must sometimes happen; but by being experienced during traditional sex, the fantasies can also increase its pleasures.

Erotic literature is an example of powerful stimulation of the imagination by a purely symbolic source. But as students cramming from textbooks will attest, not all reading has the power to stimulate the reader's imagination. When it does not, when students cannot relate what they are reading to their own framework of thinking, they are much less likely to remember the author's points. Mortimer Adler's *How to Read a Book* (1940) prescribed creative participation by readers, urging us to fill the page margins with questions and counter-arguments in imaginary dialogue with the author. Although Adler's method for stimulating the argumentative imagination is so time-consuming that we could not read many books with the diligence he recommended, following his method would make an author's ideas much more available for our own purposes.

Music is a universal stimulant for the imagination, even for the least musical. Programmatic music is composed to evoke imaginative embroidery by the listener. However, when listening to classical music that is unfamiliar and difficult, I often become engrossed in thoughts that seem completely unrelated to the music, even to the point of imagining possible solutions to technical problems that have been bothering me. A more musical listener might have richly aesthetic responses to the same pieces, with strong hedonic components evoked by the physical relationships between the musical notes. And even the least musical can experience the pleasure of singing or humming silently to oneself in what seems to be a purely imaginary activity. For maximal overall pleasure within its own domain, music must yield primarily pleasant experiences punctuated with occasional unpleasant ones, reflecting a distribution of musical events that is negatively skewed along the listener's preference dimension for musical experiences. Composers deliberately introduce frustrations to enhance the satisfaction when the melody is finally resolved. But if the stopping short of resolution is too frequent, the overall balance is likely to be negative—at least initially. It is a common observation that in music familiarity breeds *content*—what is on first hearing an exercise in frustration can, with repeated exposure, become delightfully satisfying. Experienced listeners learn to anticipate the eventual resolution, and these pleasurable anticipations can turn an initially negative hedonic balance into a positive one. Eventually, as with even one's favorite foods, there can be too much of the same music; it is then that familiarity does breed *contempt*. Experience changes the position of any particular music on the listener's scale of preference. People do not have to be told to vary their diets, culinary or musical.

Talking with other people is another, almost universal stimulant for the imagination. The gossip they relate may enhance our own self-image. Sometimes we acquire new and useful ideas, and what we hear may inspire hopes and fears about our own condition. Thus the immediate pleasures and pains of conversation may be slight in comparison with those we experience later in our own private ruminations, stimulated by something we heard or may even have found ourselves saying.

Physical adventures can also catalyze the imagination. The solitary trip in the wilderness may not have been all that satisfying, but the painful loneliness of the actual adventure can be more than balanced by the pleasures of thinking and talking about it later and looking forward to doing it again. Each year, I join a couple of friends in what cyclists call a *century*, bicycling a prescribed 100 miles up and down hills, sometimes with wind and rain. After 60 miles or so, I begin asking myself why I am doing it; after 80 miles, no longer able to locate a single part of my anatomy that does not ache, I resolve "never again!" But the next year, there I am, back again for the same ride, excited by the challenge and by memories of the previous ride that no doubt grow happier with each recollection or retelling.

Some people claim to live for their memories: the actual events may have been all too brief, but their repeated re-imaginings can make a substantial addition to happiness. It is conventional to scoff at older people when they seem to live in the past, but where is the problem if they enjoy this type of reliving? My own daydreams still tend more toward the future, anticipating the next adventure. However, these pleasures of anticipation are typically stimulated by memories, and I keep going back to the same places and activities—just as I do to the same books.

Religion provides for some people the most powerful stimulus to their imaginations. Repetitious prayer may function much like mild exercise or music, except that the images evoked are more often religious. Testimonials on the hedonic balance of religious experiences vary from one extreme to another, from the medieval Christian's emphasis on present misery to the born-again evangelical's claim to happiness at finding Jesus. In reports by medieval Christian mystics, the pleasures and pains vary with the degree of experienced closeness to God, from abject despair when feeling forsaken by God to the ecstasy of felt oneness.[8] To classify these experiences as imaginary, in the sense that others cannot share directly what the mystic is experiencing, does not make them any less real; nor should we doubt their hedonic intensity. However, the balance of ecstasy over misery would not be an attractive measure of happiness for the mystic who defines happiness as either serving or achieving unity with God.

---

[8]The *Cloud of the Unknowing* (Anonymous, @900/1957) gave a prescription for achieving the mystical state of religious ecstasy, one involving prayer, self-mortification, and long periods of misery before experiencing the sudden (but all too brief) ecstatic union with God; see also Huxley's (1937) *Ends and Means*.

Some religious sects exalt happiness in the here and now, claiming that one's own happiness is facilitated by helping others to be happy—as by living a good life. Whether people are actually happy in the religious domains of their lives is governed by the same range-frequency considerations applied to other domains. What counts is not the absolute level of altruistic deed or even the absolute level of imagined altruism, but rather the skewing of the frequency distribution of experiences in this domain, real or imaginary. Religious people can have an overall sense of praiseworthiness to the degree that they are frequently aware of the best among their own intentions and only rarely aware of the worst, even if their own best is not particularly praiseworthy by the standards of their religion. However, such a favorable balance would depend on their failure to incorporate their religion's more exalted standards into their own personal contexts for self-assessment. This suggests that even the worst sinners can, in principle, experience a gratifying sense of their own virtue. Again, there is a crucial distinction between those contexts that represent the standards of others and contexts that represent different positions on one's own scale of preference. Although we may give lip service to the standards of others or of religious institutions, it is against the backdrop of our own hedonic contexts that the drama of happiness is played out.

In this post-industrial age, as in perhaps most earlier periods of history, the imagination tends to focus less upon religion than upon the acquisition of material goods. How nice it would be to have a house of one's own, to buy a new car, to send one's children to a prestigious university! It is easy to be contemptuous of consumerism, for example of those affluent matrons in Beverly Hills who each day tour their favorite clothing stores, often without making any purchases. But such longing for more, imagining how one might look in a new dress or with new accessories, may constitute a happy domain of experience. As with every domain, it has its ups and downs. There is the pleasure of the anticipated possession, the pain of not being able to afford it or of realizing that it would not flatter one's public image. Countless advertisements on television are designed to stimulate imaginative activity about what it would be like to possess the products that are being promoted, very likely providing more stimulation for fantasy than do the regular shows these commercials interrupt. The ads try to make expensive products seem affordable, and perhaps many viewers can exclude from these fantasies the practical concern with affordability.

We can be very different in what stimulates our imaginations. As with reading, we each discover for ourselves what is most evocative and the degree to which the resulting imaginative experiences are pleasant or unpleasant. Whether stimulated by reading, television, music, adventure, conversation, religion, or proffered material goods, the possibilities for control seem to be greater than what is typically achieved in real-world domains. Events in the physical world are often beyond our control: Success is not always guaranteed by hard work and motivation, and bad luck can rob us of the fruits of our labor. However, we are free to fantasize success or love or whatever else we desire.

As illustrated by players of the computerized Happiness Game, it is not easy to recognize what maximizes overall happiness. If experienced frequently enough, pleasurable fantasies can help substantially. But even a painful scenario may be a positive factor when it extends downward the contextual range of our fantasies, thereby increasing the pleasantness of subsequent daydreams and sometimes also of real-world events. The trick is to control our fantasies so that the most frequent events, real or imaginary, are high in the contexts in which we experience them.

Isolation of Imaginary Domains

One might think that fantasies, memories, and anticipations enter the contexts for real-world judgments. This must happen, at least occasionally. Children sometimes confuse fairy stories with reality. Adults may compare their own mundane marriages with the exciting love affairs described in magazines and novels. If readers believe that the excitement portrayed in such tales could just as well be theirs, the fictional highs may be represented in their own, real-world contexts. This could reduce the excitement and pleasure of their own marriages. Unless these imaginary highpoints were experienced with relatively high frequency, their overall effect would be unhappy. However, it is also possible that, as with the TV serials centering on normal family life, this exposure to something better might actually improve the behavior of dysfunctional families, encouraging happier family life.

When a drama (or melodrama) is a powerful depiction of misfortune, it can produce the catharsis cited by Aristotle to account for the appeal of tragedy. Some women claim to feel better after "a good cry." One's own life may seem much brighter after the emotional immersion in the darkness of a more universal tragedy.

More typically, people compartmentalize such fictional representations in separate domains that do not affect their pleasures in real-world events. For example, consider the impoverished children of our inner cities, living on welfare with perhaps only a very young and marginally dysfunctional mother to guide them, children who spend the majority of their waking hours watching the television programs that so often center on upper middle-class families. Do they compare their own lot with these "role models?" How often do they entertain the possibility of such a life for themselves? Much of what they are viewing must seem so beyond the range of possibilities that it could have little effect on their own pleasures and pains. Teachers concerned to improve the chances for such children encourage them to imagine themselves successful in breaking out of their poverty. When such encouragement is unrealistic, as when students poor at math are encouraged to become doctors or when very young athletes are encouraged to aspire to professional careers in sports, it seems a recipe for disappointment. But again, it is always possible that the pleasures of imagined success outweigh the almost inevitable letdown.

Commercial television depends on selling advertising time to companies hoping to increase sales by enticing displays of their products. Do these opportunities for "window shopping" leave viewers dissatisfied with the lesser goods they already possess? My impression is that viewers' pleasurable fantasies of new acquisitions are more likely to be segregated into different contexts than those representing the hard experiences of reality. Social philosophers who bemoan the discontent that such daydreaming is supposed to generate may be endowing the advertisers with powers they do not possess.[9] This is a crucial question that readers can answer for themselves. Does the old car really seem less adequate after seeing ads for the latest models? As with other examples of relative deprivation, one is more likely to be discontent with what one already has when purchasing the new product seems entirely feasible.[10] If you believed yourself overly susceptible to such influence, the obvious defense would be to tune it out, junk the television set, and avoid people who flaunt possessions that you do not have. On the other hand, if the pleasure of imagining new possessions outweighed any resulting sense of relative deprivation, advertising would seem well designed for your happiness.

Controlling Moods

Bad moods are often initiated by experiences that are unusually painful. Other experiences then become less pleasant, even experiences in other domains. This negative cast to life may last for only a few minutes or hours, but some people suffer its ravages for days or even months. So, too, with the good moods initiated by unusually pleasant experiences that enhance the pleasantness of everything else. This reverses the usual contextual effect in which an extreme experience pushes more moderate experiences in the opposite direction. Whatever the reason for this reversal, the ability to escape bad moods and encourage good ones would be conducive to happiness.

One explanation of mood is that the initiating event combines with other events one is experiencing, pulling the preference value of the combination in its own direction.[11] For example, failing an examination can put a student in a bad mood, souring reactions to other exams, to grades, to school in general, and even

---

[9]I was surprised to be assured by a top advertising executive that 85% of ads on television are totally ineffective.

[10]See the analyses of *relative deprivation* by Crosby (1972) and by Stouffer et al. (1949).

[11]An interpretation more obviously consistent with the contextual theory is that the bad mood is due to some wonderful experience that, until dropping from the context, sours whatever else is experienced in the same context. However, most bad moods seem too pervasive for this interpretation, souring experiences in many different domains, presumably governed by an even greater number of contexts. Possibly, the bad mood might reflect a generalized disposition to add extreme upper endpoints to a great variety of contexts. Alternatively, the bad mood might be a general disposition to attend to the worst aspects of events or to evoke the most dreadful fantasies.

to other domains. When, as in this case, the initiating event is taken as a sign of more general unworthiness, it can intrude itself in any domain that evokes judgments of self-esteem. Even the pleasure of friendship with fellow students is reduced, perhaps because these friends, exuding pride in their own success, remind the student of his recent failure. The low preference value of the remembered failure is averaged with the higher preference value of friendly companionship before their joint value is judged.[12] To control this bad mood, the student would have to stop recalling his failure while with his school friends. However, he may not realize how much this memory is blending with other experiences; if he could recognize that it is the basis for his bad mood, he would be in a better position to tune it out. For example, he might spend more time with other friends who are not students. But sometimes we cannot identify the event that initiated the bad mood. It may even be a chemical condition of the body that reduces the pleasantness of whatever we are experiencing.[13]

Good moods are the other side of the coin, enhancing ordinary events that are experienced in conjunction with our memory of an extremely pleasant initiating event. This reliving in our imagination can thus "hitchhike" on other events, even those in other domains. A familiar example is the enhancement of the pleasures of male bonding by relating some success that we have had. Unless we are boring our friends, this manifestation of a good mood seems intrinsically beneficial without requiring any calculated effort; the enhancement of pleasure just comes naturally. However, if the initiating success created a new upper endpoint of the contextual range of conversations with friends, it might prove harmful in the long run—especially after it has ceased to be recalled with relish and could not be related to the same friends again without eliciting protests.

Depression.   Because depression is the extreme example of uncontrolled mood, it is tempting to apply the same sort of analysis to it. Disorders of mood have replaced schizophrenia as the favorite diagnosis for admissions to psychiatric hospitals, but problems with experiencing pleasure are also characteristic of schizophrenics. The role of heredity looms large here, and the success of antidepressant drugs encourages the belief that there is something wrong with the chemistry of such patients. If there is, it seems to result in cognitive tendencies toward self-blame and hopelessness. This comes across as paramount in the able review of the literature on depression by Gotlib and Hammen (1992). One of the cognitive interpretations that they cited, that by Rehm (1977), attributes depres-

---

[12]It has been demonstrated experimentally that the values of the component stimuli are averaged before the overall judgment is made (e.g., Anderson, 1981; Parducci, Thaler, & Anderson, 1968; Wedell, Parducci, & Geiselman, 1987). This averaging of stimuli was described by Tversky and Griffin (1991) to explain how an earlier event affects subjects' estimates of the present event, with the relative contribution of the two events depending on their similarity.

[13]The partial success of pharmacological interventions is often cited as evidence for the underlying role of body chemistry, particularly of the neurotransmitters.

sion to the setting of goals that are so unreasonably high as to be practically unobtainable. Such an interpretation would seem to treat depressives as extreme cases of a problem shared by relatively normal individuals. Most of us set goals that are unrealistically high, whether we are trying to lose weight, become rich, or stave off aging. This produces unhappiness unless the pleasures of imagined success outweigh the suffering of perpetually falling short of our own standards. But depressives seem unable to imagine success. The review by Gottlib and Hammen suggests only modest benefits from current cognitive therapies. However, they note the heterogeneous and perhaps inappropriate training of the therapists. Would depressives be helped by an understanding of the contextual theory of happiness, particularly of its implication that one's absolute level of success in any domain is not what counts for happiness and that constant highs are no more possible than constant lows?

IMAGINED MISFORTUNES AND COUNTERFACTUALS

When memory of an unusually bad experience sours events in other contexts by combining with them, the souring is due to a change in the preference value of what is being judged rather than to a change in context. This is to be distinguished from the more usual case, the one emphasized throughout this volume, in which an event that extends the contextual range downward increases the net happiness of all events experienced in the same context.[14] This extreme lower endpoint could be an outcome-evoked counterfactual, as when winning $200 in the pseudo-gambling experiment evoked the possibility of losing $200 as the opposite contextual endpoint. In the prisoner example, having one day of enforced fasting each week might evoke the possibility of an even more severe deprivation, perhaps weeks on bread and water. Imagining this extended fast might be more dreadful for the prisoner than actually having to endure it.[15] The simplest assumption is that such counterfactuals cannot enter an hedonic context unless they have already been experienced hedonically in the imagination, in this case painfully.

In the early development of psychoanalysis, Freud attributed cures to the cathartic effects of reliving painful childhood events in the imagination, even though he came to believe that these childhood events were counterfactuals—

---

[14]In a version of the computerized Happiness Game reported in chapter 9, the addition of −99 as a permanent contextual endpoint to the 0–99 distribution of outcomes yielded a cumulative average payoff of +170. This is more than three times higher than when the endpoints were fixed at 0 and 99. The cumulative average payoff would remain almost as high, +165, if the −99 also had to be experienced on 1% of the trials.

[15]In remarkable testimonial to people's powers of adaptation, dieters consuming only 400 calories a day typically report that the painful hunger pangs have largely disappeared by the end of the first week of this extreme deprivation.

that they had never occurred. When these "cures" turned out to be only temporary, he concluded that catharsis was not enough. The contextual theory of happiness suggests that the reliving of childhood trauma in these analytic sessions would make less painfully frightening anything else experienced in the same context. However, if as in a bad mood or depression the "remembered" trauma become part of how patients view their parents or how they experience other people who they identify with their parents, the overall effects may be far from beneficial. There now seems little reason to believe that simply dredging up childhood trauma, real or imagined, disposes people toward happiness.[16]

Playing Without Paying?

A contextual representation experienced only in the imagination, and then only rarely, could enhance the pleasantness of other events at the cost of relatively little pain. Consider how this might work in the computerized Happiness Game. One of the player's options is to send the hypothetical salesman off bicycling with his friends. Arising early when it is still dark and cold, the young man's expectations are low. Once on the road, these painful anticipations remain part of his context, enhancing the pleasantness of the actual ride. However, he may have paid in advance for this pleasure with his painful anticipation of how cold the ride would be. Thus, to enhance the overall balance of happiness, the painful anticipation would have to be very brief relative to the pleasures of the actual ride and any enjoyable memories the cyclist might later have of the ride.

When the ride turns out to be better than expected, the context may be augmented by the painful possibility, experienced only fleetingly, that it could just as well have been worse than expected. The bicycle rider may have thought to himself: "How lovely to have this warming sun! It could have turned out even worse than I had feared, with perhaps a freezing downpour." By extending the range much farther downward, this counterfactual enhances the pleasantness of whatever else is experienced in the same context. When the pain of establishing the new lower end point is suffered only briefly, there is considerable increase in the sum total of pleasure. The increase is greater the longer this extreme counterfactual continues to define the lower contextual endpoint for later experiences, such as other bike rides, without having to be experienced again each time.[17]

Extremely negative counterfactuals that enter hedonic contexts without ever having been experienced would seem outside our conscious control. Thus, we

---

[16]Eysenck's (1952) laudably skeptical conclusion from his review of the evidence on psychoanalytic outcomes seems not to have been outdated by subsequent research.

[17]In the test cited above in footote 14, the -99 is assumed to be always in the context but never itself experienced. If it had to be experienced every 10th trial, the cumulative average payoff would drop from $+170$ to $+118$; if it had to be experienced only every 100th trial, the drop would be only to $+165$. Both the $+170$ and $+165$ are close (but probably only coincidentally) to the level of happiness reported by the average American.

might not be able to do anything to either encourage or inhibit them. Indeed, unexperienced positive counterfactuals might be as frequent as negative ones. For example, the weather could have turned out to be much better than it actually did, perhaps with a sudden, powerful tailwind to ease the cyclist's climb up the mountain. If this logical possibility were stretching his contextual range upward, even the warming sun might not be all that delightful; thus, if he had never even experienced the pleasure of imagining this counterfactual, its contribution would be entirely negative. Computer simulation of such nonexperienced counterfactuals that temporarily extend *both* ends of the context illustrate a remarkable dampening of feeling, with much less use of extreme categories. Although producing a more believable frequency distribution of category use, the net effect is to shift the overall balance of happiness toward neutral.

Perhaps at least some pain must be experienced if a counterfactual is to become the lower endpoint of an hedonic context. Once it is represented in the context, it may keep its place there indefinitely, with only very occasional and very brief experiences of pain. The end of this chapter is concerned with how a realistic attitude toward the possibility of misfortune might foster the presence of such counterfactuals, improving the overall balance by providing extreme lower endpoints with relatively little pain.

If the imagined misfortune must be experienced in all its horror before it can be incorporated into an hedonic context, then this pain must be averaged in with the pleasures that it enhances in the assessment of the overall effect upon happiness. I can still remember what happened after a minor accident in my childhood. A teenage uncle undertook to treat my small cut with tincture of iodine, a disinfectant I greatly feared because of its painful sting. To mask this sting, he pinched my arm ferociously at the exact moment of applying the iodine. Then, to mollify my resulting outrage, he pointed out that I had not even felt the sting! But I could not see any gain in the tradeoff, the pinch hurting as much as the sting that it was masking. This is the problem with deliberately exposing oneself to painful and potentially tragic events in the hope of improving the rest of life; and because the conditions for tragedy persist and their pain is experienced much longer than a pinch, they can tip the balance much farther toward unhappiness.

There are many types of information that, although apparently relevant, do not affect our judgments. We read about the wealth of an Arabian oil sheik without feeling deprived ourselves. This is especially true if we are not Arabian, are not in the oil business, and never had the opportunity to enter it. In the more humble case of the possibility that the sun would not have come out, the cyclist cannot miss the pertinence of this possibility to his own situation. The sun might well not have come out for this particular ride which could have been spoiled by a freezing rain.

Pollyanna's "Game."   We sometimes think we feel better after deliberately imagining something worse that could really have happened but did not. This is like the game played by the fictional Pollyanna who eased the burden of her own misfortunes by imagining how much worse off others were. This notion is so simple and so analogous to downward-looking social comparisons that it must have been tried by everyone. If it were clear that it worked, would we not all be playing Pollyanna's game rather than smiling condescendingly when someone else tries to be a Pollyanna? Instead, we have learned that merely imagining the misfortunes of others is not enough. In the contextual theory of happiness, this could be because their mere imagining does not bring these misfortunes into the context in which our own, lesser misfortune is experienced.

Perhaps the relatively painless approach used by Polyanna does work in cases where the counterfactual, the terrible alternative that has never actually happened to us, seems a real possibility; but when its possibility seems remote, it is unlikely to affect how we experience anything else.[18] Reminding well-fed children that the starving waifs of Africa would be grateful for the food they refuse to eat will not improve its taste. The well-fed child can hardly believe that he or she could just as well be among the starving. But knowing full well how freezing it would be outside, the same child might derive enhanced pleasure from snuggling beneath a down comforter on a cold winter night. There would have been ample experience with cold, perhaps as recently as when first slipping down between the cold sheets. However, it may not be necessary to have had a recent experience; it might suffice to know what it would be like without the comforter, a knowledge supported by much earlier suffering from the cold. In this case, the lower contextual endpoint established by the counterfactual was not completely without cost because the pain was actually experienced—although very much earlier. If such an occasional or distant bad experience sufficed to support this kind of counterfactual, the exchange could still be favorable. The experimental evidence suggesting that endpoints remain in the context much longer than do intermediate experiences encourages belief in the staying power of this kind of counterfactual.

The more serious problem with the Pollyanna technique for extending the contextual range downward is that such judgments tend to be purely cognitive, with no hedonic component. We may recognize intellectually that our own circumstances are much better than those of the less fortunate; but if this recognition does not evoke real pain in the empathic contemplation of the misfortunes of others, it is unlikely to become part of any hedonic context and thereby enhance our pleasure in our own good fortune. In concentrating on happiness, the contextual theory may inadvertently reinforce an exaggerated conception of the pervasiveness of intense pleasures and pains in everyday life.[19]

---

[18]Although in the opposite direction from the relative deprivation analyzed by Crosby (1972), the same principles ought to apply.

[19]Diener, Sandvik and Larsen (1985) concluded that subjects persuaded to record their feelings at random moments "reached an extremely happy state about once a week and for about one per cent of their waking time" and that intensely happy moods could be expected to occur even less frequently for older people (in Diener et al., 1991).

Encouraging Helpful Counterfactuals

Admittedly, the postulation of counterfactuals that extend downward the ranges of hedonic contexts without their own pain having to be experienced regularly may seem like an appeal to a *deus ex machina*, a miraculous entity brought in to hold open the possibility of a happiness more in line with most people's claims or hopes. But let us speculate freely about the sorts of strategies that might encourage such happy contexts.

Suppose that you are investing your savings in the commodity market. Respectable economists warn that commodities are notoriously volatile, with rapid, unpredictable changes in their prices. However, like so many other gamblers, you cannot accept such skepticism. You believe that you have sufficient insight to profit from trading in futures on corn or hog bellies. The odds may be overwhelmingly against you, but our concern here is not with your financial return but with the overall balance between pleasure and pain in this market domain of your experience. Although you will be more pleased when you gain money than when you lose it, your net pleasure or pain will be largely determined by the skewing of the frequency distribution of these returns. It will also be affected by social comparisons, how your earnings compare with the commodities market as a whole—particularly with the earnings of those other speculators with whom you can identify most closely.[20] Your optimistic faith in your own insight, though satisfying in itself, may not be an entirely positive factor. Insofar as pleasing anticipations of high profits enter this context, your satisfaction from real monetary returns will be lowered. And if you should lose all your capital, your fantasies of winning with commodities are likely to vanish under the harsh light of reality. It would seem difficult to find happiness in such a chancy domain.

This somber picture can be brightened by bringing in our *deus ex machina*, a very negative counterfactual. Insofar as it is possible to win heavily in commodities, it must also be possible to lose heavily—in fact to lose everything. Of course, the type of person who concentrates upon possible losses would be unlikely to have become involved with commodities in the first place. Nevertheless, your present context might include this logical possibility without your having to regularly reexperience its dreadfulness. The facilitating attitude here might be one of openness to the inexorable logic of the situation but with a determination not to dwell upon it. This sounds like wisdom, a wisdom that seems as likely to pay off in hedonic gain as in reduced financial loss.

Examples can be found in other domains. You could suddenly lose the one you love most. Life is short. Count your treasures while you can! This philosophical awareness of the awful possibilities should be distinguished from the "tragic

---

[20]See Frank (1985) for an engaging explication of the role of social comparisons in making economic choices (which would otherwise seem contrary to the neo-classic economic theory so popular today).

romanticism" against which Russell inveighed in *The Conquest of Happiness* (1930). Russell was attacking what too often passes for philosophic profundity— the view of life as a vale of tears, the claim that only a fool could be happy in such a cruel world. This type of tragic romanticism encourages repeated anticipation of the awful possibilities, suffering from them as though they were already happening. It is only to the degree that the negative counterfactual is not itself suffered repeatedly that it boosts the overall balance of happiness.

Consider a common enough example from the domain of health, the case of a woman who, although occasionally suffering from flu or a bad cold, much more regularly experiences a zestful sense of her own healthy vigor. This seems a happy balance, with experiences from the upper part of her context for health vastly more frequent than experiences from the lower part. However, as she slips into middle age, she becomes aware of new physical limitations, perhaps of feeling exhausted in situations that formerly would scarcely have tired her. She becomes resigned to these increasingly restrictive limits, but often feels depressed by a growing awareness of aging. Friends begin to suffer more serious health problems, disabilities, even terminal illnesses. Insofar as she suffers in empathy with them, her balance of pleasure is further reduced.

Here is where the tragic sense of life's limitations could help. Although it is crucial that this still healthy woman avoid the morbid fear of falling ill, she would be happier if she occasionally reminded herself of the real possibility of debilitating illness. Like most of us who naturally avoid recognizing the wretched possibilities, this woman finds reasons why her friends' misfortunes could not just as well have happened to her: unlike them, she takes good care of herself, she does not smoke, both of her parents are still alive. Although reducing her fears for her own health, such defenses may preclude any painful recognition of its precariousness. A tragic sense of this precariousness could provide an extreme lower endpoint of her context for health, increasing the pleasure she derives from her actual state of health. Arthritis, lower back pain, chronic fatigue, the various ailments that become the almost inevitable concomitants of aging, all are more supportable when experienced in a context that includes the occasional painful recognition of the much more dreadful possibilities.

So, too, with other important domains of experience. In our work, in our loves and friendships, in our family life, even in our recreations, the balance of pleasure over pain depends upon where what we experience falls within its own hedonic context. There must be a worst in each of these contexts. The further this worst is below the great bulk of events experienced in the same context, the greater the overall balance of pleasure over pain.

If most of these hedonic events are imaginary, the worst is also likely to be imaginary. In our work, we can imagine complete failure. Business people can lose their businesses, employees can lose their jobs. Among younger academics, there is the fear of not getting tenure; among older academics, the fear of a life's work proving worthless. Even when such fears are irrational, they can enhance the pleasantness of whatever else is experienced within the same context. The businessperson who has a well-controlled sense of what it would be like to fail, takes greater pleasure in anticipations of success. The academic's anticipations of the pleasures of security are enhanced by a well-controlled sense of insecurity. To be well-controlled means that, although painful when imagined, it is experienced no more frequently than is necessary to hold its place in its context of success and failure. When we find ourselves getting less pleasure in our work, it may be a sign that the tragic extreme has dropped from the hedonic contexts of that domain.

Our pleasure in the happiness of our children can also be enhanced by the occasional fear that their lives will turn out badly. But children are not above providing us with a rational basis for such fears—so that the pain can come to outbalance the pleasure. In this case, there is a tendency for the tragic sense to get out of hand. There is also the danger of negative moods spoiling our pleasure in our children by blending these worst possibilities into our better perceptions and hopes about how well they are doing.

More generally, our happiness can profit from an occasional reminder that, however wonderful life is, it can be snatched away in an instant, that any of us can be the victim of factors outside our own control. The Greek tragedians ascribed such misfortune to fate or to the capriciousness of the gods. Dostoevsky ascribed it to a flaw in the Karamazov character, an inherited lack of restraint that was a prescription for disaster. Whatever the ascribed causes of misfortune, the tragic sense must not be allowed to inhibit our savoring the great joys of life.[21] We must not apply brakes to our ecstasies by consciously reminding ourselves that they are transitory. The tragic sense that would make for happiness keeps the worst almost completely hidden away in the context, without its misery having to be re-experienced again and again. This is a key part of what has always been regarded as being realistic. It is a type of realism that, by acknowledging the potential for tragedy, even experiencing it in very small doses, enhances the joys of everyday experience.

SUMMARY

Examples from everyday life illustrate the pervasive contributions of imagination to happiness. With the overwhelming majority of our pleasures and pains occurring in the imagination, happiness depends on how we control the hedonic contexts for these imaginary experiences. As measured by summing pleasures over a particular duration, happiness can be increased by packing in more he-

---

[21]As an example, consider that when the context represented the 10 most recent outcomes from the test distribution in chapter 9, the modest measure of happiness (+29) would actually have dropped into the negative without the 6% of the payoffs that were *very, very pleasant*.

donic experiences—especially more of those pleasures of the imagination that we can enhance by selecting appropriate sources of stimulation from reading, cinema, television, music, conversation, religion, and even the possibilities for material acquisitions. These daydreams or fantasies do not necessarily influence the pleasures of real-world events because they are often in different contexts. But in one common type of mood, a memory or anticipation combines with whatever is currently experienced, shifting its hedonic level to reflect the place of the combination in the context. With extended bad moods, as in severe depression, there is the added problem of standards too unrealistic to be regularly experienced as pleasant fantasies but nevertheless present in hedonic contexts, robbing life of its pleasures.

The contextual theory of happiness prescribes a negatively skewed distribution of events, whether real or imaginary, allowing no possibility for events so isolated as not to be experienced in a context of related events. Pleasant fantasies are the stuff of happiness, but the overall balance can also be enhanced by extremely negative counterfactuals. This is different from the Pollyanna game of always trying to imagine something worse, for the actual pain must be experienced at least occasionally. Indeed, the crucial consideration for optimal control of imagined misfortunes is that they be experienced much less frequently than are other events represented in the same hedonic contexts. A paradoxical consequence is that cultivating a rarely experienced but nevertheless enduring sense of tragedy can provide an important foundation for happiness—but only if it is not invoked as a dampener of ecstasy.

12 Social Planning: Utopia Destroyed

A CASE HISTORY OF MICRONESIA

The mystique of the South Pacific is the essence of a romantic tradition, a dream in which many of the more unpleasant parts of life are happily absent. On these islands of perpetual summer, breadfruit and fish are free for the taking. Shelter is constructed of palm fronds in an afternoon. Work, at most, need be only occasional. Children are easy to raise and universally desired. And best of all for the promiscuous male, women are extraordinarily available and passionately devoted to the pleasures of love. Food, shelter, children, and sex—the basics of life are readily satisfied. Truly Utopian!

I once met a man who after describing to me the joys of his life in Tahiti admitted that he was moving to Israel. When I asked why he was leaving paradise, he answered: "You must understand that I am a Polish Jew. If there is one thing that a Polish Jew needs, it is worries. In Tahiti, I have no worries."

This presumed limitation illustrates a fundamental flaw in Utopian writing.[1] Utopias never ring true because a crucial ingredient seems lacking—worries. The contextual theory of happiness assumes that regardless of how happy a life may be, there must always be a worst, some part of it that is least preferred, and

---

[1] Another example comes from a description of the indigenous people of Baja California by Father Jacob Baegert, a Jesuit missionary there during the early 18th century:

> "They are much happier than people in Europe, even happier than the rich and comfortable. The native sleeps better on hard ground than a rich man does on his feather bed. In all his life, the California native never has, or learns, anything to worry or distress him or to destroy his joy in life . . . . (in Bowden, 1992, p. 15)

184

that this worst, however it might seem to an outsider, is truly unbearable to the person who is experiencing it. Even my emigre from Tahiti was leaving behind some "worsts." They may not just have been worries, and they were unbearable enough that he was ready to risk the uncertainties of life in a new and highly pressured country.

Consider what these worsts might be in the real life of the South Seas, beginning with a relatively simple physical phenomenon, the weather. By picking the right latitude, one can be assured of temperatures that always remain in the 80's (27 to 32 degrees, Celsius). In the context of a more varied climate, this range might seem ideal. Many would choose it in preference to yearly swings from bitter cold to suffocating heat, and tourists find the tropical climate a major attraction. But what about the natives, those whose experiences have always been limited to this ideal range? These minor variations in climate, imperceptible to us, are among their favorite topics of conversation. There are "cold" days, "bitterly cold," when the trade winds howl down from the east. The natives complain about these winds from which they must seek protection behind screens of woven pandanus. It is true that the temperature may still be above 80, but that does not make the wind seem less cold. And when drenched by the spray while sailing or fishing off the reef, the cold may be as painful to them as the worst we experience in our more temperate climes.

This is not to say that one suffers more from the cold in the South Seas, but only that the Utopia of a tropical climate does not ring true unless we are given insight into how the worst of its features are experienced. Utopias often seem monotonous because their authors do not take this relativism into account.[2] The variations in what might seem to be a perfect climate add up to overall satisfaction only insofar as the worst of its weather occurs rarely, the best much more often.

A similar analysis might be applied to the alleged sexual freedom of island life. It seems likely that when fewer hours have to be devoted to providing for food and shelter, sexual encounters may occupy a much greater proportion of one's time. However, like the weather, courting must also have its bad moments. Infidelity, jealousy, malicious gossip, rejection, feelings of being trapped—any of these seem likely. It is harder for an outsider to know about the islanders' private sexual lives than about their weather, but even a Utopian scenario should include some of the ups and downs of love. The young man who seems to be intimate with so many of the island maidens may be most attracted to the very one who rejects him. The sense of belonging and trust cannot be experienced unless there is the possibility of loss and rejection. Again, it is the outsider who, coming from a different context, finds social life in the islands attractively free. We cannot know how it is actually experienced in the context of those growing up in the South Seas.

---

[2]Huxley's (1976) *Island* and Skinner's (1948) *Walden Two* are striking examples of this point.

These contextual considerations have a moral, not just for writers of Utopias, but also for those outsiders dedicated to improving the lives of island peoples. One might wonder who would presume to improve upon paradise. Unfortunately, there is no shortage of idealists, especially among the bravest and the finest in the United States Government. Starting with the Kennedy Administration in the early 1960s, thousands of Peace Corps volunteers were sent out to the American Trust Territory of the Pacific which included most of Micronesia. Centered slightly north of the equator, Micronesia is not in the traditional South Seas, but its small coral islands fit our romantic visions of paradise more closely than even the better known islands of Polynesia to the southeast. This is in part because the little coral islands of Micronesia remained much more isolated than Polynesia and, as a consequence, retain more of their traditional culture. I made several visits to Micronesia during the 1970s and early 1980s, particularly to the Truk district. The rest of this chapter uses these experiences to illustrate how the contextual theory of happiness applies to problems of social planning.

Truk: Man in Paradise is the title of a charming book by the anthropologist, Gladwin, and the psychologist, Sarason (Gladwin & Sarason, 1953). The great Truk lagoon, where their study was conducted, lies 8 degrees north of the equator in the far western Pacific, north of New Guinea, east of the Philippines, and an 11-hour flight southwest from Hawaii. Approaching from the air, one sees a small group of green-covered islands, the tops of sunken mountains, surrounded by a coral reef which encloses a circular lagoon, some 40 miles in diameter. The colors are almost too rich, too romantically saturated, to be real. Approached on a small sailboat, as I once did, the reef seems hardly to rise above the sea, so that one's first impression is of a sudden calm as one leaves the ocean swells behind by sailing through one of the several passes into the relative flatness of the lagoon. Each of the volcanic islands is populated, each with its own culture that anthropologists claim is distinct from the cultures of its neighboring islands. Most of the population is located on Moen, one of the larger islands, where the United States established its Administrative Center. It is here that the influence of industrial civilization is most evident, with trucks and autos, several miles of roads, a dock for cargo ships, and a scattering of western-style stores. Other islands in the lagoon have no cars, few of the modern amenities, and much less apparent attachment to the things that money can buy: Farther from the administrators of U.S. largess, they have less money and hence less chance of participating in the market economy.

Even within the Truk lagoon, one can see something of what life must have been like during the half-dozen centuries separating the islands' first settlement and the coming of outside control. On my 16' Malibu outrigger, I sailed alone to an island barely 2 miles long, inhabited by scarcely 30 souls. These kindly people did not want me to sleep on my boat, warning of evil spirits. Although land and building materials were free for the taking, several generations lived crowded together in a single room. They had no electricity and few manufactured goods. Theirs was a subsistence economy, breadfruit, taro, and fish. But they had all been to the District Center. One young man had recently returned from the United States. He asked me whether I thought he could readapt to island life. That, indeed, was what I was there to study. My advice, perhaps premature, was that adaptation would be easier if he could stay away from the District Center.

Outside the Truk Lagoon, some 200 miles to the west, there is a chain of coral atolls called the Western Carolines, with Puluwat the best known among them.[3] As Gladwin described it, Puluwat fits closely our conception of a tropical paradise. And with my interest in sailing, it had for me the special attraction of being one of the few places in the world where people still navigate the high seas in small sailing vessels, constructed entirely of indigenous materials, just as they have done for hundreds of years. I had planned to sail to Puluwat in my little outrigger, copied after the design of their own *proas*. Intimidated by the unexpected strength of the tradewinds, I instead made the voyage on a 23' sloop, with another American and a youth from Puluwat as crewmates. It was my first experience with navigation, a particular challenge because the highest points on a coral atoll, the tops of the coconut trees, are not visible beyond 10 miles. Miss your destination by only a dozen miles, and the next landfall might be China! This gives some sense of the traditional isolation of these islands.

Once safely anchored in the Puluwat Lagoon, we moved in with the family of our young crewmate. It seemed a romantic dream come true. All the elements of idyllic island life were there—virtually complete self-sufficiency, absence of apparent problems of health, food for an entire family collected with perhaps 10 hours of work each week, lovely bare-breasted maidens giggling provocatively beneath the coconut palms, and for me, the great adventure of the small sailing outriggers being prepared for the open sea. How could anyone want to improve on this paradise?

The history of the Micronesian Islands is one of resistance to improvement. The Truk warriors had a fearsome reputation, fearsome enough to discourage the Yankee whalers from putting in for fresh water—insufficient for ships' needs anyway. This spared the Trukese the smallpox and venereal disease that wrought havoc across the South Seas. Missionaries, Catholic priests and then Protestants, brought a written alphabet so that the *Bible* could be read in the Trukese language. An added benefit, not anticipated by the missionaries, was that written love poems now became an important adjunct to courting. Traders arrived at the volcanic islands, exchanging some of the more dubious benefits of civilization (including guns) for *copra*, the dried meat of the coconut. Spain was apparently a passive proprietor until the late 19th century, when the Germans brought a true benefit of discipline by collecting every last gun. After the German defeat in

---

[3]Thanks to a later anthropological study by Gladwin (1970), this one largely devoted to the remarkable system of navigation by which the islanders sail, without sextant or compass, to little atolls hundreds of miles away.

World War I, the Japanese administered the islands until the end of World War II, when the United States assumed control. The American mandate from the United Nations was to improve on paradise, hence the Peace Corps.

The primary mission of the Peace Corps volunteers in Micronesia was education. The logic of their enterprise went roughly like this: The Micronesians do not know about the rest of the world; only through education can they acquire the knowledge necessary for intelligent choices about their future. Their most important choice, presumably, was whether to go for the possible benefits of the industrial revolution or to continue with their subsistence economy, living as they had lived for centuries.

There was no shortage of skeptics, especially among the idealistic young Peace Corps volunteers. The skeptics understood that once the prospect of modern material goods was revealed, there would be no choice at all. Better to leave the Micronesians alone. Let the United States Navy continue its protective mission, cordoning off the islands from outsiders.

Others ridiculed the skeptics, accusing them of wanting to treat the natives like *animals in a zoo*, on display for the amusement of visiting anthropologists. Government apologists argued that the Micronesians had the right to knowledge. Like everyone else, they had the right to make their own mistakes.

I side with the skeptics, believing that the zoo analogy obscures the conditions determining the choice. Once a boy has been shown his first internal combustion engine, whether an outboard or a car, he wants it. Although he may be free (in some philosophical sense) to turn it down, what people has in fact done so? One could have predicted, with perfect confidence, that the Micronesians would opt to enter the 20th century, an option that a traditional American education would hardly prepare them to reject. It was also predictable, although with perhaps less than perfect confidence, that their choice to enter world competition would produce a profound sense of their own inadequacy, that they could not possibly compete successfully in distant foreign markets and that all attempts to do so would fail.

It was the decision to educate the Micronesians that prevailed. Peace Corps volunteers were sent out in unprecedented numbers, one or two for each little atoll. They came mostly as teachers, providing basic primary school education. What incentive could the natives have for schooling? In spite of the idealism of many of the volunteers, the most effective incentives proved to be economic: Imported foods, such as canned fish, were distributed free at the schools as a daily reward for attendance. When a shipping strike prevented deliveries of canned goods, the schools had to shut down for lack of students. Children had been sent to school so that they could bring home these imported foods for which their parents had acquired a compelling fondness.

Later, an even more powerful economic incentive for schooling became apparent. Any student who completed primary school was immediately hired as a teacher. With a real cash income, perhaps $1,200 a year, the first big purchase was achieved—an outboard motor! Outboards were not entirely new. The Japanese soldiers had had them. But such social comparisons shift one's values only when there is a real possibility of acquiring for oneself what the other person already has. When one of your own, not a Japanese soldier, not even a government official, but someone just like you, acquires this most desirable of all objects, your range is quickly extended upward.

Imagine the first time a local youth speeds across the lagoon in his newly purchased outboard, leaving in his wake the sweating paddlers of canoes! No advertising is necessary to promote this product. Each paddler wants one. Each spectator viewing the scene from the shade of the coconut palms wants one. And how is this marvelous product, now absolutely essential for happiness, to be gotten? By completing primary school, that was the obvious inference.

The psychology of the islanders is no different from that of the Americans, the Europeans, or anyone else who sees a school diploma as a crucial step toward the acquisition of the material goods they have learned to want. As I write this, 250,000 students are marching in the streets of Paris, protesting the remote possibility that educational standards might be raised enough to exclude them from some of the material benefits of contemporary French consumerism.

In Micronesia, during the early years of the Peace Corps effort, there was a teaching job for each new graduate of primary school. Later, when most of these positions had been filled by islanders, the requirement was raised to completion of junior high school (which typically meant living several years on a different atoll where a junior high school was located), then to completion of high school at the District Center. When I was last in Truk, some college training outside Micronesia had become a virtual requirement for a teaching position. This escalation of credentials is a common experience in the United States and Western Europe. It is the law of supply and demand. As the supply of qualified applicants outgrows the demand for teachers, the competition for positions increases. It is only when education creates new jobs that this imbalance between the numbers of candidates and openings can be avoided. Because the total income of Micronesia was largely determined by appropriations from the United States Congress and the level of these appropriations remained relatively constant, there were few new jobs.

Such were the economics of the situation. What about the psychology? In this case, it seems to me that psychology followed from economics in a highly predictable way. The Trukese do not have a heritage of formal education. To go to school constituted a disruption of their traditional way of life. But since the economic incentives were so great, large numbers did go to school and did respond to the escalation of credentials. It may have been hard for parents to see their 12-year-old children taken away in ships for junior high school and later high school, but the expectation of material gain was enough to make the separation seem worthwhile.

I asked a priest who had helped to found the elite Catholic high school for boys in Truk whether he had any reservations about what had been accomplished. He said he had none. He thought it was good for a boy's soul to learn some Latin, even if the boy never really mastered it, would never have occasion to read it again, and if it did not help him gain regular employment. As a sometimes idealistic professor, I should be sympathetic to this view of education for its own sake; but I am not. In this case, elite education fosters expectations that are doomed to disappointment. The students expect to get high-paying jobs. Their parents and home community are also counting on this source of cash income, for there is traditionally much sharing of personal property in Truk, particularly among family members. But few of these graduates will ever be employed. For them, and for those who had been counting on them, the consequence is a painful frustration of aspirations.

Consider the plight of the "educated" lad, diploma in hand, who returns, jobless, to his home island. He comes back as a failure. Whatever he has learned of Latin or English or mathematics insures him no status on his home island. He is just another boy (young men are neither given nor take much responsibility in Truk) who must do the bidding of his elders, with the added burden of knowing that he has somehow let everyone down. In a real sense, his situation is much worse than it would have been had he never been to school. And the worst part of it is that his psychological context for self-esteem has been expanded to include a vision of himself as the great provider, not to mention the great consumer, of foreign goods. So close but yet so far!

What is it that he will never have? First, there is the cash income that he might have earned as a teacher. This had been the major incentive for leaving his home island in the first place. At high school in the district center, he acquired tastes for new things that a cash income can buy. Beer and western-style foods, shoes, trousers, sun glasses, wrist watches, radios, taped music, perhaps even video tapes—any or all of these can become accessible to young people on Moen, particularly if they have relatives there with cash income. He will also have ridden in trucks, perhaps even in a private car. To some degree, he has become accustomed to these material commonplaces of the wider world. And he has understood that they can all be his, providing he finishes school and secures a paying job. Because he is clearly better educated than many of those who have already secured employment, it even seems that he is entitled to these new luxuries—a perfect prescription for a profound sense of relative deprivation (cf. Crosby, 1972).

What we have here then is an upward extension of the range, an expanded context that includes many possibilities not in the traditional context of island life. We saw that extension of the psychological range comes easily, restriction comes much more slowly—and, in this case, painfully. Can the young people adjust to the harsh reality that they will never have what formerly seemed almost within their grasp?

I asked this question of Francis Hezel, the Jesuit philosopher who was principal of the Catholic high school in Truk. He thought that the adjustment could be much easier than I imagined. Citing the case of an outstanding student who had been expelled in his senior year for having been caught drinking, he predicted that if I were to sail to the distant atoll to which this young man had returned, I would not be able to pick him out from those of his age group who had never left home. Like them, he would be lolling around in the traditional *thu* (a red loincloth), teasing with the girls, occasionally participating in sailing adventures on the outriggers. His experiences on Moen would have faded into the past, like an almost forgotten dream.

I believe that such complete readjustment may well be possible, particularly when, as in this example, it quickly becomes clear that there is little possibility of ever receiving a cash income. It is harder while the door to employment still seems open. This is the condition for those students who do not return to their native atolls, electing to remain instead at the District Center on Moen where they may be supported by relatives in government agencies while they still hope to find the jobs that seem rightfully theirs. Evidence for the hardness of their condition seems everywhere apparent on Moen. Angry young men congregate morosely on the streets, often drunk, sometimes dangerous. Alcoholism quickly became the local plague, the Western-supplied substitute for the diseases that had earlier decimated Polynesia.

And what of those relatives who earlier found paying jobs in one of the agencies established by the United States Government. They certainly acquired the material goods. They live in concrete-block houses, with many of the material acquisitions enjoyed by working members of industrialized societies. Are they to be envied? Psychologically, they may be living near the top of their own contexts for success, doing better than their friends and family. But like all of us, they have their own problems, their worsts. They find themselves caught between two cultures. Trukese culture requires them to share their good fortune with family and friends. "People from my home island can't appreciate how expensive it is to live on Moen," one man complained to me. "They think that because I am earning money, I have plenty left over for them." Western culture requires these working Trukese to keep up with those of their neighbors who also have paying jobs. There never seems to be enough money.

Other aspects of this "success" also tip the balance toward unhappiness. Working for a government agency puts the native alongside American technical experts who are much better prepared for this type of work, the island education hardly sufficing for the demands of such a career. Put in a position for which they are grossly unqualified, the "lucky" employees must somehow live the sham of pretended participation. This must be a demeaning experience. One of these government employees told me, "I wish I could go back to my little island, back with the boys sitting all day under the coconut trees, doing a little fishing, a little chopping of coconuts, but mostly just relaxing with the boys."

Because it is so remote and exotic, one thinks of Micronesia as a special case. But my impression is that this sad affair, with minor variations, often gets played out where social planning is dedicated to improving conditions in an absolute sense, without thinking through how the improvements will change the contexts for judgment. As in our own lives, upward extensions of context are fervently desired and immediately gratifying. It is when people cannot regularly experience the new best that happiness is actually reduced. This seems to have been the case with Micronesia—a paradise, at least to outsiders, before the "improvements" were undertaken. However, even if life had not seemed so good, our efforts should have been guided by a greater concern for the contextual consequences.

13 Thoreau: A Message for the Very Strong

In the early 19th century, Henry David Thoreau borrowed an ax and went to live in the woods beside Walden Pond, near Concord, Massachusetts. His objective was to discover how simply he could live and whether one could be happy in such a life. *Walden*, Thoreau's (1854/1973) personal account of this 2-year experiment, is a beautiful testimonial to simplicity. It is an American classic, a blend of social criticism and humanistic psychology, a charming application of Emerson's transcendentalist philosophy.

Walden exerts an extraordinary influence on the romantic strain in American culture. This is perhaps best illustrated by our system of National Parks. The preservation of some of the most beautiful areas of the American wilderness owes much to the writings of Thoreau and Emerson, particularly through their effects on John Muir who personified, in his outdoor adventures in the California Sierra and other wild places, the life of freedom in nature advocated by Thoreau. And solace for the soul *is* imbibed from the natural scenic wonders of the parks: Each year, millions of visitors from all over the world emulate, for a week or two, this return to a more primitive, outdoor life. In varying degrees, these vacationers hope to capture the sense of freedom and independence that is so characteristically an American ideal.

Thoreau's message was simple and direct. In his criticisms of the economic life of early 19th century America, Thoreau asserted that the benefits of civilization were too costly in lost freedom. Thoreau exalted the sense of freedom he experienced by escaping these material entrapments.

Thoreau addressed himself particularly to young people who, like himself, were distressed by the prospect of having to earn a living. He had tried teaching school but preferred an outdoor life, sauntering through the New England woods and meadows, communing with nature, thinking about what to him seemed most important. Was such a life practical? Would he need a cash income? Could he live happily in relative independence from the economy of the marketplace? His experiment at Walden Pond was designed to test his hypothesis that "a man is rich in proportion to the number of things which he can afford to let alone" (p. 82).

Insofar as his 2-year experiment in the woods supported this hypothesis, it seemed to provide a unique answer to the problems facing many young people. Forget about preparing for a job, stop thinking about a career; instead, devote each moment of your life to doing what seems most important to you! By deliberately choosing what the world calls "less," you will find yourself in possession of that most valuable of riches: freedom.

Walden is a grand testimonial to the success of Thoreau's experiment, apparently demonstrating that he, at least, could live the simple life, answering to nobody, happy in his freedom. The account of his two years at Walden Pond fairly bursts with enthusiasm and a sometimes delirious sense of freedom. As he described his experiences there, his economic arguments seem confirmed by the psychological consequences of pursuing their implications.

The logic of Thoreau's economics goes like this: The products of the industrial revolution can only be enjoyed at the price of a disproportionately large amount of freedom-sapping labor. Thoreau used the railroad as an example. Traveling to Boston by train, instead of walking, would require the price of a ticket which could be earned only by working more hours than the time saved by the train. But Thoreau did not count walking as work; he felt freer, more alive, when walking and observing nature leisurely, at close hand, than when sitting trapped as a passive passenger on a rushing train.

This example may seem dated by a century and a half of increasing material productivity, but current examples can be found to illustrate the same argument. My son, when he was a student at the University, once asked me what would be wrong with his buying a car. "Loss of freedom" was my Thoreauean answer. Citing government figures for the total cost of car ownership, I calculated that my son would have to work 20 hours a week (at student wages) just to support a car. "Would it be worth all that drudgery?" After carefully considering my argument, he concluded that it would be! Months later, when the new car was stolen, I felt reassured that he did not use the insurance money to replace it.

Thoreau demonstrated that he could build his own shelter and then grow his food with only several weeks of farming each year, producing enough surplus to exchange for clothes and simple material luxuries, perhaps including an occasional visit to the tea shop in Concord. Free land may be harder to come by today, but the abandoned packing boxes that he recommended as shelter for those less skilled at carpentry might still be available. The same amount of manual labor today would afford a level of material luxury that would have seemed like conspicuous consumption to Thoreau, and our present system of social supports would provide emergency backups unavailable in the 19th century.

THOREAU'S PSYCHOLOGY OF FREEDOM

It may be easier to accept Thoreau's economics than his psychology. As he described it, his experiment at Walden Pond demonstrated that if material needs could be reduced, one would live more happily, with a greater sense of self-fulfillment and freedom. However, Thoreau was testing his own preconceptions, and some readers may be skeptical of this self-auditing of his hedonic accounts. Transcendentalists did not report their pains. Muir, after a long, freezing October night without blankets on the top of 12,000' Mt. Ritter, gave only the subtlest hint of his suffering—that it was with gladness that he welcomed the morning star! So too, Thoreau may have greeted the sun with enthusiasm after a cold, solitary night in his thinly walled cabin. If a few moments of jubilation were achieved at the expense of a long night of suffering, the exchange may have been no better than the bad bargains he thought others were making to gain the doubtful benefits of consumerism.

What light can be thrown on the psychological interpretation of Thoreau's experiment by the contextual theory of happiness? As with so much of Utopian writing, it is distressing that Thoreau does not refer to his psychological lows, the moments when he felt hopelessly trapped—terrible moments that made possible his experiences of exalting freedom. The argument is made in chapter 12 that this same neglect reduces the psychological credibility of other examples of Utopian writing.

In interpreting Thoreau, we should try to distinguish between freedom in an absolute sense and freedom in the relativistic, psychological sense. The inmates of prisons are not free in an absolute sense, but it is possible that a prisoner might feel free, might indeed be free, in a psychological sense—or so Boethius (524/1969) claimed in *The Consolation of Philosophy*.

We can easily appreciate how free were Thoreau's days at Walden Pond, in the absolute sense: Thoreau arranged his life there so that he could spend most moments exactly as he pleased. What is less clear, in spite of his eloquent testimonial, is how often he actually experienced his exalting sense of freedom, and whether such moments of feeling free greatly outweighed the agonizing moments of feeling trapped. In the popular song *Me and Bobby McGee*, Kris Kristofferson wrote that "freedom is just another word for nothing left to lose," implying that in such a state of absolute freedom one may feel anything but free. Many might fear that that is what would happen to them should they follow Thoreau's prescriptions to reduce their material and social dependencies. But they would be approaching their own Walden Ponds with their own hedonic contexts, different from Thoreau's, with different beliefs and preferences concerning what is necessary for life.

Let us try to reconstruct the ups and downs of Thoreau's own feelings of freedom and lack of freedom. If there had not been at least some misery, some sense of powerlessness or entrapment, freedom would not have been such an important domain of his life, perhaps not even an hedonic domain at all. Just as we can appreciate that children growing up in wealthy families might never experience a sense of affluence (never having experienced its absence), we can imagine Thoreau eventually taking his absolute freedom as a matter of course, as though forgetting that he had ever been shackled to the demands of a market economy. But Thoreau went to Walden Pond from a condition of psychological servitude, a condition in which he felt oppressed by the need to earn a living. Perhaps he had doubts about whether he could get his cabin built by winter, whether the beans he planted would actually grow, whether he could support the relative isolation from other people. It must have been very satisfying when each of these obstacles was overcome. At such times, like his chanticleer in the morning, he could crow his ode to freedom.

Suppose that Thoreau sometimes did feel trapped by his experiment, feeling forced to live alone, deprived of foods and companionship that he remembered with longing. In principle, he could have reported such feelings, either while thinking to himself, while recording experiences in his journal, or even in conversations with his occasional visitors. He apparently did not. But this does not contradict the assumption that he sometimes experienced an extreme loss of freedom. To assert that he did feel trapped implies only that he would have characterized himself as unfree if his actual internal judgments, his feelings of being trapped, were articulated honestly—either to himself or to others.

We cannot know with certainty that Thoreau ever felt trapped at Walden Pond. His context for judging his relative freedom there may have continued to include his oppressive earlier experiences as a schoolteacher. Because he apparently began his experiment on the debit side, the balance at Walden Pond may have proved very positive so long as these earlier experiences remained in the context. His sense of freedom at Walden Pond was also supported by the knowledge that he would have to return to the wage slavery he despised, were he to succumb to marketplace consumerism.

There is a misanthropic tone to some sections of *Walden*, suggesting that Thoreau might have taken a certain satisfaction in the enslaving conditions suffered by others. For example, there is his evocative description of the poor Irish, weighed down by their furniture as they moved from one shanty to another, oppressed by having to earn their rents laying down railroad tracks, each tie the tombstone for another Irishman. These desperate laborers could have escaped their misery by switching to a subsistence economy, just as he did. But Thoreau's analysis was more often turned against middle-class citizens, people whose lives were closer to the life he would have lived if he were not at Walden Pond. In his reflections on how trapped they felt by their material desires, he may have been keeping in his context something of his own past entrapment—without actually having to endure its misery. This would have helped to tip the balance positively in the domain of freedom.

Later, as the restricting experiences of his previous life dropped from his context, the balance between feelings of freedom and feelings of entrapment would have become more level. Thoreau's departure from Walden Pond was consistent with this possibility. He wrote that he left because he had "several more lives to live" (p. 323). But it may have been the withering of his sense of personal freedom that made other lives seem more attractive.

We need not be so skeptical with respect to the psychological success of Thoreau's experiment. It may be that he discovered an effective condition for happiness. His prescription to reduce one's demands rather than continue struggling to meet them sounds like good contextual relativism, reflecting a belief that it is not the absolute level of anything that counts. And the things that he most liked to do—long rambles through the woods, speculative discourses with himself—these were pleasures that he could repeatedly indulge. His escape from the demands of regular employment, his living alone in the woods, his devotion to his journal in which he recorded his own ruminations—these would all seem to facilitate the imaginative life. And, as far as we can infer from his journal, Thoreau was very much in control of his imagination. In the transcendentalist tradition, he dwelt on the wonders of nature the more religiously oriented would identify as manifestations of God and spiritual blessedness. Thus, the events at the top levels of his hedonic contexts, real or imaginary, may have come relatively often, the sine qua non for happiness.

Contrast Thoreau's freedom with that of a prosperous philosopher, such as Emerson. Having a respectable income, the philosopher can satisfy the material needs that the average person thinks essential. Being a philosopher, he does not imagine that additional wealth could buy him greater happiness. He sees no gain from the fulfillment of new and more demanding needs. Is not such a person in a Thoreau-like situation, living the life of Thoreau, although at a more luxurious material level? Thinking relativistically, there seems to be no essential difference between the two lives. Each can experience a surplus of pleasure over pain, feeling free more often than feeling restricted. Where Thoreau's pleasures came from the wilderness, living alone, pursuing his own ruminations without external pressures, the philosopher's may come from splendid conversations, delivering popular lectures, listening to music, or even from a slowly acquired collection of stamps.

A mistake that many readers make with *Walden* is to tie its message to the particular experiment that Thoreau described: living alone in the wilderness, doing without many of the usual material amenities, displaying a naturalist's interest in plants and animals. This misses what is essential in Thoreau, his belief that happiness comes not from achieving some absolute material level, but rather in living so that one feels free to pursue one's own interests. This is not a complete protection against disappointments, frustrations, and an occasional sense of failure—all of which must be experienced at least occasionally, regardless of how one lives. It is, however, a tempting prescription for minimizing the relative frequency of unhappy experiences. Less can be more when it facilitates living near the top of one's hedonic contexts.

Reading *Walden*, one can be caught up in Thoreau's desire to live *deliber-*

ately, that is, to live more fully. He proclaimed himself ready to experience the utter truth of life; and if it proved bitter, to experience that bitterness in all its depths. When analyzed in terms of the conceptual theory of happiness, this seems directed toward increasing the proportion of experiences that are genuinely hedonic—even if the distribution of genuine pleasures and pains remained unchanged. By reducing the proportion of zeros representing nonhedonic experiences, Thoreau would raise the overall average, the theory's measure of happiness.

For Thoreau, living deliberately meant choosing those activities that give free play to one's imagination. Thoreau assumed that the drudgery of the workaday world was unnecessarily restricting. It was while sauntering through the woods and across the meadows, sitting by the pond, struggling to articulate his impressions and ideas, reliving and sharpening them for his journal, that he reaped the fruits of his freedom. The transcendentalist philosophy that discouraged dwelling on one's miseries might also have kept the overall balance positive. Thoreau's way involves a liberation from the deadening habit of stifling one's fantasies for fear they would interfere with worldly success. Above all, the quest for simplicity is to cut down on the distracting, nonhedonic elements of experience that reduce our possibilities for happiness. What is left is an enhanced opportunity to discover which activities work best for us, to deliberately choose to live happily rather than just to live.

A LESSON FOR TODAY?

In the recent past, the United States and Western Europe have seen many failed attempts to fulfill the Thoreauean dream. Thoreau could have been the patron saint of the hippy generation that came of age in the 1960s. Like Thoreau, the hippies wanted the freedom to live deliberately; perhaps even more than Thoreau, they wanted to escape the constraints of social convention. Happiness was to be achieved here and now, not put off for some future that might never come. In their articulated, existentialist desire to seize control of their own lives, some sounded very much like Thoreau. However, most of them failed so dismally in this quest for freedom that the next generation resolved not to repeat their mistakes. Rejecting Thoreau's ideals, many students of the 1980s set prosperity as their professed goal, convinced that their future happiness depended upon financial success.

What went wrong with the hippy experiments? I believe that it was primarily a case of Thoreau's dream being pursued by the wrong people. One must be strong, very strong, to live happily at Walden Pond. One must have secure principles to keep the beat when one "hears a different drummer" (p. 326). But far from being stronger than others, hippies tended to be weaker, too ready to sacrifice the beauty of life for the ugliness of drugs. In some cases, the drugs weakened minds that were already marginal. The goal of a continuous high could not be achieved; indeed, the contextual theory of happiness implies that it can never be achieved. Strong drugs like heroin came increasingly to provide only temporary escape from the misery of physical withdrawal. Marijuana, LSD, amphetamines, and cocaine seemed to weaken the aptitude for practical affairs. Some hippy communes were plagued by hepatitis, spread by inadequate sanitation and unsterilized hypodermic needles. It was a disaster, destroying lives rather than saving them.

We tend to underestimate individual differences in capacity. This underestimation is made even by experienced university lecturers in introductory science courses who try, in a hapless exercise in frustration, to instruct in the same classroom students with widely varying aptitudes and preparation for mathematics. And so it is with the ability to stand up against the values of one's society, sticking by one's own standards, avoiding the invidious social comparisons that would demean one's deviant way of life. Comparing their own dismal existence with that of mainstream America, many hippies sank into despair. Many lacked a coherent philosophy or the strength to stick with it. Although their revolt against society could be initially satisfying, with its loose sex and drugs, there was no method for ensuring that these satisfactions would endure and predominate.

Those communes that did endure were based, in most cases, on religious principles, communicated by very strong leaders who enforced rigid standards of behavior. Although often living at a very low material level, the members of these more successful communes could hardly have enjoyed the personal freedom celebrated by Thoreau. On the contrary, even their ideas were tightly controlled by the social group and its leader. Fear was often the instrument of control, whether fear of the outside world, of the devil, of disapproval from other members, or even of punishment by the leader.

This control becomes so extreme in some of the contemporary cults that they are widely believed to brainwash their members. Psychologists have had little success in understanding this type of control, and there still seems no clear demarcation between it and less extreme methods of influence: religions, moral philosophies, even training programs in the sciences try to shape how people think and act. Although *Walden* was a magnificent effort at persuasion, it encouraged the very opposite of brainwashed passivity, instead asking us to make our own decisions, to live deliberately.

Obtaining the absolute biological necessities for survival may be much easier today than in the mid-19th century. This, could make it easier to establish a Thoreauean independence. However, Thoreau was not so besieged by the media of our contemporary consumerism. Television encourages those social comparisons most inimical to Thoreau's philosophy of simplicity, that one is rich in the things one can do without. Television teaches what goods are available, that others like oneself already possess these goods, and that their possession is a passport to happiness. The quest for a simpler, freer life is not encouraged by this kind of information. People may not be any more materialistic today, but pursuit of a less materialistic life may require greater strength of character.

What is this less materialistic life? In terms of the contextual theory of happiness, it is a life in which one can be happy with whatever material conditions one has achieved. It is less materialistic in the sense that one is not frustrated by the disparity between what one has and some higher material level that one has either deliberately forsaken or cannot manage to attain. *Walden* argued that, at least for people as strong as Thoreau, happiness can be consistent with a material level far below that experienced by all but the poorest of contemporary Americans. But his message should be equally tempting for the wealthiest who may nevertheless feel frustrated by the disparity between what they have and what they would like to have. Regardless of one's absolute level of wealth, Thoreau's message was that that level can be adequate for a happy life.

To achieve the understanding that would make possible his kind of life, Thoreau emphasized simplicity. Insofar as we can simplify our lives, we will be surprised at how readily the laws of nature will be revealed to us—or so he asserted. This is extraordinarily similar to the credo of experimental scientists who, by simplifying the natural confounding of conditions, hope to eliminate alternative interpretations. And it is an experiment with our own lives that Thoreau advocated, an experiment in which we simplify life's conditions so that we can come to understand what is essential.

Of all the people I have known, the one who seems most successful in simplifying life's material conditions is an extraordinarily strong woman known as Sister Chantal who has lived for the past 20 years as a hermit in a small cave in the south of France. She had studied to become a nun, but left on her own (as she explained it) "to experience a closer, more loving relationship to God, without the distracting intellectual dogma of the monastic order." Although she is not a mystic, she has tried to arrange her life so as to maximize her experienced love for God.

In its more material aspects, Chantal's life seems simple indeed. Once a month, she hitches a ride for the 7 miles to the nearest town where she sells the several pairs of woolen socks that she knitted since her last market day. This earns her the equivalent of about $30, enough for all of her worldly needs for the month to come! However, she describes herself as neither an ascetic nor a saint, "just a little girl to whom God has said, 'I love you'." Where the transcendentalist Thoreau sought to be close to nature, Chantal sees the world outside her cave as a distracting complication. Therefore, she remains in her cave most of the day, leaving it only to tend her vegetable garden, to carry water from a nearby spring, and for other essential needs. Much more than with Thoreau's naturalistic pursuits, this concentrates her attention upon her private experiences, what in this volume is called the imagination. Indeed, Thoreau's consuming interest in the natural phenomena of his New England woods must often have distracted him from his private ruminations. But it is only in the sense that Chantal's experienced relationship to God is not experienced directly by others that we relegate it to her imagination: For Chantal, the presence of God is as real as the stone walls of her cave—not as a schizophrenic who hears voices or has visions but as a sensible woman who experiences this presence as a private, subjective experience. And it is while engaging in the highly automatized activity of knitting that she most often experiences this presence. The rest of her life, the relative isolation from other people, the living in a cave, the minimal participation in the market economy, all of this simplifies her concentration upon her loving relationship with God.

Simplification is a relational concept. Thoreau simplified his material conditions when he established himself at Walden Pond, divesting himself of the distracting concerns with earning a living. However, after a couple of years there, he may have adapted to the point where the details of daily living absorbed much of his attention, interfering with his freedom to spend each moment as he wished. So, too, with Chantal: Although her 2 Waldenesque years have stretched to 20, we cannot know whether the restricted world of her cave does not often seem too complex, too distracting from her religious purposes.

The deliberate specification of purposes is perhaps the most difficult part of Thoreau's message for those attracted to his way of life. Let us presume, although with some trepidation at our presumption, that Thoreau's purpose was to immerse himself in his own internal life—his imagination—rather than in his external circumstances. Simplifying the external was a means to enriching the internal. Where Chantal seeks a religious experience of love, Thoreau sought intellectual understanding.

Many of us, even if we were to think deeply about our fundamental purposes, might find our goals to be as different from Thoreau's as Chantal's appear to be. But insofar as our own purposes are satisfied primarily in our imaginations, the methods employed by these "simplifiers" could also prove useful to us as well. In trying to apply them, we should not think that we have to live alone in the woods or in a cave. Rather, we should try to identify the distractions that interfere with our imaginations and to experiment with eliminating them. For some people, obvious steps toward simplification might be to get rid of the television set, the daily newspaper, even certain friends. We can adopt an experimental attitude in evaluating the results. We might find, for example, that control of our imaginations actually decreased with the loss of some sources of external stimulation. Certain books, certain people, certain worldly activities might turn out to be essential stimulants for our imaginative life.

This book concentrates on happiness. Neither Thoreau nor Chantal have identified happiness as the goal of their experiments. But the contextual theory presented here could just as well be about the psychological experience of freedom or of love. The same psychological principles would apply. There would be the same speculation about which conditions would facilitate experiences that are high in their contexts, regardless of their absolute levels. What the example of these strong experimentalists who have lived so simply can give us is the inspiration to experiment for ourselves, inspiring us to try different methods for gaining control of our own hedonic experiences.

Glossary

The following definitions conform to the most formal use of terms in this book, with the caveat that some of these terms are also used in their different everyday meanings:

category rating: Overt expression of a dimensional judgment, sometimes numerically, but usually in terms of one of a set of ordered verbal labels, such as *unpleasant*, *neutral*, *pleasant*.

context (frame of reference): The set of events, real or imaginary, determining the judgment of any particular event; the cognitive representation of that set; more loosely, the standards for a dimensional judgment.

contextual endpoints: The lowest and highest representations in a context, the least and most preferred members of an hedonic context.

contextual range: The difference between the two endpoints of the context, as on a scale of preference.

contextual representation: Hypothetical values, usually unconscious, representing conscious experiences of those real or imaginary events that determine the judgment of any particular event.

counterfactual: An imaginary event that has not occurred in real life but that could be represented as a contextual endpoint.

domain: A broad class of experiences, such as work or play, in which hedonic judgments are made, typically in many different contexts.

event (stimulus): Some physical change in the environment, real or imaginary, eliciting a judgment, such as sweetness or pleasantness (e.g., a sip of lemonade, a fantasy of success).

frequency value: What the judgment would have been if equal differences in judgment corresponded to the same number of contextual representations, in accordance with the frequency principle.

happiness: The theoretical algebraic sum of all hedonic judgments, divided by the total time period in question.

hedonic judgment (pleasure): A judgment of degree of pleasantness or painfulness, relative to a context of preference values.

imagination (fantasy, memory, anticipation): Experience of private events, in contrast to experience of real-world events—those that can be experienced by others.

judgment (dimensional judgment): An internal or covert evaluation on a bipolar scale, such as pleasure-pain or love-hate; this evaluation is experienced as an attribute (e.g., the pleasantness) of what is being judged.

living more fully: A life in which a higher proportion of all experiences are hedonic.

pain (suffering): A phenomenal experience, the opposite end of the scale of judgment from pleasure.

pleasure (satisfaction): A phenomenal experience identified here with a judgment made in a context varying on a preference scale.

preference-scale value (utility): A theoretical value assigned to to reflect the relative degree of preference for an event.

psychophysical (stimuli and experiments): Simple perceptual events, like auditory tones of differing loudness; experiments employing such stimuli, often for purposes of simplicity in interpreting the results.

range-frequency compromise: Location of each judgment halfway between its range and frequency values.

range value: what the judgment would have been if judgments divided the contextual range into equal subranges, in accordance with the range principle.

skewed distribution: Systematic imbalance of the relative frequencies with which events occur in different parts of the range (of outcomes or their contextual representations); when events occur more frequently or are more closely packed in the lower or less preferred parts of the range, the distribution is positively skewed; when the higher values predominate, the skewing is negative.

References

Adler, M. J. (1940). *How to read a book*. New York: Simon & Schuster.

Anderson, N. H. (1981). *Foundations of information integration theory*. New York: Academic Press.

Andrews, F. M., & Withey, S. B. (1976). *Social indicators of well-being: Americans' perceptions of life quality*. New York: Plenum.

Anonymous. (1957). *Cloud of unknowing* (I. Progoff, Trans). New York: Julian. (original work published @900)

Argyle, M. (1987). *The psychology of happiness*. Oxford, England: Oxford University Press.

Aristotle (1986 trans.). *Nicomachean ethics* (M. Ostwald, Trans). New York: Macmillan. (original work published @340BC)

Attneave, F. (1959). *Applications of information theory to psychology*. New York: Holt, Rinehart, & Winston.

Bartlett, J. (1982). *Familiar quotations*. Boston: Little, Brown & Co.

Barrow, R. (1980). *Happiness and schooling*. New York: St. Martin's Press.

Beebe-Center, J. G. (1929). The law of affective equilibrium. *American Journal of Psychology, 41*, 54–69.

Beebe-Center, J. G. (1932). *The psychology of pleasantness and unpleasantness*. New York: Van Nostrand.

Bentham, J. (1948). *An introduction to the principles of morals and legislation*. New York: Hafner. (original work published 1789)

Bevan, W., & Pritchard, J. F. (1963). The effect of subliminal tones upon the judgment of loudness. *Journal of Experimental Psychology, 66*, 23–29.

Birnbaum M. H. (1974). Using contextual effects to derive psychophysical scales. *Perception and Psychophysics, 15*, 89–96.

Birnbaum, M. H. (1982). Controversies in psychological measurement. In B. Wegener (Ed.), *Social attitudes and psychophysical measurement* (pp. 401–485). Hillsdale, NJ: Lawrence Erlbaum Associates.

Boethius (1969). *The consolation of philosophy* (V.E. Watts, Trans.) New York: Penguin Books. (original work published in 524)

Bouchard, T. J. Jr., Lykken, D. T., McGue, M., Segal, N. L., & Tellegen, A. (1990). Sources of human psychological differences: the Minnesota study of twins raised apart. *Science, 250,* 223–228.

Bowden, D. (1992). *The Sonoran desert.* New York: Abrams.

Braida, L. D., & Durlach, N. I. (1972). Intensity perception II: Resolution in one-interval paradigms. *Journal of the Acoustical Society of America, 51,* 483–502.

Brickman, P., & Campbell, D. T. (1971). Hedonic relativism and planning the good society. In M.H. Appley (Ed.), *Adaptation-level theory* (pp. 287–301). New York: Academic Press.

Broadbent, D. E. (1958). *Perception and communication.* London: Pergamon Press.

Brown, D. R. (1953). Stimulus similarity and the anchoring of subjective scales. *American Journal of Psychology, 66,* 199–214.

Browning, R. (1939). Pippa passes. In O. J. Campbell, H. Craig, J. F. A. Pyre, & J. M. Thomas (Eds.), *Great English writers* (Vol. 2, pp. 525–546). New York: Crofts.

Campbell, A. (1981). *The sense of well-being in America.* New York: McGraw-Hill.

Campbell, A., Converse, P. E., & Rodgers, W. L. (1976). *The Quality of American Life.* New York: Russell Sage Foundation.

Campbell, D. T., Hunt, W. A., & Lewis, N. A. (1957). Effects of assimilation and contrast in judgments of clinical materials. *American Journal of Psychology, 70,* 347–360.

Cantril, H. (1965). *The pattern of human concerns.* New Brunswick, NJ: Rutgers University Press.

Carr, H. A. (1925). *Psychology.* New York: Longman.

Centers, R. (1947). The American class structure: A psychological analysis. In T. M. Newcomb and E. L. Hartley (Eds.), *Readings in social psychology* (pp.481–493). New York: Holt.

Cowan, J. L. (1968). *Pleasure and pain.* New York: St. Martin's Press.

Crespi, L. P. (1944). Quantitative variation of incentive and performance in the white rat. *American Journal of Psychology, 55,* 467–520.

Crosby, F. (1972). A model of egoistical relative deprivation. *Psychological Review, 83,* 85–113.

Csikszentmihalyi, M. (1990). *Flow: The psychology of optimal experience.* New York: Harper & Row.

Csikszentmihalyi, M. (1993, August 12). Relax? Relax and do what? *New York Times,* p. A15.

Csikszentmihalyi, M., & LeFevre, J. (1989). Optimal experience in work and leisure. *Journal of Personality and Social Psychology, 56,* 815–822.

Csikszentmihalyi, M., & Massimini, F. (1985). On the psychological selection of biocultural information. *New Ideas in Psychology, 3,* 115–138.

Dermer, M., Cohen, S. J., Jacobsen, E., & Anderson, E. A. (1979). Evaluative judgments of aspects of life as a function of vicarious exposure to hedonic extremes. *Journal of Personality and Social Psychology, 37,* 247–260.

Diener, E. (1984). Subjective well-being. *Psychological Bulletin, 95,* 542–575.

Diener, E., Larson, R., & Emmons, R. (1984). Persons X situation interactions: Choice of situations and congruence models. *Journal of Personality and Social Psychology, 47,* 580–592.

Diener, E., Sandvik, E., & Larsen, R. J. (1985). Age and sex effects for emotional intensity. *Developmental Psychology, 21,* 542–546.

Diener, E., Sandvik, E., & Pavot, W. G. (1991). Happiness is the frequency, not the intensity, of positive versus negative affect. In F. Strack, M. Argyle, & N. Schwarz (Eds.), *Subjective well-being.* Oxford, England: Pergamon.

Dostoyevsky, F. (1991). *The brothers Karamazov.* (R. Pevear & L. Volokhonsky, Trans.). New York: Vintage Classics. (original work published 1880)

Easterlin, R. A. (1973). Does money buy happiness? *Public Interest, 30,* 3–10.

Eysenck, H.J. (1952). The effects of pscyhotherapy: An evaluation. *Consulting Psychology, 16,* 319–324.

Eysenck, M. W. (1990). *Happiness: Facts and myths.* Hillsdale, NJ: Lawrence Erlbaum Associates.

Fabre, J.-M. (1987). *La relativisation des jugements.* Thèse d'Etat. Université de Provence, Aix-en-Provence.

Fabre, J.-M. (1993). *Contexte et jugement.* Paris: Presses Universitaires de Lille.

Fechner, G. (1966). *Elements of psychophysics* (D. H. Howes, Trans.). New York: Holt, Rinehart & Winston. (original work published 1860)

Frank, R. L. (1985). *Choosing the right pond: Human behavior and the quest for status.* New York: Oxford University Press.

Freedman, J. L. (1978). *Happy people.* New York: Harcourt Brace.

Garner, W. R. (1962). *Uncertainty and structure.* New York: Wiley.

Gergen, K. J. (1984). Experimentation and the myth of the incorrigible. In V. Sarris & A. Parducci (Eds.), *Perspectives in psychological experimentation: Toward the year 2000* (pp.17–26). Hillsdale, NJ: Lawrence Erlbaum Associates.

Gladwin, T. (1970). *East is a big bird.* Cambridge, MA: Harvard University Press.

Gladwin, T., & Sarason, S. B. (1953). *Truk: Man in paradise.* New York: Wenner-Gren Foundation for Anthropological Research.

Gotlib, I. H., & Hammen, C. L. (1992). *Psychological aspects of depression.* New York: Wiley.

Gravetter, F., & Lockhead, G. R. (1973). Critical range as a frame of reference for stimulus judgment. *Psychological Review, 80,* 203–216.

Green, D. M., & Swets, J. A. (1966). *Signal detection theory and psychophysics.* New York: Wiley.

Gutek, B. A., Allen, H., Tyler, T. R., Lau, R. R., & Majchrzak, A. (1983). The importance of internal referents as determinants of satisfaction. *Journal of Community Psychology, 11,* 111–120.

Harvey, O. J., & Campbell, D. T. (1963). Judgments of weight as affected by adaptation range, adaptation duration, magnitude of unlabeled anchor, and judgmental language. *Journal of Experimental Psychology, 65,* 12–21.

Haubensak, G. (1982). An Extension of Parducci's range-frequency theory of absolute judgments. In H.-G. Geissler & P. Petzold (Eds.), *Psychophysical judgment and the process of perception* (pp. 262–282). Berlin: VEB Deutscher Verlag der Wissenschaften.

Haubensak, G. (1992). The consistency model: A process model for absolute judgments. *Journal of Experimental Psychology: Human Perception and Performance, 18,* 303–309.

Helson, H. (1938). Fundamental problems in color vision. I: The principle governing changes in hue, saturation, and lightness of non-selective samples in chromatic illumination. *Journal of Experimental Psychology, 23,* 439–476.

Helson, H. (1947). Adaptation level as frame of reference for prediction of psychophysical data. *American Journal of Psychology, 60,* 1–29.

Helson, H. (1964). *Adaptation-level theory.* New York: Harper & Row.

Hollingworth, H. L. (1910). The central tendency of judgment. *Journal of Philosophy, Psychology, and Scientific Method, 7,* 461–469.

Houston, J. P. (1981). *The pursuit of happiness.* Glenview, IL: Scott, Foresman.

Hull, C. (1943). *Principles of behavior.* New York: Appleton Century Crofts.

Hunt, W. A. (1941). Anchoring effects in judgment. *American Journal of Psychology, 54,* 395–401.

Hunt, W. A., & Volkman, J. (1937). The anchoring of an affective scale. *American Journal of Psychology, 49,* 88–92.

Huxley, A. (1937). *Ends and means.* London: Chatto & Windus.

Huxley, A. (1976). *Island.* St. Albans: Triad/Panther.

Illich, I. (1975). *Medical nemesis.* London: Calder & Boyars.

James, W. (1890). *Psychology.* New York: Henry Holt.

Johnson, D. M. (1949). Learning function for a change in the scale of judgment. *Journal of Experimental Psychology, 39,* 851–860.

Johnson, D. M. (1955). *The psychology of thought and judgment.* New York: Harper.

Kahneman, D., & Miller, D. T. (1986). Norm theory: Comparing reality to its alternatives. *Psychological Review, 93,* 136–153.

Kahneman, D., & Varey, C. (1991). Notes on the psychology of utility. In J. Elster & J. E. Roemer

(Eds.), *Interpersonal comparisons of well-being*. Cambridge, England: Cambridge University Press.

Klusky, J. I. (1990). Toward a theory of hedonic judgment: The effect of context in nonmonotonic domains. *Dissertation Abstracts International, 51*, 02B. (University Microfilms No. 90-22016)

Krantz, D. L., & Campbell, D. T. (1961). Separating perceptual and linguistic effects of context shifts upon absolute judgments. *Journal of Experimental Psychology, 62*, 35–42.

Krech, D., Crutchfield, R. A., Livson, N., Wilson, W. A., & Parducci, A. (1982). *Elements of psychology*. New York: Knopf.

Kuhn, T. S. (1970). *The structure of scientific revolution* (2nd ed.). Chicago: University of Chicago Press.

MacQueen, J. B. (1966). Some methods for classification and analysis of multivariate observations. *Proceedings of the Fifth Berkely Symposium on Mathematical Statistics and Probability* (pp. 281–297). Berkeley: University of California Press.

Marsh, H. W., & Parducci, A. (1978). Natural anchoring at the neutral point of category rating scales, *Journal of Experimental Social Psychology, 14*, 193–204.

Marsh, H. W., & Parker, J. W. (1984). Determinants of student self-concept: Is it better to be a relatively large fish in a small pond even if you don't learn to swim as well? *Journal of Personality and Social Psychology, 47*, 213–231.

McGarvey, H. R. (1943). Anchoring effects in the absolute judgment of verbal materials. *Archives of Psychology, 39*, No. 281.

Mellers, B. A. (1982). Equity judgment: A revision of Aristotelian Views. *Journal of Experimental Psychology: General, 111*, 242–270.

Mellers, B. A. (1990). A psychophysical theory of equity. In H.-G. Geissler (Ed.), *Psychophysical explorations of mental structures*. Toronto: Hogrefe & Huber.

Mellers, B. A., & Birnbaum, M. H. (1982). Loci of contextual effects in judgment. *Journal of Experimental Psychology: Human Perception and Performance, 8*, 582–601.

Mellers, B. A., & Cooke, A. D. J. (in press). Tradeoffs depend upon attribute range. *Journal of Experimental Psychology: Human Perception and Performance*.

Mill, J. S. (1939). Utilitarianism. In E. A. Burtt (Ed.), *The English philosophers from Bacon to Mill*. New York: Random House. (original work published 1863)

Miller, G.A. (1956). The magical number seven plus or minus two: Some limits on our capacity for processing information. *Psychological Review, 63*, 81–97.

Miller, G. A. (1962). *Psychology, the science of mental life*. New York: Harper & Row.

Myers, D.G. (1992). *The pursuit of happiness*. New York: Morrow.

Osgood, C. E., Suci, G. J., & Tannenbaum, P. H. (1955). *The measurement of meaning*. Urbana: University of Illinois Press.

Parducci, A. (1956). Direction of shift in the judgment of single stimuli. *Journal of Experimental Psychology, 51*, 169–178.

Parducci, A. (1963). The range-frequency compromise in judgment. *Psychological Monographs, 77* (2, Whole No. 565).

Parducci, A. (1965). Category judgment: A range-frequency model. *Psychological Review, 72*, 407–418.

Parducci, A. (1968). The relativism of absolute judgment. *Scientific American, 219*, 84–90.

Parducci, A. (1973). A range-frequency approach to sequential effects in category ratings. In S. Kornblum (Ed.), *Attention and performance symposium*. New York: Academic Press.

Parducci, A. (1974). Contextual effects: A range-frequency analysis. In E. C. Carterette & M. P. Freidman (Eds.), *Handbook of perception: Vol. II*. New York: Academic Press.

Parducci, A. (1976). Grades, standards, and happiness, *UCLA Educator, 18*, 28–32.

Parducci, A. (1982). Scale values and phenomenal experience: There is no psychophysical law! In H.-G. Geissler, P. Petzold, H. F. J. M. Buffart, & Yu. M. Zabrodin (Eds.), *Psychophysical judgment and the process of perception* (pp. 11–16). Berlin: VEB Deutscher Verlag der Wissenschaften.

Parducci, A. (1983). Category ratings and the relational character of judgment. In H.-G. Geissler, P. Petzold, H. F. J. M. Buffart, E. L. J. Leeuwenberg, & V. Sarris (Eds.), *Modern trends in perception* (pp. 262–282). Berlin: VEB Deutscher Verlag der Wissenschaften.

Parducci, A. (1984a). Perceptual and judgmental relativity. In V. Sarris & A. Parducci (Eds.), *Perspectives in Psychological Experimentation: Toward the Year 2000* (pp. 135–149). Hillsdale, NJ: Lawrence Erlbaum Associates.

Parducci, A. (1984b). Value judgments: Toward a relational theory of happiness. In R. Eiser (Ed.), *Attitudinal Judgment* (pp. 3–21). New York: Springer.

Parducci, A. (1989). Hedonic judgments for Aristotelian domains. In G. Canevet, B. Scharf, A.-M. Bonnel, & C.-A. Possamai (Eds.), *Fechner Day 89* (pp. 36–41). Cassis, France: International Society for Psychophysics.

Parducci, A. (1990). Response bias and contextual effects: When biased? In J. P. Caverni, J.-M. Fabre, & M. Gonzalez (Eds.), *Cognitive Biases* (pp. 207–219). New York: North-Holland.

Parducci, A. (1992a). Comment on Haubensak's associative theory of judgment. *Journal of Experimental Psychology: Human Perception and Performance*, *18*, 310–313.

Parducci, A. (1992b). Elaborations upon psychophysical contexts for judgment: Implications of cognitive models. In H.-G. Geissler, S. W. Link, & J. T. Townsend (Eds.), *Cognition, information processing, and psychophysics: Basic issues* (pp. 207–223). Hillsdale, NJ: Lawrence Erlbaum Associates.

Parducci, A., Calfee, R. C., Marshall, L. M., & Davidson, L. P. (1960). Context effects in judgment: Adaptation level as a function of mean, midpoint, and median of the stimuli. *Journal of Experiemntal Psychology*, *60*, 65–77.

Parducci, A., & Fabre, J.-M. (1995). Contextual effects in judgment and choice. In J.-P. Caverni, M. Bar-Hillel, F. H. Barron, & H. Jungermann (Eds.), *Contributions to decision making* (pp. 97–109). Amsterdam: Elsevier Science Publishers.

Parducci, A., & Haugen, R. (1967). The frequency principle for comparative judgments. *Perception and Psychophysics*, *2*, 81–82.

Parducci, A., & Hohle, R. (1957). Restriction of range in the judgment of single stimuli, *American Journal of Psychology*, *70*, 272–275.

Parducci, A., Knobel, S., & Thomas, C. (1976). Independent contexts for category ratingss: A range-frequency analysis, *Perception & Psychophysics*, 1976, *20*, 360–366.

Parducci, A., & Marshall, L.M. (1961). Context effects in judgments of length. *American Journal of Psychology*, *74*, 576–583.

Parducci, A., Marshall, L. M., & Degner, M. (1966). Interference with memory for lifted weight. *Perception & Psychophysics*, *7*, 83–86.

Parducci, A., & Perrett, L. F. (1971). Category rating scales: Effects of relative spacing and frequency. *Journal of Experimental Psychology Monograph*, *89*, 427–452.

Parducci, A., Thaler, H., & Anderson, N. H. (1968). Stimulus averaging and the context for judgment. *Perception & Psychophysics*, *3*, 145–150.

Parducci, A., & Wedell, D. H. (1986). The category effect with rating scales: Number of categories, number of stimuli, and method of presentation. *Journal of Experimental Psychology: Human Perception and Performance*, *12*, 496–516.

Pater, W. (1963). *Marius the epicurean.* New York: Dutton. (original work published 1934)

Peale, N.V. (1952). *The power of positive thinking.* Englewood Cliffs, NJ: Prentice-Hall.

Perrett, L. F. (1972). Contextual Effects in Clinical Judgment. *Dissertation Abstracts International*, *32*, 07B. (University Microfilms No. 72–02,951).

Peter, L. J. (1969). *The Peter principle.* New York: Morrow.

Peters, H. N. (1935). The judgmental theory of pleasantness and unpleasantness. *Psychological Review*, *42*, 354–386.

Plato. (1892). *The dialogues of Plato* (B. Jowett, Trans.), New York: Random House. (original work published 360BC)

Popper, K. R. (1959). *The logic of scientific inquiry.* London: Hutchinson.

Porter, E. H. (1913). *Pollyanna.* Boston: Page.

Poulton, E. C. (1989). *Bias in quantifying judgments.* Hillsdale, NJ: Lawrence Erlbaum Associates.

Powys, J. C. (1935). *The art of happiness.* New York: Simon & Schuster.

Priestley, J. B. (1937). *Self-selected essays.* London: Heinemann.

Proust, M. (1922). *Swann's way.* London: Chatto & Windus.

Raiffa, H. (1968). *Decision analysis.* Reading, MA: Addison-Wesley.

Rehm, L. P. (1977). A control model of depression. *Behavior Therapy, 8,* 787–804.

Riskey, D. R., Parducci, A., & Beauchamp. G. K. (1979). Effects of context in judgments of sweetness and pleasantness. *Perception & Psychophysics, 26,* 171–176.

Russell, B. (1945). *A history of western philosophy.* New York: Simon & Schuster.

Russell, B. (1975). *The conquest of happiness.* London: Unwin. (original work published 1930)

Russell, J. A., & Fehr, B. (1987). Relativity in the perception of emotions in facial expressions. *Journal of Experimental Psychology: General, 116,* 223–237.

Ryle, G. (1949). *The concept of mind.* New York: Barnes & Noble.

Sandusky, A., & Parducci, A. (1965). Pleasantness of odors as a function of the immediate stimulus context, *Psychonomic Science, 3,* 321–322.

Sarris, V. (1967). Adaptation-level theory: Two critical experiments on Helson's weighted-average model. *American Journal of Psychology, 80,* 331–334.

Sarris, V., & Parducci, A. (1978). Multiple anchoring of the neutral point of category rating scales, *Perception & Psychophysics, 24,* 35–39.

Savage, L. J. (1950). *The foundations of statistics.* New York: Wiley.

Schoemaker, P. J. H. (1982). The expected utility model: Its variants, purposes, evidence and limitations. *Journal of Economic Literature, 20,* 529–563.

Scitovsky, T. (1982). *The joyless economy.* New York: Oxford University Press. (original work published 1976)

Shakespeare, W. (1936). Hamlet. In W.A. Wright (Ed.), *The complete works of William Shakespeare* (pp. 733–782). Garden City, NY: Doubleday. (original published in 1602)

Skinner, B. F. (1948). *Walden two.* New York: Macmillan.

Skinner, B. F. (1971). *Beyond freedom and dignity.* New York: Knopf.

Smith, T. V. (1934). *Philosophers speak for themselves.* Chicago: University of Chicago Press.

Smith, R. H., Diener, E., & Wedell, D. H. (1989). Intrapersonal and social comparison determinants of happiness: A range-frequency analysis. *Journal of Personality and Social Psychology, 56,* 317–325.

Solomon, R. L. (1980). The opponent-process theory of acquired motivation: The costs of pleasure and the benefits of pain. *American Psychologist, 35,* 691–712.

Solzhenitsyn, A. (1963). *One day in the life of Ivan Denisovich* (H. T. Willetts Trans.). New York: Dutton.

Solzhenitsyn, A. I. (1986). *The gulag archipelago* (T.P. Whitney Trans.). New York: Harper & Row. (original work published 1974)

Spinoza, B, (1994). *A Spinoza reader: The ethics and other works* (E. Curley Trans.). Princeton, NJ: Princeton University Press. (original work published 1677)

Stevens, S. S. (1957). Adaptation-level vs. the relativity of judgment. *American Journal of Psychology, 71,* 633–646.

Stevens, S. S. (1971). Issues in psychophysical measurement. *Psychological Review, 78,* 426–450.

Stevenson, C. L. (1944). *Ethics and language.* New Haven, CT: Yale University Press.

Stouffer, S. A, Suchman, E. A., Devinney, L. C., Star, S. A., & Williams, R. M. (1949). *The American soldier: Adjustment during army life* (Vol. 1). New York: Wiley-Princeton University Press.

Strack, F., Schwarz, N., & Gschneidinger, E. (1985). Happiness and reminiscing: The role of time perspective, affect, and mode of thinking. *Journal of Personality and Social Psychology*, *49*, 1460–1469.

Swets, J. A., Tanner, W. P., & Birdsall, T. G. (1961). Decision processes in perception. *Psychological Review*, *68*, 301–340.

Taylor, S. E. (1980). *Positive illusions*. New York: Basic Books.

Terkel, S. (1972). *Working*. New York: Ballantine Books.

Thoreau, H. D. (1973). *Walden*. Princeton, NJ: Princeton University Press. (original work published 1854)

Thorndike, E. L. (1911). *Animal intelligence: Experimental studies*. New York: Macmillan.

Thurber, J. (1945). The secret life of Walter Mitty. *Thurber carnival* (pp. 47–51). New York: Harper.

Thurstone, L. L. (1927). A law of comparative judgment. *Psychological Review*, *34*, 273–286.

Tiger, L. (1992). *The pursuit of pleasure*. Boston: Little, Brown.

Tolman, E. C. (1950). Cognitive maps in rats and men. *Psychological Review*, *55*, 189–208.

Tolstoy, L. (1887). *The Cossacks*. New York: P.F. Collier.

Torgerson, W. S. (1958). *Theory and methods of scaling*. New York: Wiley.

Tulving, E., & Schacter, E. L. (1990). Priming and human memory systems. *Science*, *247*, 301–306.

Tversky, A., & Griffin, D. (1991). Endowment and contrast in judgment of well-being. In F. Strack, M. Argyle, & N. Schwartz (Eds.) *Subjective well-being* (pp. 101–108). Oxford, England: Pergamon.

Twain, M. (1962a). Comments on the killing of 600 Moros. In J. S. Smith (Ed.), *Mark Twain on the damned human race*. New York: Hill & Wang.

Twain, M. (1962b). The mysterious stranger. In W. Blair (Ed.), *Selected shorter writings of Mark Twain* (pp. 290–388). Boston: Houghton Mifflin. (original work published 1916)

Upshaw, H. S. (1969). The personal reference scale: An approach to social judgment. In L. Berkowitz (Ed.), *Advances in experimental social psychology* (pp. 315–371). New York: Academic Press.

Veenhoven, R. (1984a). *Conditions of happiness*. Boston: Reidel.

Veenhoven, R. (1984b). *Data book of happiness*. Boston: Reidel.

Volkmann, J. (1951). Scales of judgment and their implications for social psychology. In J. H. Rohrer & M. Sherif (Eds.), *Social psychology at the crossroads* (pp. 279–294). New York: Harper & Row.

von Neumann, J., & Morgenstern, O. (1947). *Theory of games and economic behavior*. New Jersey: Princeton University Press.

Wallach, H. (1948). Brightness constancy and the nature of achromatic colors. *Journal of Experimental Psychology*, *38*, 310–324.

Watson, J. B. (1913). Psychology as a behaviorist views it, *Psychological Review*, *20*, 158–177.

Wedell, D. H. (1984). A process model for psychophysical judgment. *Dissertation Abstracts International*, *45*, 3102B (University Microfilms No. 84 28,589).

Wedell, D. H. (1990). Methods for determining the locus of context effects in judgment. In J.-P. Caverni, J.-M. Fabre, & M. Gonzalez (Eds.), *Cognitive biases* (pp. 285–302). New York: North Holland.

Wedell, D. H., & Parducci, A. (1985). Category and stimulus effects: A process model for contextual memory in judgment. In G. d'Ydewalle (Ed.), *Cognition, information processing, and motivation*. (pp. 55–70). New York: North-Holland.

Wedell, D. H., & Parducci, A. (1988). The category effect in social judgment: Experimental ratings of happiness. *Journal of Personality and Social Psychology*, *55*, 341–356.

Wedell, D.H., Parducci, A., & Geiselman, R.E. (1987). A formal analysis of ratings of physical attractiveness: Successive contrast and simultaneous assimilation. *Journal of Experimental Social Psychology*, *23*, 230–249.

Wirtz, W. (1977). *On further examination: Report of the Advisory Panel on the Scholastic Aptitude Test Decline*. New York: College Entrance Examination Board.

Wolfe, T. (1987). *The bonfire of the vanities*. New York: Farrar, Straus, & Giroux.

Woodrow, H. (1933). Weight discrimination with a varying standard. *American Journal of Psychology*, *45*, 391–416.

Zaidel, D. (1971). A judgmental approach to decision analysis. *Dissertation Abstracts International*, *31*, 10B. (University Microfilms No. 71–09,264).

Zoeke, B., & Sarris, V. (1983). A comparison of "frame of reference" paradigms in human and animal psychophysics. In H.-G. Geissler, H. F. J. M. Buffart, E. L. J. Leewenberg, & V. Sarris (Eds.), *Modern issues in perception* (pp. 283–317). Amsterdam: North Holland.

Author Index

Subject Index